Philosophy of Religion for OCR

This resource is endorsed by OCR for use with specifications H173 and H573 AS and A Level GCE Religious Studies.

In order to gain OCR endorsement, this resource has undergone an independent quality check. Any references to assessment and/or assessment preparation are the publisher's interpretation of the specification requirements and are not endorsed by OCR. OCR recommends that a range of teaching and learning resources are used in preparing learners for assessment. OCR has not paid for the production of this resource, nor does OCR receive any royalties from its sale. For more information about the endorsement process, please visit the OCR website, www.ocr.org.uk.

Copyright © Dennis Brown and Ann Greggs 2018

The right of Dennis Brown and Ann Greggs to be identified as Authors of this Work has been asserted in accordance with the UK Copyright, Designs and Patents Act 1988.

First published in 2018 by Polity Press

Polity Press
65 Bridge Street
Cambridge CB2 1UR, UK

Polity Press
101 Station Landing
Suite 300
Medford, MA 02155, USA

All rights reserved. Except for the quotation of short passages for the purpose of criticism and review, no part of this publication may be reproduced, stored in a retrieval system or transmitted, in any form or by any means, electronic, mechanical, photocopying, recording or otherwise, without the prior permission of the publisher.

ISBN-13: 978-1-5095-1797-8
ISBN-13: 978-1-5095-1798-5 (pb)

A catalogue record for this book is available from the British Library.

Library of Congress Cataloging-in-Publication Data

Names: Brown, Dennis, 1955- author.
Title: Philosophy of religion for OCR : the complete resource for component 01 of the new AS and A Level specifications / Dennis Brown, Ann Greggs.
Description: Medford, MA : Polity, 2018. | Includes bibliographical references and index.
Identifiers: LCCN 2017048522 (print) | LCCN 2018007097 (ebook) | ISBN 9781509518012 (Epub) | ISBN 9781509517978 (hardback) | ISBN 9781509517985 (pbk.)
Subjects: LCSH: Religion--Philosophy--Textbooks.
Classification: LCC BL51 (ebook) | LCC BL51 .B77 2018 (print) | DDC 210.76--dc23
LC record available at https://lccn.loc.gov/2017048522

Typeset in 9.5pt on 13pt Utopia by Servis Filmsetting Ltd, Stockport, Cheshire
Printed and bound in Great Britain by CPI Group (UK) Ltd, Croydon

The publisher has used its best endeavours to ensure that the URLs for external websites referred to in this book are correct and active at the time of going to press. However, the publisher has no responsibility for the websites and can make no guarantee that a site will remain live or that the content is or will remain appropriate.

Every effort has been made to trace all copyright holders, but if any have been inadvertently overlooked the publisher will be pleased to include any necessary credits in any subsequent reprint or edition.

For further information on Polity, visit our website: politybooks.com

PHILOSOPHY OF RELIGION FOR OCR

DENNIS BROWN AND ANN GREGGS

THE COMPLETE RESOURCE FOR COMPONENT 01 OF THE NEW AS AND A LEVEL SPECIFICATION

polity

Dennis dedicates this book to his brothers Robin and Brian, and to the memory of our parents, Robert and Jean Brown

Ann dedicates her first book to her son, Billy, with all of her love and her apologies that it is not a Pokémon book

Contents

Acknowledgements	vi
Foreword	vii
How to Use This Book	ix
Philosophers' Timeline	x
Introduction	1

SECTION I PHILOSOPHICAL LANGUAGE AND THOUGHT — 7

1	Ancient Philosophical Influences: Plato	9
2	Ancient Philosophical Influences: Aristotle and Causation	24
3	Soul, Mind and Body	39

SECTION II THE EXISTENCE OF GOD — 55

4	Teleological and Cosmological Arguments	57
5	The Ontological Argument	84

SECTION III GOD AND THE WORLD — 95

6	Religious Experience	97
7	The Problem of Evil	115
8	God's Attributes	133

SECTION IV RELIGIOUS LANGUAGE — 159

9	God-Talk: Negative, Analogical, Symbolic	161
10	Challenges to Religious Language	185

Study Skills and Assessment	208
Glossary of Key Terms	221
Illustration Credits	225
Index	227

Acknowledgements

This book is the result of an interesting journey for the authors – at times enjoyable, stimulating, frustrating and all-consuming. We could not have completed it without the help of many people. We would like to thank everyone at Polity Press who has been involved in the project, especially Pascal Porcheron, Ellen Macdonald-Kramer, Neil de Cort and Leigh Mueller, who have worked tirelessly with us and have shown enthusiasm, creativity and patience in their editorial and production roles at every stage. The book is much better for their input.

Thanks are also due to Polity's anonymous readers for their helpful comments on various chapters in the early stages, as well as our long-suffering 'guinea-pigs' – sixth-form students at The Manchester Grammar School (MGS) who have played a valuable part in the book's evolution, providing us with honest and sometimes forthright feedback, and sharpened the book's clarity and exercises.

Ann would like to thank Dennis for his continued friendship, support and patience throughout the writing process – without him, she would not have had this opportunity. Ann also thanks her friends Michael, Gemma and Melanie for their unwavering ability to make her laugh. She also pays homage to her family, Patricia, Robert, Jaqueline, Paul, Thomas, Heather, Colette and Adrian, and thanks them for always believing in her, no matter what.

Dennis would like to thank Ann for her agreement to write half the book in half the time, for her intelligence and her determined and practical approach to the dynamics of writing under pressure. He would also like to thank members of the Religion & Philosophy department at MGS for various conversations on aspects of the book, in corridors on the way to lessons, in classrooms or in the department office. Their advice was always germane and their understanding of topics perceptive.

The authors and publishers are grateful to all who gave permission to reproduce copyright material. While every attempt has been made to acknowledge all the sources we have drawn upon, we would like to apologise if any omissions have been made and would invite any such copyright holders to contact Polity Press, so that these may be rectified in future editions.

Foreword

Why should you study the Philosophy of Religion? A simple and quick answer is that you have chosen to take Religious Studies at AS or A Level and Philosophy of Religion is on the specification. A longer and more interesting answer is that philosophy of religion is concerned with some of the most important and enduring questions that human beings ask.

Philosophy of religion used to be thought of as an activity that only theologians engaged in, who used it as a means of justifying their belief in God, in particular the Judaeo-Christian God. During the twentieth century, however, it began to be associated with a more philosophical, rational approach that took it away from purely 'religious' discussions, whose purpose was to justify belief in God, towards a non-confessional approach that focused on philosophical thinking about religion. The outcome of this shift was that philosophy of religion began to be studied by people who had no religious beliefs at all, and is now studied in the same way as the philosophy of science or the philosophy of psychology.

As you will soon discover in this book, Philosophy of Religion studies the ideas and belief systems of religions, and asks whether God's existence may be proven, what God's defining characteristics may be, about the relationship between God and the world – including the question of human suffering – and the nature of and difficulties with religious language. It has a very long history, reaching back, in the western tradition, to Plato and his student Aristotle. These two philosophers have had a fundamental and long-lasting influence on the development of Christian philosophy and belief. To take just one example, Aquinas was particularly influenced by Aristotle's theory of causality and he developed this in the direction of the Cosmological argument for God's existence. Aquinas, in his turn, has been hugely influential concerning more modern discussions relating to how religious believers talk about God and whether religious language holds any real meaning.

As you work your way through this book, you will be faced with technical terms that you may not have come across before, but you will find help with these in the definition boxes and in the glossary at the end of the book. Initially, you may find it difficult to understand what the philosophers are saying because their language is different from yours, but you will soon learn to understand what they mean. Perseverance will bring benefits. Do not give up!

We hope that you will find your journey into philosophy of religion interesting, stimulating and challenging. By the end of your study of philosophy of religion, we trust that you will have learned something about this subject and, perhaps, about yourself. Good luck!

How to Use This Book

It should be clear to you that the authors want you to enjoy reading this book and learning about philosophy of religion. We have designed it so that it will help you not just to pass the AS / A Level exam you are studying for, but to achieve the highest grade you are capable of. The chapters follow the structure of the AS and A Level specification very carefully and each chapter is designed to be relatively self-contained and to cover the knowledge and skills you will need to succeed in the Philosophy of Religion section of the course.

To this end, we have highlighted important terms in the margins. They are also included in a comprehensive Glossary at the end of the book. You should use these for consolidation of your learning and also for revision purposes, when you are preparing for your examination. The list of Further Reading at the end of each chapter will point in the direction of specific sources of information on individual topics – following these up will be an excellent way of extending your knowledge and understanding and also of exploring in further detail the topics that interest you.

The chapter summaries outline the key points that you need to know after studying each chapter and you can use these as revision checklists as you complete the work in each chapter. If you do not feel confident about everything outlined in the summary, you should read back through the chapter again to refresh your memory. At the end of each topic, some 'thought points' are included to help you revise the topic. You should attempt these as they will really help you practise for your exams and also give you an indication of how ready you are.

Each chapter also contains a number of exercises to get you thinking about the topic in question, and for you to talk through with your fellow students and your teacher. These are important, as you will consolidate your learning as you work through the chapters and debate some of the arguments and counter-arguments throughout the course. This practice really is the best way to learn about the topics and to work out your own opinions on the areas covered in the course.

Websites

There are a number of websites mentioned in the book and, while you should always proceed with caution when using resources from the internet, they can provide a valuable resource to further your knowledge and understanding of topics.

Philosophers' Timeline

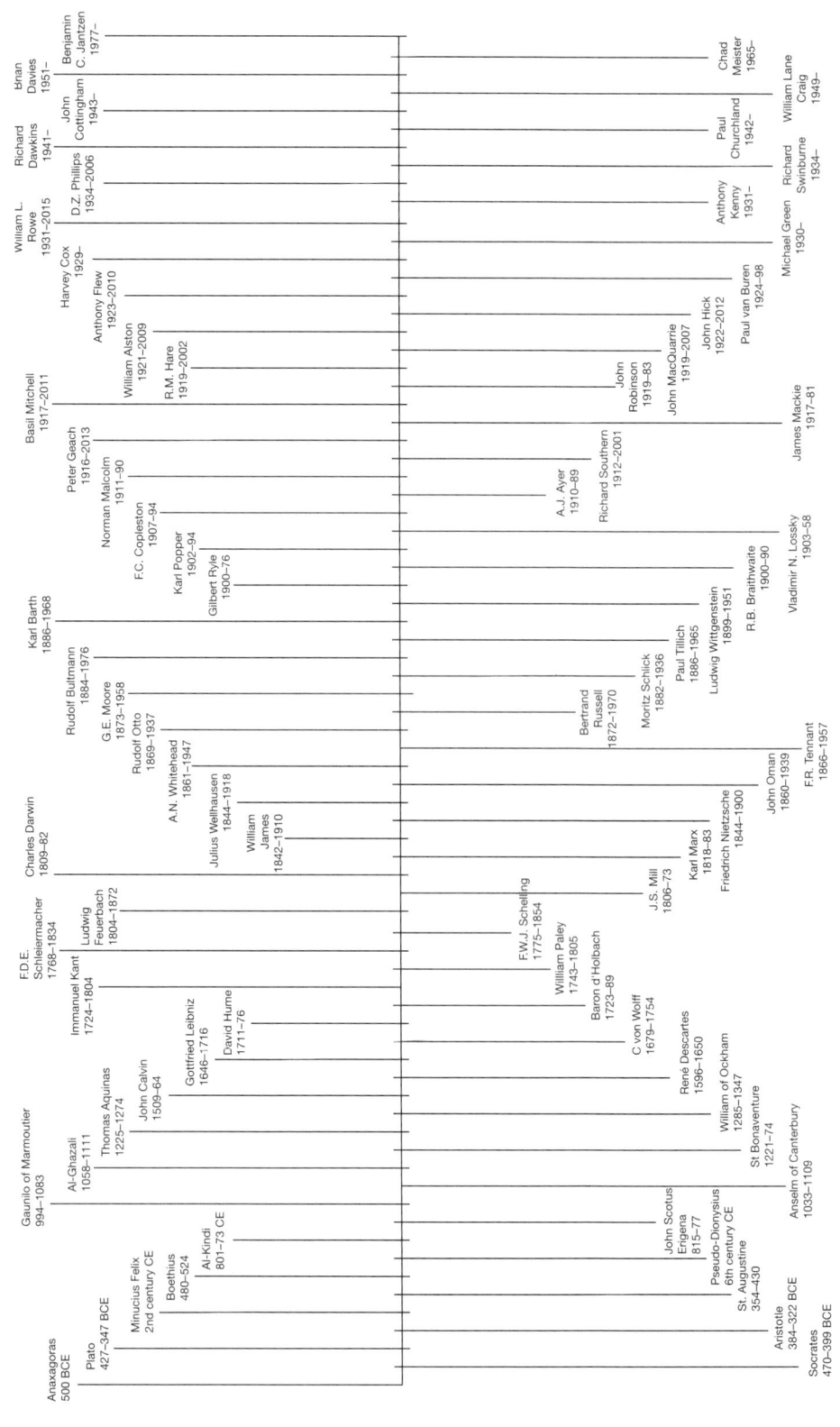

Introduction

Philosophy of Religion

Welcome to your course in Philosophy of Religion for OCR. Philosophy of Religion is a flourishing field of study in schools and universities and contains a varied range of topics. Though there is considerable debate about the nature and scope of the subject, we may define it as 'philosophical reflection on religious ideas'. Philosophical reflection involves the analysis of words and sifting of the evidence for arguments and claims. Underlying these debates are important issues about what reality is like and how much we can know about it. With this definition, we are implying that Philosophy of Religion is primarily about rational argument. For others, however, especially those who come to Philosophy of Religion from their own faith perspective, they may place less importance on logical arguments and more on their own personal experience of God in the ways in which they engage with other people and with the world.

As you will learn from this book, philosophy of religion has been studied and discussed for thousands of years across the world and in different cultures, from the Indus Valley civilization, Asia, China, Greece and Rome, worldwide through Christianity and Islam and into the modern world. During the last 100 years, there have been a number of interesting developments in the Philosophy of Religion that have stimulated philosophers to re-engage with the ancient debates and formulate answers that will satisfy 21st-century minds. Possibly the most significant development has been the Logical Positivist movement, which declared that all language, not just religious language, was only meaningful if it could be 'verified', or was able to be checked using **empirical** evidence. Philosophers of religion, such as John Hick and Alvin Plantinga, developed arguments attempting to justify the continuing value of religious language. In your course, you will be studying some of these ancient debates and their more recent developments.

Philosophy and the history of ideas

One distinctive feature of this textbook lies in its attention to the history of ideas.

Ideas are not treated as though they float around in the abstract. They emerge from and give impetus to movements and periods of change. Technology such as the printing press at the time of the Protestant Reformation was to distribute ideas across Europe at a pace that had never been seen before. Just think that, a little

Introduction

over 100 years after Karl Marx's death, one-third of the world's population is living under the influence of his thought. Attention to the history of ideas, along with the analysis of primary texts, is central to the study of Philosophy at university. But even in A Level study, understanding how the biographies, times and ideas of key thinkers interact can bring Philosophy of Religion to life. So, you should keep in mind the flow of ideas and a sense that thinkers are often moved to write in opposition to influential movements or writers of their day. Kant, for example, wrote that Hume awoke him from his 'dogmatic slumbers'. He was moved to justify his knowledge claims and to meet Hume's scepticism. As you read through the chapters, try to situate thinkers in their periods and enquire into the changing times in which ideas emerge. Often it is the artists, poets, engineers and inventors who innovate change. The philosophers articulate new social, political, religious or cultural movements in language, and make these ideas more clearly understood. So, you should refer back to the timeline on page x as you read through this book and seek to build up a mental picture of when key thinkers were writing and how their context may have shaped their ideas or account for what they were reacting to.

Before we begin the journey, however, there are some important technical terms in Philosophy of Religion that are widely used in discussion of the topics you have to study and which you are expected to know and understand. It is worth giving some information about them here so that you will be able to recognize their meaning when you encounter them in individual contexts throughout the book.

Arguments

One of the important topics you will cover in your course concerns arguments for the existence of God, but arguments will be central in discussion of any idea in any of the topics you will study. Before you look at those, it is important that you are aware of how the word 'argument' is used in philosophical debate. Many arguments have been proposed throughout the ages in attempts to persuade or prove that God exists or that God does not exist. The word 'argument' has several meanings. It can mean a synopsis of a longer piece of work – you summarize its 'argument'. More commonly, it can mean a disagreement you might have with someone else. You might think that it was a 'good' argument, or a 'bad' one, depending on whether you 'won' it or not. You might have lost your temper, shouted, lied, said hurtful things about the other person or forced your view on them. As you might guess, this is not the sense in which a philosophical argument would proceed. An argument in the philosophical or logical sense is about producing reasons in favour of your point of view and reasons against that of your opponent.

Philosophical arguments are made up of reasoning that is set out clearly in various steps. For instance, if I were to argue that it would be a bad idea to pour marmalade into my car engine, my reasoning would involve my knowledge of the

Introduction

detrimental effect of marmalade on sophisticated machinery. The steps of the argument would be:

1. If you pour marmalade into your engine, it will not work
2. If you cannot drive your car, you will be miserable
3. **Therefore**, if you pour marmalade into your engine, you will be miserable.

Certainly, this is a silly example, and philosophical arguments tend to be much more sophisticated and complex, as you will see.

In philosophy, there are two kinds of argument – **deductive** and **inductive**. Deductive arguments can either be **valid** or **invalid**. 'Valid' is a term used to show that the argument is logically consistent. Deductive arguments are thought to be valid if and only if the conclusion follows automatically from the premises, and the premises imply no other possible conclusion. Consider the following simple example:

> **Deductive argument:** An argument where the premises lead to the only possible conclusion.

All Scotsmen wear kilts
Donald is a Scotsman
Therefore, Donald wears a kilt.

> **Inductive argument:** An argument in which the premises lead to a conclusion that is probable, not conclusive.

If we put this argument into a symbolic form, it becomes:

All Ps are Q
R is a P
Therefore R is a Q.

It does not matter what is substituted for P, Q and R. The result will always be a valid argument. If the premises are also factually correct (**sound**), the conclusion is 100 per cent certain. This is called a **proof**. Philosophers of religion who have searched to find a 'proof' of the existence of God must have a logically valid argument as well as sound premises. This is an extremely difficult task – some would say an impossible one – as a proof is a rare thing.

Inductive arguments are different. To begin with, the truth of the premises of an inductive argument do not entail the truth of the conclusion, but instead they create a greater or lesser probability that the conclusion is true. Inductive argument is the sort of reasoning that a detective would use to gather evidence in solving a crime.

The following is an example of inductive reasoning:

1. Ronnie Stash cannot produce an alibi for the night of the robbery.
2. Large amounts of money and a bag full of tools useful for a burglary were found hidden in his flat.
3. Ronnie Stash has previous convictions for breaking and entering.
4. A man matching his description was seen loitering near the crime scene late on the night of the robbery.
5. Therefore Ronnie is guilty of robbery.

Now, these four premises do not provide us with 100 per cent certainty that the conclusion 'Ronnie is guilty' is true.

Notice that the conclusion does not follow automatically from the premises. The premises could all be true, yet the conclusion false. For example:

(a) It could all be a coincidence. He could have won the money on the horses, and he could be doing carpentry at evening classes.
(b) Somebody could be trying to frame Ronnie for a crime he did not commit, by planting the gear in his flat.
(c) Somebody closely resembling Ronnie could have been loitering at the scene of the crime.

You may decide, on balance, that it is more probable that Ronnie is guilty. Perhaps you may feel that realistically the weight of evidence outweighs the possibility of him being innocent. Whatever decision you come to, you are, in this case, using inductive reasoning. Notice, however, that none of this evidence makes his guilt or innocence 100 per cent certain. Strictly speaking, inductive arguments cannot provide us with proof, nor can they be described as valid or invalid. Inductive arguments are simply stronger or weaker depending on how well they provide evidence for their conclusion.

> **St Thomas Aquinas (c.1225-74)** is one of the most important philosophers and theologians of the medieval period. His thoughts and writings have had an enormous influence on Christians for over 700 years. He was born into an aristocratic family in Roccasecca in Italy and decided at a young age that he wished to join the Dominican Order of Friars. His parents disagreed, however, wanting him to become a Benedictine monk and imprisoned him for more than a year, hoping that he would change his mind. His family finally relented and allowed him to leave. He studied at the University of Naples and then entered the Dominican Order. Nicknamed the 'dumb ox', perhaps because of his size and possibly his weight, his academic ability soon became evident. At his death, aged no more than fifty, he had penned around 8 million words in commentaries and works of **Natural Theology**. His *Summa Theologica* was to synthesize the scientific reason of Aristotle (on whose works Aquinas had written commentaries) with Christian teaching on faith and scripture. He wanted to integrate **revelation** and human reason and see them as compatible. Many truths (including knowledge of the existence of God) can be arrived at through human reason and logic, independent of revelation. Thomism (the name for his school of thought) still remains central to Roman Catholic theology.

Thomas Aquinas introduces the two kinds of argument in relation to God's existence: 'Demonstration [of God's existence] can be made in two ways: One is through the cause, and is called a priori ... The other is called a demonstration a posteriori' (*Summa Theologica*, 1, 2, 2).

Natural Theology: The attempt to use rational, scientific evidence about the world to argue for the existence of God.

1 A priori

This is a Latin phrase and means 'from what comes before'. It refers to knowledge that is not dependent on sense experience. For instance, 'a triangle has three sides'. This is obviously a sentence that does not need to be checked by looking for evidence. It is a tautology and therefore true by definition.

In terms of the Philosophy of Religion, it is particularly linked with the **Ontological** argument for God's existence (see chapter 5 pages 84–8). The term has a long history in philosophical discussion, from its use by Euclid in his book *Elements* in *c.*300 BCE,

Revelation: A divinely given disclosure of information to humans.

through several philosophers in the Middle Ages – such as Albert of Saxony in the fourteenth century – to Kant in the eighteenth century. Since Kant's time, it has been used widely.

2 A posteriori

This is another Latin term, meaning 'from what comes after', and is also a way of thinking. A posteriori knowledge is dependent on sense experience and is usually called empirical knowledge. If I were to say 'it is raining today', anyone listening would be able to check whether this was correct by looking at the sky. We can make observations like this by using our senses and this is the normal way that almost everyone operates. We can make judgements on the basis of sense experience and these judgements may be factually correct or incorrect. The difficulty with a posteriori arguments is that conclusions based on them may change. For instance, at one time, the statement 'the earth is flat' would have been correct, but it is not today. Another difficulty with it is that we can never be sure that what we perceive with our senses is the same as what someone else perceives. This is particularly noticeable with perception of colour, where I may see a wall as red, while someone else may see it as a different shade of red or even pink. In this sense, then, a posteriori arguments can only ever be partially persuasive, never wholly convincing. There will always be some level of doubt in such an argument. This will be especially important to remember when we look at the **Teleological** and **Cosmological** arguments for God's existence.

Argument Terms

Term	Meaning
A priori	A type of argument that reaches a conclusion based only on reason
A posteriori	A type of argument that reaches a conclusion based on observation and experience
Deductive	An argument where the premises lead to the only possible conclusion
Inductive	An argument where the premises lead to a conclusion that is probable, not conclusive
Valid	An argument where the premises lead to a logical conclusion
Invalid	An argument that does not make logical sense
Sound	A valid argument that is also factually correct
Proof	There can be only one conclusion from the argument, so it must be true
Therefore	Signals the conclusion of an argument
Empirical	Making use of evidence from the world

Exercise

1. Finish the following arguments to make them valid.

    All frogs are purple
    Gertrude is a frog

    If I am thinking then I must exist
    I am thinking

2. Which of the following deductive arguments is: (a) invalid, (b) valid but not a proof, and (c) a proof?

    All three-sided shapes have internal angles of 180 degrees
    Triangles are three-sided shapes
    Therefore triangles have internal angles of 180 degrees.

    All fish like chips
    Andy is a fish
    Therefore Andy likes chips.

    All taxi drivers have long noses
    Geoffrey has a long nose
    Therefore Geoffrey is a taxi driver.

3. Explain how inductive arguments are different from deductive arguments.

4. Produce inductive arguments that support the following conclusions.

    (a) Cows are mammals.
    (b) Smoking is bad for your health.
    (c) The earth is being visited by extra-terrestrial life forms.

SECTION I
PHILOSOPHICAL LANGUAGE AND THOUGHT

CHAPTER 1
Ancient Philosophical Influences: Plato

LEARNING OUTCOMES
In this chapter you will learn about
- Plato's philosophical views
- his understanding of reality
- the Theory of Forms
- the analogies of the Cave, the Sun and the Divided Line
- Plato's reliance on reason rather than the senses

Forms: Plato's doctrine that there was an ideal, eternal, spiritual world that is 'real' and that existed above our world. The Forms are found in the Realm of the Forms, and included Forms of Beauty, Justice and Truth, among other ideals.

Introduction

Plato was taught by the first great western philosopher, Socrates, and it is through his teachings and values that Plato came to his key idea, the **Theory of Forms**. Socrates famously held the belief that 'True knowledge exists in knowing that you know nothing.' Although Socrates was known to be a very wise man, he did not hold the belief that he knew all of the answers to deeper philosophical questions; however, he knew that nobody else did, either. He would question concepts such as friendship, courage or beauty, and challenge anyone who thought they knew the answer by subjecting their

10 PHILOSOPHICAL LANGUAGE AND THOUGHT

> **Plato (c.427–c.347 BCE)** came from a noble family who had political and poetic ambitions for him. He opted instead for philosophy and became a devoted pupil of Socrates, whose unjust death sentence at the hands of the Athenian court in 399 caused Plato to leave Athens. He was motivated to seek the perfect form of justice and attempted to train philosopher-kings who would implement this. Socrates speaks in most of Plato's dialogues and it is difficult to distinguish the thought of one from that of the other. Plato founded the Academy, a school of philosophy in Athens. This is seen as the first university and it sought unchanging truth, mathematics being central to this quest as it offered knowledge unspoilt by the changing physical world. For this reason, Plato placed the command 'let no-one who is ignorant of geometry enter here' above the entrance to the Academy. His work, *Republic*, has a legitimate claim to being the most important political text in history. The questions he raised and his influence on Christian, Jewish and Islamic thought, not to mention western philosophy and politics, led Alfred North Whitehead to comment that western philosophy is merely 'a series of footnotes to Plato'.

response to a series of searching questions, which brought out subtleties of meaning, demonstrating that the original answers were defective. This had a dual effect:

1. It exposed the ignorance of people who thought they were wise enough to know all of the answers.
2. It aroused interest in philosophy among ordinary people.

Socrates was not arrogant enough to believe that he had all the answers himself to the questions he asked. He knew that true knowledge could only be found after thorough questioning. He taught that we must question everything. This belief eventually led to his arrest on charges of corrupting the youth of Athens, and impiety (not believing in the gods of the city). Socrates was tried, found guilty and given two options – to renounce his beliefs or drink a cup of hemlock (poison). Socrates held firm to his principles and died in 399 BCE.

Plato

Socrates was hugely influential in the life and works of Plato. He had a huge impact on Plato's writings, which showed Socrates to be a wise protagonist. Initially, his writings stayed true to Socrates; however, as Plato's writings developed, so did the beliefs he held on knowledge, and this led to one of the earliest and most famous attempts to explain certain kinds of knowledge – the Theory of Forms. Plato developed this idea as a result of studying Pre-Socratic thinkers such as Heraclitus and Cratylus, who argued that everything is constantly in flux and nothing ever remains the same, hence the idea 'You cannot step into the same river twice.' For Cratylus, everything is evolving and becoming and by the time you have begun to understand one concept fully, the meaning will have changed so you can never achieve a true understanding of anything. Plato argued that the result of this thinking was that genuine, true knowledge becomes impossible. How can one ever understand what 'x' is if 'x' is constantly changing? Plato refutes these ideas and suggests that there

Ancient Philosophical Influences: Plato

is something permanent beyond the physical realm of observable change, in which we can gain true and certain knowledge.

Plato also developed the ideas of Pythagoras, who stated that mathematical/geometrical ideas are fundamentally different from the ideas we have of the objects around us. These ideas are timeless and immutable, whereas the world of our experience is not. Whereas our experience of mathematical truth is certain and arrived at through thought and deduction, our 'knowledge' of the sensible world – arrived at with the use of our senses – is not, and is therefore inferior as it cannot be seen to be certain. Plato was deeply influenced by Pythagoras and extends the latter's ideas, stating that there is an unseen realm of eternal truths which underpins and explains the realm of the senses. Plato suggests that the world we live in is a world of appearances, but that true knowledge of the real world belongs in a world of ideas which he calls the 'Forms'.

For Plato, a major part of his activity is the search for true knowledge (here, venturing away from the teachings of Socrates) despite the fact that, for Socrates, the search for knowledge was arguably unsuccessful. As I. M. Crombie states:

> In practice, the point of (Plato) writing the dialogue (Republic) was not to fail to define knowledge, nor to show that it cannot be defined, but to illuminate certain other matters. Perhaps, the chief of these is that our knowledge of the external world is not a matter of undergoing 'sense data' but of interpreting them. This result emerges from a long and complicated discussion which distinguishes sensation from judgement.
> (I. M. Crombie, *An Examination of Plato's Doctrines: Plato on Knowledge and Reality*, Routledge, 1962, p. 3)

Plato suggests that there are all kinds of everyday knowledge that we hold. For example, you can recognize a dog because you have an awareness of what attributes a dog has – your knowledge of what a dog actually is precedes your awareness of the dog in the present context. However, when it comes to defining concepts such as beauty, justice or goodness, then we may all have an idea of what these concepts involve; indeed, we may even be able to recognize these attributes in other people or other scenarios, but would we be able to formulate an exact definition of them, or are these concepts entirely subjective? For example, I may hang a painting in my home, which I think is beautiful, but another person may not see the same beauty and would not want it on display in their home. So, how then may we have knowledge of such concepts if they are entirely subjective? For Plato, we have eternal knowledge of these concepts through the Realm of the Forms.

> **Exercise**
> What do you understand by the term 'Beauty'? Do you think it is an objective term? Whatever your view, explain your answer.

The Forms

In order to gain a full understanding of what Plato means when he discusses the Forms, we must look at Book V of the *Republic*, in which Socrates tries to persuade Glaucon that a beautiful object can be seen to be ugly – or that 'Beauty is in the eye of the beholder.' He argues that beauty is purely subjective and entirely limited. One may look at a flower that from afar appears stunningly beautiful, but upon closer inspection you may notice torn petals, dying leaves or perhaps insect bites taken out of the flower – in which case, there may be another flower which holds a more perfect form of beauty than the original. The same can be said in terms of concepts such as 'short' or 'tall' – a giraffe may be tall in comparison to a human, but then compare it to Mount Everest and it is tiny. In order to understand concepts such as these we have to accept that we have no firm knowledge from our senses as they are all subjective and qualitative. Plato argues instead that there must be something which is quantitative, measurable and immutable – therefore, there must exist a world of Forms in which justice is *always* just, beauty is *always* beautiful, small is *always* small, and so on.

If we take *beauty* as a class concept and make the following two statements,

1. That is a beautiful person
2. That is a beautiful statue

both of these statements can be true, but only in very different senses. Both can 'participate' in the common property of 'beauty' despite being quite different in reality. Plato calls the common property 'beauty itself', meaning it is distinct from the particular beauty of the woman, or indeed the statue. If we are to have an understanding of what we mean when we say 'This statue is beautiful', then we must have some prior knowledge (temporal – of this world, not spiritual) or understanding of beauty. If not, how can we know this statement is true? How are we able to rank beauty? For Plato, neither the person nor the statue can be perfectly beautiful. They will have factors which share in the concept of beauty with other beautiful things, but it is the ultimate standard of beauty by which we judge a beautiful thing, and this is the idea – the Form of beauty. In reality, then, what does this mean with regards to our knowledge? If concepts such as 'beauty' and 'justice' are merely names and not realities, how can any of our moral judgements be true? For example, the statement 'Paying debts is just' cannot be evaluated as being either true or false. There is a difference between *perception* and *knowledge*. If knowledge is the truth of what really exists, then would there ever be anything to know? What we call the 'real world' is not 'real' at all – it is merely a world of appearance. For Plato, the only reality is that within the Realm of the Forms.

The world in which we live is merely a 'sensible' realm – a world in which we perceive by our senses. The sensible realm is not reality – it is merely a shadowy reflection of the perfect world in the Realm of the Forms. We live in a world of false appearances. Everything we perceive is encountered by our senses and these will change, develop and die. However, what makes something what it is belongs to our knowledge of it in the Realm of the Forms. By 'Form', Plato is referring to the essence of a thing. For example, although there are many breeds of dog, whether you see a Dalmatian or a Pug you automatically reference the 'Form' of a dog. You do this regardless of the fact that they look nothing alike, because both animals conform to some degree of what our concept of a dog is – four legs, hairy, tail and bark. Objects 'participate in' or 'reflect' the Forms. However, Plato's argument is that we must have prior knowledge of what a dog is, so the Form of a dog must exist somewhere – and for Plato that existence is in the world of the Forms. The Forms are unchanging, hence they will always be our reference point for true knowledge of our earthly senses. Our learning is quite simply remembering the knowledge gained by our immortal soul when in the Realm of the Forms.

Plato was not overly concerned with the Forms of tangible objects such as desks, sofas or shelves. Instead, he was more concerned with the Forms of such concepts as truth, beauty and justice. The world of Forms was more true and real for Plato than the 'sensible' realm, as the Forms are the unchanging, timeless and true versions of the imperfect 'shadows' on earth. Although nothing in our world reflects the perfect version of the Forms, they are present in all things – for example, the true Form of beauty is reflected in a beautiful flower. Our world is constantly changing and we rely on our senses to understand what is going on around us. For example, you are not the same person you were three years ago, or even three minutes ago. Cells are forever changing, and different ideas and understanding flit through our minds. The real world is unchanging and eternal. It is the world of ideals, not senses, where there are perfect Forms of the things we know on earth.

Plato was a Dualist. As Andrew Lawless describes: 'He (Plato) posits the existence of two *irreducible* kinds of things: the mental (or intelligible) and the physical (or visible). . . . Whatever consciousness is, however supervenient (dependent) on the body it may be, it nonetheless cannot be reduced to, or described as, a purely physical event. Nor, of course, can physical events be reduced to mental ones' (Lawless, *Plato's Sun – An Introduction to Philosophy*, University of Toronto Press, 2005, p. 34).

Plato's Dualism

The concept of **Dualism** is important when considering Plato's theory, for the following reasons:

- Plato was a Dualist – he distinguishes between body and soul.
- He holds firm to the belief that we all have immortal souls.
- These immortal souls belong to the world of the Forms before being born into a physical body and placed in a physical realm.
- The soul, when in a body, has vague recollections of the true world of the Forms from its experience before personhood.
- This is the reason why young children can have basic knowledge of concepts such as truth, beauty, justice, etc., without ever being taught them.

So, apart from the 'sensible realm', there is an 'Intelligible Realm' populated by Forms – ideals and universals. For Plato, this is the 'real' realm and the sensible realm is just a mere imitation of this. The only way to encounter this realm is through the

14 PHILOSOPHICAL LANGUAGE AND THOUGHT

use of thought and reason. This realm can also be thought of as transcendent and is sometimes referred to as a 'spiritual' realm. It is immutable and all true knowledge comes from the realm of the Forms. In this realm, the most important and fundamental Form is the Form of the Good.

The Form of the Good

Goodness is arguably the most difficult concept to understand – I can say that ice cream is good, but too much of it can have detrimental consequences for my health, so it cannot be entirely good. In the 'sensible' realm, we can label things as 'good', as most things known to us can be classed as 'good', e.g. a 'good' holiday, a 'good' TV programme, a 'good' mark for your essay. Ideal Forms all have one thing in common, which is that they all have the presence of Good in them. Plato states that all Forms stem from the Form of the Good and that this Form sustains them all. It is said that the Form of the Good 'illuminates' all other Forms: it enables us to gain knowledge of them, and without the Form of the Good we have no knowledge of anything. For Plato, this Form is seen to be the ultimate object of enquiry and is far superior to all other Forms in terms of reality and perfection. There is a hierarchy, as seen below:

It can be argued that the ultimate goal of Philosophy is to gain true knowledge of the Good. To explain this Form, Plato refers to three analogies: the Cave, the Sun and the Divided Line. Each of these will be explained in more detail below.

Form of the Good: This Form is seen to be the ultimate object of enquiry and is far superior to all other Forms in terms of reality and perfection in Platonic thinking.

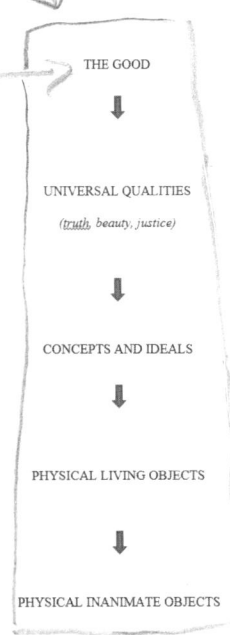

THE GOOD
↓
UNIVERSAL QUALITIES
(*truth*, beauty, justice)
↓
CONCEPTS AND IDEALS
↓
PHYSICAL LIVING OBJECTS
↓
PHYSICAL INANIMATE OBJECTS

The Analogy of the Cave

An analogy is a comparison between one thing and another for the main purpose of clarification, or to explain a point in more depth. It incorporates two meanings – a literal meaning and a symbolic meaning. For example, in the film *Forrest Gump*, the famous quote 'Life is like a box of chocolates – you never know what you're going to get' compares the unknown elements of surprise in life to eating a box of chocolates without the description of what is inside.

Plato's Analogy of the Cave is one of the most well-known passages from his *Republic*, in which he discusses the ideal society and who should rule over it. He spends time reflecting on the sort of education and upbringing that the ruler would need in order to rule over society to make or keep it just and moral. The analogy works on several levels – at its simplest, it is merely a story about prisoners being held captive in a cave, yet at its most complex it examines the progress of the mind from the lowest stages of understanding reality to a complete and enlightened understanding of the real world. For Plato, this enlightened understanding of reality is the knowledge of the Good represented by the brilliant light of the sun outside. Plato used this story to illustrate his understanding of the Forms, although the interpretation of the analogy is widely debated amongst scholars and philosophers.

Analogy: An analogy is a comparison between one thing and another for the main purpose of clarification or to explain a point in more depth.

Ancient Philosophical Influences: Plato

Summary of Plato's Analogy of the Cave

Plato asks us to imagine a group of prisoners who have spent their whole lives chained up near the back of a cave, at the bottom of a steep slope. They are facing the rear wall and are unable to turn around to see anything other than the back wall of the cave.

The only thing the prisoners are able to see is a series of shadows that are cast on this wall by a fire that burns far behind them, providing the only light available in the cave. Immediately behind the prisoners, between them and the fire, is a low wall, behind which people are moving about and talking, while holding a variety of different objects above the wall. It is these objects that form the shadows on the back wall of the cave and the only thing that the prisoners can see. To the prisoners, the shadows seem real as they are not aware of what is happening behind them.

Plato goes on to say that if one of the prisoners were to be set free the first thing he would feel is pain and confusion. Blinded by the fire, he would be unable to see the objects clearly and, in the dazzling light, the familiar shadows he has become accustomed to would seem much more comforting and real. If he were then taken from the cave into the sunlight, he would be even more dazzled and confused. Initially, he may seek the shadows and reflections in order to find comfort, and go back to the world he had become accustomed to and comfortable in. However, slowly his eyes would get used to the amazing clarity of real colours, objects and animals. Finally, he would emerge from the cave and see the sun for what it really is – the source of life – including (indirectly) the shadows formed in the cave. It would be then that, for the first time, the prisoner would understand the truth about knowledge and reality.

The prisoner who made this journey would no longer care to return to the world of shadows from which he came. If he were to go back to the other prisoners to tell them what he had found, they would consider him insane. They would also notice that his journey had weakened his ability to predict the movement of the shadows, and after spending time in the sunlight he would find it more difficult to become accustomed to the darkness of his old life. If he were to try to convince the others to join him, he would be put to death for leading them astray (note here the similarities between the reaction to the returning prisoner and the reason Socrates was put to death, as explained earlier).

16 PHILOSOPHICAL LANGUAGE AND THOUGHT

> **Exercise**
> 1. What comparisons can you draw between the cave and the world we live in?
> 2. To what extent do you agree with the picture painted here of reality?
> 3. What does this say about the human condition?
> 4. Is reason or experience more important when seeking the truth?
> 5. Does this analogy sufficiently incentivize people to seek the truth or does it miss the argument that 'ignorance is bliss'?

Explanation of the Analogy of the Cave

- *The Chained Prisoners* The prisoners represent mankind, chained up and trapped by the superficial world of desires and temptations. People are told what to think by their culture, language, experience, politicians, etc. They have never tried to discover true knowledge, nor do they have a desire to, as it does not even occur to them that there could be more to life than what they see before their eyes.
- *The Shadowy Play* The shadows are created by 'real' objects being paraded behind the wall and in front of the fire, reflecting the shadowy images onto the cave wall in front of the prisoners. As the prisoners' heads are chained so that they are only able to see the shadow on the wall and not the actual object, they only see a mere shadow of the perfect image (for example, a shadow of a book as opposed to a real book). In the same way, we acquire knowledge of concepts by our experience of the physical object but are mistaken if we think that the concepts we grasp are the same as the real thing (i.e. the Form).
- *The Cave* The cave may be seen as a symbol of our imprisoned, immortal soul. Everything we need to become enlightened and achieve true knowledge is within us already – we just have to work to unlock it.
- *The Journey Out of the Cave* The journey out of the cave describes the struggle for the soul to become enlightened with true knowledge – just as the prisoner's eyes becoming accustomed to the light is hard, so is our journey from comfortable ignorance to wisdom. There is a suggestion that, for some, the journey will not be completed as it is too difficult – the pain may be too much to bear and they might return to the comfort of what they already 'know' to be true. However, for others, the force compelling them to seek true understanding helps them to break through the pain and discomfort and make a discovery of knowledge.
- *The Sun* The last thing the escaped prisoner accustoms his eyes to is the bright light of the sun. Here, the sun represents the Form of the Good, which for Plato is the ultimate truth/knowledge. Once he sees the sun, he realizes that life in the Cave was an illusion and that any achievements made there are meaningless as they do not represent reality in any way.
- *The Outside World* Once the prisoner has left the cave, he will be blinded by the sun and will not be able to see anything. However, his eyes will become accustomed to the brightness eventually, and he will slowly begin to see shadows and outlines of objects, before developing the ability to see clearly and

Ancient Philosophical Influences: Plato

distinguish one object from the next. This represents the fact that true knowledge may be scary and alarming at first, but we become accustomed to it and it soon sits comfortably in our mind.

- *The Return of the Prisoner* Although the prisoner may want to remain outside the cave and bask in the sun's rays (or his newfound knowledge), Plato states that he has a *duty* to return to the cave and let others know the truth, even though he will stumble in the dark and his words will make no sense to the other prisoners. Although returning to the people in the cave (ignorant people) will be difficult – some may mock him, others may fear him, some may even want him dead because he is trying to bring about change – it is a necessary task. The enlightened must learn how to see in the dark again in order to communicate with the other prisoners – or the enlightened must be able to view the world from the standpoint of ignorant people in order to communicate and lead them from the darkness of the cave (ignorance) to the light of the sun (knowledge).

Plato uses this analogy to illustrate his Theory of the Forms; however, not every point is explained by him and some aspects are open to interpretation. He is presenting his Dualistic view of the world through the World of the Forms and the natural, observable world of our senses.

The Meaning of the Analogy of the Cave

Plato's analogy emphasizes the difference between the appearance of the world (as represented by the scene inside the cave) and the reality behind this appearance (represented by the outside world). Each feature within the analogy develops this contrast in order to convince the reader of the importance of making the effort to discover reality, by making the point that everybody is convinced that what they are looking at is real. The prisoners' knowledge is based exclusively on their sense of sight and sound and, as this is all they have ever known to be true, they accept it without question.

Plato's analogy teaches that empirical knowledge (knowledge gained through the senses) is flawed. It does not show the true reality of things – appearances can be deceptive. By contrast, the escaped prisoner has discovered reality. After emerging into the real world outside the cave, his power of reasoning leads him to a philosophical understanding of the truth. This is a priori knowledge based on reason alone and not making any references to (arguably) flawed sense perception. Plato can be seen to be pointing out the need to distinguish between the two very different realms of appearance and reality. He uses this analogy to show that the situation the prisoners are in is no different from the situation we are in – humans are prisoners, trapped within a world of flawed sensory 'knowledge', and we need to be set free in order to see the Forms clearly. However, we are so bound by our own way of thinking by using sense experience that we are unable to see the Forms clearly. It would take a very wise and enlightened being to be able to see the Forms and free themselves from the prison of the physical world.

Plato believes that the people carrying the objects behind the wall are just as ignorant as the prisoners. They too are bound to believing that they are playing a part in the real world; however, the things they are carrying are still mere reflections of the Forms and this shows that these people have no more knowledge of truth than the chained prisoners. Plato uses this analogy to criticize leaders (politicians and philosophers) by arguing that they are trying to lead people towards the truth when they have no knowledge of the truth themselves.

When the prisoner is released, he is blinded initially by the light of the fire; then, as he emerges from the cave, it becomes more and more unbearable as the glare of the sun blinds him. Here, Plato is showing that at times people can be reluctant to be taught and to gain knowledge. It is much easier to sit in the comfort of your own ignorance than be blinded by true knowledge. It can be difficult for both the teacher and the person being taught – at times, the teacher may have to drag people out of their ignorance and into the shiny bright light of true knowledge. However, just as the prisoner's eyes slowly adjust to the glare of the sun and he begins to see the 'real' world for what it truly is, we also come round slowly to the glare of true knowledge and become more comfortable with our understanding of reality.

There is a sense that, once the prisoner has become accustomed to the glare of the sun, he wants to remain on the 'outside' and never return to the cave (remain in knowledge and never return to ignorance). He feels a sense of duty to return to the prisoners to tell them what they are missing and try to free them, so that they too can escape the ignorance of life inside the cave and achieve true knowledge of the outside world. When he returns below the ground once again, he has difficulty seeing – illustrating the difficulty of seeing the mere reflection of the Forms in the sensory world. Although the released prisoner is the only person who knows the truth, on his return the others mock him. Plato states that they would kill him if they could, possibly referring to the fact that the general view of philosophers in Ancient Greece was that they were odd and were to be mocked. He may also be referring again to the death of his teacher Socrates here, as Socrates put his own knowledge of truth before his life.

Although it is in the prisoner's own interests to remain outside the cave, he returns to lead others out. It is this quality, according to Plato, that makes a true leader – a person with knowledge who puts the interest of others first, rather than leading for the sake of having power and furthering their own interests.

Not only does the Analogy of the Cave raise questions about true Forms of knowledge, it also raises questions regarding who is the most suitable ruler of society (given Plato was distrustful of politicians at the time, as they had sentenced Socrates to death). He also raises the issue of the fact that, at times, some people are very happy and comfortable to remain living in ignorance without true knowledge of the Forms, and distinguishes between the wise who struggle for knowledge and the ignorant who remain living in a mere shadow.

> **Exercise**
>
> Why would anyone want to live in ignorance of the way things really are in the world? Team up with a classmate and create a short dialogue to explain both sides of the argument.

Ancient Philosophical Influences: Plato

The Analogy of the Sun

The second analogy Plato uses to explain the Form of the Good is the Analogy of the Sun. Take a moment to look around the room you are in. Make a list of what you see. Think about the colours observed, different patterns, shapes, outlines, shadows. Then ask yourself this: what do you need in place to be able to see all of these things?

For Plato, three things needed to be in order:

1. An object to be seen
2. Eyes to see the object
3. Light to illuminate the object

Just as in the physical, observable world there are objects that can be seen using the medium of all of the above, so in the intelligible world there are things that can be seen though the soul or the 'mind's eye'. Sun is to sight and physical objects as the Good is to thought and intelligible objects.

In Plato's Analogy of the Sun, he says that the Form of the Good is the source of all knowledge. Without the Form of the Good, there can be no other Forms in existence (as all other Forms have an aspect of the Form of the Good associated with them).

Taking this further, you could attempt to look around a room when all of the lights were off, in the dead of night, when it is plunged into darkness. It would be impossible to see anything clearly at all without the light of the sun guiding your vision. Equally, without the 'bright light' of the Form of the Sun guiding your path to knowledge, one is unable to see clearly and nothing will be known as truth. For Plato, for anything to be known at all it has to be understood in light of the Form of the Good. As a result of everything participating in the Form of the Good, there is an ultimate aim to return to this Form, bringing an ethical approach to Plato's understanding. Knowledge of the Form of the Good enables the philosopher to seek out the good in all situations – good actions, good morals – and ultimately an understanding of the Form of the Good will lead one to aim to become a better (or 'good') person.

> **Exercise**
> How would you define the word 'good'? What kinds of thing might it refer to? Give reasons for your views.

The Analogy of the Divided Line

The Analogy of the Divided Line is a continuation of the Analogy of the Sun and is meant to be read and understood with reference to the Analogy of the Cave.

20 | PHILOSOPHICAL LANGUAGE AND THOUGHT

The Divided Line analogy uses a literal 'divided line' to discuss four different types of 'object' and the way in which we come to have any kind of empirical or a priori knowledge of what exists (or, indeed, how we form opinions on what exists).

As represented by the diagram below, line AB is the line representing conjectures. Line BC is representative of our knowledge of the physical world. Line CD is knowledge of mathematical 'truths' (shapes, trigonometry, etc.) and line DE represents our knowledge of philosophical ideals – especially those of the Forms, focusing on the most important: the Form of the Good.

According to Plato, the lengths of the lines differ in size according to the importance of the knowledge gained. As seen in the diagram, line AB is the shortest line, insinuating that beliefs are the lesser form of knowledge. This line would be represented by the prisoners in the cave who had no knowledge of the outside world and who spent their lives believing that the only reality was what was in front of their eyes.

Lines BC and CD are longer than AB, showing that, although empirical knowledge of the physical world and mathematical 'proofs' are more important than belief, they are of equal value to one another and therefore can be seen to be co-dependent on each other. This would be represented by the people (politicians, perhaps?) holding the objects behind the prisoners and in front of the fire. They have a certain amount of developed knowledge – they certainly have more understanding of reality than the chained prisoners – but they are still living in an artificial world of ignorance.

The longest line, and therefore the most highly rated, is line DE – the line representing philosophical knowledge. This relates to ideals such as knowledge of the Realm of the Forms, philosophical enquiry and debate. As one may guess, this line is represented by the escaped prisoner who seeks the truth and returns to share the light of knowledge with those who are bound by their ignorance.

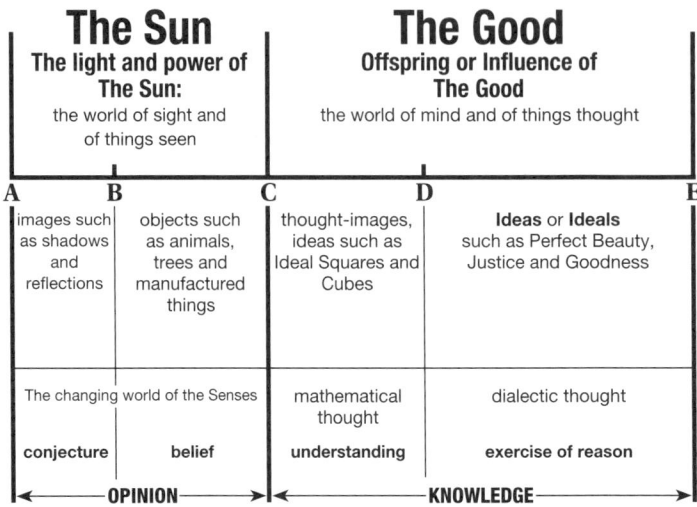

Problems with the Theory of Forms

Is there such a thing as an 'absolute good'?

Central to Plato's theory is the existence of the 'Form of the Good' – an eternal and immutable standard of moral goodness which can be achieved using a priori reasoning. Once individuals have achieved full knowledge of this goodness (which is a possibility for Plato), then there would be no debate over moral issues as there would be a firm agreement across the board over what is right and wrong.

This may be questioned by people who hold a more relativist view and do not ascribe to the belief that there are certain and absolute rights and wrongs. They argue that moral goodness is a posteriori (through experience) and that there can be no absolutes. For example, something that is deemed as rude in one culture may, in a different culture, be regarded as polite. The morals of society change with the development of the modern world and our understanding of moral goodness needs to change along with these developments. The rise in feminism is one example of this change – in the early 1900s, women were not expected to work, they were not allowed to vote and their sphere was restricted to the home. This was widely accepted by society as that was the 'role' of the woman, whilst the man went out to work to earn money. Fast-forward to the year 2017 and this concept is simply outdated, immoral, illegal and deplorable for many, as it is now widely accepted that women are equal to men and have the same rights.

The Forms and the physical world

Throughout Plato's theory, there appears to be no clear link between the Realm of the Forms and the world which we only know of by appearances – the 'imitation world of shadows'. There appears be a sense of 'gloom in ignorance' – that the world we live in is compared to a cave in which prisoners are chained by their ignorance. Here, Plato is seemingly ignoring the concept that at times people may agree with the saying 'Ignorance is bliss.' Even if our sensory world is not reality, it does not mean to say that it cannot be enjoyed in full. In his book *The Open Society and its Enemies* (vol. I: *The Spell of Plato*, Routledge, 1945), **Karl Popper (1902–94)** argues that Plato is trying to find some comfort in absolute certainty – that by holding on to absolute and immutable concepts, Plato is simply hiding away from the fact that the world is an unknown entity, and whilst this lack of certainty can be terrifying, it makes more sense to find true knowledge in our world of changing reality, rather than seeking an immortal world of Forms.

Materialist view

There is an argument stating that, although Plato references the Realm of the Forms, there is no empirical evidence of such a world. Materialists (who support the idea that there is nothing else in existence other than physical matter – see chapter 3, p. 41)

22 PHILOSOPHICAL LANGUAGE AND THOUGHT

would argue that, without such evidence, Plato's theory can never be proven and, as such, is wrong. As W. S. Wilson states in *Reclaiming Communist Philosophy*:

> The dialectical materialist view, in opposition to Platonic mysticism, is that form and matter are inseparable but at the same time distinct. The form that matter takes may be the form of beauty. Beauty exists, but never apart from beautiful things. Goodness exists, but never apart from good people. Thought exists, but not apart from brains.
> (Wilson, *Reclaiming Communist Philosophy: The Dialectics of Nature*, Information Age Publishing, Inc., 2016, p. 33)

Here, we see a suggestion that, although there is no argument as to the non-existence of concepts such as beauty, thought and goodness, there is an argument to suggest that such concepts only exist when attached to a physical entity, therefore negating the requirement for Plato's Realm of the Forms. Our only true knowledge comes from what we can experience. We can have no knowledge of anything beyond our realms of understanding.

Are there real forms of everything?

Plato argues that the world of the senses is a mere shadow of the real world in the Realm of the Forms. Everything we can see around us is a pale imitation of the perfect object in the Forms. If this is the case, could it be argued that there are Forms for absolutely everything we come across in our sensual world, including nonsensical items such as a shoe, a box or a cushion? Plato does not really reflect on the existence of such mundane material objects, preferring to focus on concepts such as beauty, goodness and truth. However, **Bertrand Russell (1872–1970)** states:

> (Plato) expounds the theory of ideas (forms); he is sure that there are ideas of likeness, justice, beauty, and goodness; he is not sure that there is an idea of man; and he rejects with indignation the suggestion that there could be ideas of such things as hair and mud and dirt – though, he adds, there are times when he thinks that there is nothing without an idea. He runs away from this view because he is afraid of falling into a bottomless pit of nonsense.
> (B. Russell, *History of Western Philosophy*, Routledge, 1991, p. 127)

Here, we see that even Plato struggled with his theory – at times suggesting that there has to be a Form for everything, yet at other times he does not seem so sure.

This may also raise the question of whether there has to be a perfect Form of such things as hate or disease? However, applying Augustine's logic of evil as a privation, we can skirt around this question with the suggestion that such negative concepts are merely the privation of the Form of the Good, which we turn away from due to the ignorance of humanity.

Awareness of Forms

Arguably, if one were to accept that there was an eternal world of Forms containing the ultimate truth, how would one ever come to a comprehensive understanding of these whilst living in the world of the senses? If our only true understanding of the

Ancient Philosophical Influences: Plato

Forms is from our soul living amongst the realm before achieving bodily existence, how are we able to gain sufficient knowledge of such concepts as truth, beauty and goodness for it to have any positive impact on our lives as we live them now?

FURTHER READING

Julia Annas, *Plato – A Very Short Introduction*. Oxford University Press, 2003

Roy Jackson, *Plato: A Complete Introduction: Teach Yourself*. Teach Yourself Books, 2016

Rebecca Newberger Goldstein, *Plato at the Googleplex: Why Philosophy Won't Go Away*. Atlantic Books, 2015

Thomas Taylor, *An Introduction to the Philosophy and Writings of Plato*. Aeterna Press, 2015

William A. Welton (ed.), *Plato's Philosophy – Varieties of Interpretations*. Lexington Books, 2003

Thought Points

1. Summarize Plato's Theory of Forms, then explain it to someone else.

2. Explain what you think are the major criticisms of the Theory of Forms.

3. Draw your own diagram of the Analogy of the Cave.

4. Explain how the analogies of the Sun and the Divided Line relate to that of the Cave.

5. 'Universals do not exist.' Do you agree? Give reasons for your answer.

6. 'Plato's Theory of Forms provides everything we need for understanding the development of western philosophy.' Discuss.

CHAPTER 2

Ancient Philosophical Influences: Aristotle and Causation

LEARNING OUTCOMES

In this chapter you will learn about
- the philosophical views of Aristotle, in relation to
  - his understanding of reality
  - the four causes (material, formal, efficient and final)
  - the Prime Mover (and connections between it and the Final Cause)

Introduction

Aristotle was a pupil of Plato, as Plato had been a pupil of Socrates. His philosophical works are noted for the extraordinary variety of subjects he wrote on, and are characterized by careful observation of the physical world around us. He paid close attention to defining and classifying data. He was very highly regarded in his field, and Dante describes him as: 'a master of those who know, sitting amid his family of Philosophers' (Dante Alighieri, *Inferno*, Penguin, 2006, p. 131).

Ancient Philosophical Influences: Aristotle and Causation

Aristotle (384–322 BCE) was born in Stagira at the northern periphery of the Greek Empire. His father was the physician to the King of Macedonia and wanted his son to be a doctor too. At the age of 18, Aristotle joined Plato's Academy. Through his connections, he became a personal tutor to a 13-year-old who would become Alexander the Great, and Aristotle was later to set up his own school, the Lyceum, in Athens in 334 BCE. By this time, he began to diverge from Plato's ideas. Following Plato's death, his nephew became head of the Academy, rather than Aristotle. This may have been because Aristotle was a non-citizen and could therefore not own property in the city. Aristotle is seen as an early empiricist. He comes to base judgements more on sense perceptions than on pure reason, pioneering the study of biology and classifying types of objects in the natural world. Where Plato's students had focused on geometry or the harmonics of sound, Aristotle was more practical, performing dissections (his father may have given him some lessons in medicine, perhaps even surgical techniques) and categorizing knowledge in a more systematic way. In some ways, Aristotle was a precursor to science and he wrote hundreds of books on a very wide variety of subjects, including physics, biology, economics, logic, ethics, zoology, music and poetry. While some of these may now be obsolete, his ideas on philosophy are still relevant and influential today.

Although Aristotle had been a pupil of Plato's, he rejected Plato's concept of two worlds, the other being inhabited by objects of knowledge. Aristotle taught that there is only one world – the world of our experience – a world of inexhaustible fascination and wonder. He believed that whatever was outside the realms of our experience is utterly irrelevant to us. As we have no way to validate what is outside our experience, so we have no way of referring to it or talking about it, therefore it cannot (and, indeed, should not) enter into our discourse. He held firm to the belief that all of our knowledge begins with an examination of the world around us.

Aristotle's Empiricism and Plato's Rationalism

Aristotle was born fifteen years after the death of Socrates, so although Socrates' work did influence Aristotle to some extent, it did not have the same profound impact as it did on Plato. Aristotle held a very deep respect for his teacher, Plato, although he profoundly disagreed with him with regards to the Theory of Forms, and is believed to have said 'Plato is dear to me, but dearer still is truth'.

In Part One of his book *Metaphysics*, Aristotle introduces his work by stating the following:

> All men by nature desire to know. An indication of this is the delight we take in our senses; for even apart from their usefulness they are loved for themselves; and above all others, the sense of sight. For not only with a view to action, but even when we are not going to do anything, we prefer seeing (one might say) to everything else. The reason is that this, most of all the senses, makes us know and brings to light many differences between things.

(Aristotle, *Metaphysics*, 1)

In this opening paragraph, we can note a very different approach to philosophy from that taught by Plato. Indeed, it is recognized that Aristotle was one of the first Empiricists (people who believe all knowledge is ultimately based on sense experience). Whereas Plato sought a realm outside the sensible world (world of our senses) to understand our existence, Aristotle found this understanding by conducting a detailed examination of the world. He makes use of the senses and empirical evidence in the world around him to reach his conclusions.

The method Aristotle uses is *per genus et per differentia* (meaning 'through type and difference') as a method for defining things. For example, suppose I looked at a goldfish. The first thing I would use to define the creature would be my sight to decide which type of animal it was – in this instance, a fish. This would be its type (or genus). I would then compare it to other types of fish and note the differences it has from fish such as clown fish or catfish. The more closely I examined all of these differences, then the greater my knowledge would become of all the fish studied in this process of definition. This slow and careful process of categorization would lead me to a closer understanding of the creature in question. J. S. Mill supported Aristotle's theory, stating: 'Definitions of this kind are what logicians have had in view when they laid down the rule that definitions should be per genus et per differentiam. "Differentia" seldom being taken to mean the peculiarities constitutive of the species' (Mill, *A System of Logic*, CreateSpace Independent Publishing Platform, 2016, p. 95).

Another difference in style from Plato is in Aristotle's view of how we achieve knowledge. For Plato, there is one type of certain knowledge and this is achieved through a full understanding of the Forms. This type of knowledge is strictly theoretical and intellectual. For Aristotle, this is not the case. Aristotle does not believe that our knowledge comes through our soul having memories of concepts from its time in the Realm of the Forms. He believes that we achieve knowledge through being taught and shown skills. We are taught mathematics and develop our skills as musicians through learning, hard work and practice. As opposed to knowledge being innate within us and education being the simple drawing out of our prior knowledge from the World of the Forms, for Aristotle, learning is observing and repeating what we have seen. However, he does not believe there is only one kind of knowledge. As David Bronstein states: 'To have unqualified... knowledge of x is to know that y... is the cause of x... Aristotle does not mean this to define knowledge (*gnosis*) in general, but a specific kind of knowledge: scientific knowledge (*epistemē*)... For one thing, the objects of scientific knowledge are necessary, whereas the objects of other types of knowledge (e.g. perception) are contingent' (Bronstein, *Aristotle on Knowledge and Learning*, Oxford University Press, 2016, p. 36).

We see here that, for Aristotle, knowledge was based on so much more than just one theoretical point. There are different ways of learning – through theory *and* practice. For example, just because I have a lot of theoretical knowledge about music and I have the ability to read sheet music, it does not automatically follow that I am an excellent pianist. To achieve that skill would take years and years of practice and much time spent observing and listening to others play. Aristotle believed that different types of knowledge required different skill sets – for example, the knowledge of a musician varies hugely from that of a scientist, and is different again from that of a mathematician. These different forms of knowledge are distinct – it is quite often the case that those who are especially gifted in the sciences are not gifted in the same sense with the humanities (and vice versa).

One of Aristotle's greatest discoveries was his demonstration of the fact that the Earth was a sphere. Using empirical observation, he observed the moon eclipse, watching the shape of the shadow moving across the face of the moon. Beginning with his observation, he was able to reflect on what could cause the shape of these shadows. He concluded that the only possible object between the moon and the sun was the Earth, and so came to the conclusion that the Earth had to be spherical in order for the eclipse to happen, thus providing empirical evidence for the shape of the Earth. Arguably, this knowledge could never have been reached by Plato's theoretical means, so this empirical method appears more successful in discovering knowledge about the 'sensible' world we live in.

[annotation: evaluative point & implications in showing it to be more applicable]

The Four Causes

> **Exercise**
> Explain how each of these objects came into existence. Identify and list as many contributing factors as you can.

A major part of Aristotle's philosophy was concerned with the nature of things and how we explain the way things came into existence. In the above task, you probably noted a number of factors through which the objects came into existence, from the materials used to put them together, to the design by which they were made, to the original purpose intended for the products. Clearly, having flour, sugar and eggs sat separately is very different from having a sponge cake.

Although Aristotle rejected Plato's theory that all things are how they are because they belong to the 'Form' of that thing (for example, a dog is an imperfect reflection of the perfect dog in the world of the Forms), Aristotle was still concerned with *why* things exist as they do. As Jonathan Lear states of Aristotle: 'The expression "the why" is suggestive of the intimate link Aristotle saw between man and the world. Man is by nature a questioner of the world: he seeks to understand the world the way it is. The world for its part reciprocates: it "answers" man's questions' (Jonathan Lear, *Aristotle: The Desire to Understand*, Cambridge University Press, 2011, p. 26).

This interest in the 'why' of the world led Aristotle to suggest that there are four different types of cause (or explanation) regarding why any object exists in the world.

PHILOSOPHICAL LANGUAGE AND THOUGHT

In modern philosophy, these explanations have come to be referred to as the '**Four Causes**'.

As stated above, Aristotle, unlike Plato, did not believe there are two separate realms. As an empiricist, he believed that the world we live in is the only place in which we can have true knowledge. This is because it is through our sense experience that we come to a full understanding of how and why things are the way they are.

- **Form:** Whereas Plato believed 'Form' was an ideal separate from a substance itself, Aristotle believed that form was found within the item itself. Form is the item's structure and characteristics and can be perceived through our senses.
- **Substance:** Aristotle referred to substance as the material from which things are made. This differs from form as form is the *essence* of an object (i.e. that a table has four legs and a flat surface on the top), whereas substance is what the object is *made* from (i.e. a table is made from wood, nails and glue). This can also be referred to as *matter*.
- **Prime Matter:** Prime matter refers to anything that lacks a well-defined form – it is not organized into any particular structure. It has *matter* but no *form*.

> **Four Causes:** The term given to Aristotle's theory that there are four different kinds of cause to explain why things exist.

After considering the facts of the above, Aristotle was led to one of the most important aspects of his philosophy, that of the development of potentiality and actuality. This then provided the basis from which to discuss the beginning of all things – The Four Causes:

1. The Material Cause
2. The Formal Cause
3. The Efficient Cause
4. The Final Cause

The Material Cause – *What is it made of?*

The Material Cause is the substance from which a thing is made or created. All matter has the potential to change. If we use the example of a book – a book is made of paper. The paper used (the matter) had the potential to be a number of other things – fuel for a fire, torn into confetti, etc. However, in this instance, the matter was used to write on and create a book. Aristotle uses the following examples to illustrate this cause:

> The bronze is the material cause of a statue.
> The silver is the material cause of a bowl.
> The letters are the material cause of a syllable.
> The parts are the material cause of the whole.
> The premises are the material cause of the conclusion.
> (Aristotle, *Physics*, Green Lion Press, 1999, p. xxv)

> **Material cause:** The substance from which a thing is made or created.

Having the knowledge of what something is made of, however, does not give us all the necessary information for full knowledge of the thing. We may understand that the book is made from paper, ink and glue, but this knowledge gives us no understanding of what exactly a book is.

The Formal Cause – *What are the characteristics?*

Formal Cause: The characteristics of an object.

In order to understand this, it is helpful to think of it as the question 'What form does it have?' For example, a silver bowl does not become a bowl because it is made of silver (it could be made of a number of different properties). It is a bowl because the material is shaped into the *form* of a bowl. If it were not shaped into this form, the material would simply be a lump of silver.

It is important not to confuse Aristotle's 'form' with the Forms in Plato's writings. For Aristotle, *form* is not a transcendent concept in which all other parts are mere imitations, as in Plato's thinking. *Form* for Aristotle is **immanent** (of this world). For example, a sculptor may have an idea about what he wants to create – this idea would be classed as the Formal Cause.

Immanent: God existing within and sustaining the universe.

The Efficient Cause – *How does it happen?*

Efficient Cause: How an object comes into being.

If we are to keep the example of the statue (from above), once the sculptor has the idea for the characteristics of the statue (Formal Cause) and has collected materials such as bronze (Material Cause), does the statue then create itself? The answer is a resounding 'no'. There has to be an 'Efficient Cause' to turn the material and ideas (potentiality) into a statue (actuality). In this example, it would be the sculptor. A statue is a statue because it is in the form of a statue made by somebody – leading to the idea of cause and effect. Aristotle referred to this cause as the *primary source of change*. He was also aware that Efficient Causes can be found in nature too. The natural process of growth and change may be said to be the Efficient Cause of a rose bush.

Teleology: The English word 'teleology' comes from the Greek word *telos*. *Telos* means 'aim' or 'purpose', or the 'result' of a course of action.

The Final Cause – *What is it for? What is its purpose?*

Final Cause: The purpose of an object.

Helen Lang states: 'The most obvious locus of Aristotle's **teleology** is his doctrine of the final cause, the goal, purpose, end, or that for the sake of which. The final cause, by any of its names, is the end of all motion within things . . . in short, the final cause is in every sense the most important of the four causes' (Helen Lang, *Aristotle's Physics and Its Medieval Varieties*, p. 124).

This cause is arguably the most difficult to understand. If we consider the notion of 'cause and effect', we can see a relationship between events or things where one thing or action comes about as a result of another. It is the idea that, for every action, there is a reaction (illustrated by a domino rally – once one domino is pushed, it causes another to do so, and another, until all of the dominos have fallen).

Aristotle, however, thought differently. He understood the purpose for which something exists as a cause. A sculptor makes a statue for the viewing pleasure of others or to commemorate a special event. The statue is made for the sake of its use – to fulfil its ultimate purpose (or *telos*). For Aristotle, the nature of everything is 'purposive'. We can understand this because, generally, anything we do as humans is to fulfil a purpose. Take the following example:

- You make detailed notes in class for the purpose of revision . . .
- For the purpose of passing your exams . . .
- For the purpose of gaining a place at university . . .
- For the purpose of gaining a good degree . . .
- For the purpose of getting a good job . . .

The list could continue on for many more points. The purpose of me listening to music is for my enjoyment. I make cakes for the purpose of eating them. As humans, we can grasp this concept of purpose easily as it is something that makes sense to us.

This theory (like any which centres its judgements of reality based on purpose) is *teleological* in nature (coming from the Greek word *telos* meaning 'end', 'purpose' or 'goal'). Aristotle believed everything in nature had a purpose, or end goal, and that if we were to examine the human body we would find purpose to all of its parts. For example, without nerves we would not feel pain and may therefore cause damage to our body without realizing. Without eyelids, we would constantly get dust and grit in our eyes which would cause damage to our eyesight. Given the belief that all parts of a person serve a purpose, one can see how Aristotle jumps to the conclusion that each person as a whole has a purpose, and a good human is one who has fulfilled this purpose.

> **Exercise**
>
> Try to identify the four causes of the following:
> - Cup
> - Chair
> - Clock
> - Gun
> - Watch
> - Computer
> - Dog
> - Robot

The Prime Mover

Just as Aristotle suggested that everything within the universe had a purpose, he followed this by assuming that the whole universe has a purpose (connecting this to the idea that, just as each part of a person has a purpose, so must a person as a whole). Like his predecessor Heraclitus, Aristotle believed that the world was in a state of constant flux. He observed that, in order for movement to occur, then there has to be a mover, and for Aristotle, movement meant more than simply travelling from A to B.

Ancient Philosophical Influences: Aristotle and Causation

It could also include changing, cooling, melting, etc. Aristotle argued that, behind every chain of events, there has to be a cause of these events that has caused all of the movement within the universe.

For Aristotle, the Final Cause of the universe must be the Prime Mover. David Bradshaw puts Aristotle's Argument in the following way:

> The argument [for a Prime Mover] can be summarized as follows. (1) Time cannot come into being or pass away, for that would involve the paradox of a moment before time or a moment after time. (2) Given Aristotle's own definition of time as 'the number of motion in respect of before and after' or any other definition linking time inseparably to motion, motion also cannot come into being or pass away, and so must be continuous. (3) There must be a mover to cause this continuous motion. (4) The mover cannot merely be something capable of causing the motion but must actively do so. (5) Even for the mover to act continually is not sufficient if its substance includes potency or is potency, for then the mover could possibly not be, and so could not guarantee eternal motion. (6) Therefore, the very substance of the mover must be actuality.
> (David Bradshaw, *Aristotle East and West: Metaphysics and the Division of Christendom*, Cambridge University Press, 2008, p. 25)

Here, we must note that the concept of the Prime Mover is what Aristotle views to be God. Upon further examination of the Prime Mover, one must see that the Prime Mover is distinct from, and certainly different from, the concept of God within the Abrahamic religions.

Whereas the God of the Abrahamic religions is both immanent and transcendent, perfect, eternal and everlasting, having an intimate relationship with his creation, the Prime Mover is decidedly different. For one, the Prime Mover is transcendent and not the immanent God involved with creation that Abrahamic religions believe in. God does not listen to prayer as he is not interested in the world, as the Prime Mover is seen to be pure actuality and therefore incapable of change. In contemplating the world and being concerned with the requests of human beings, that would mean the Prime Mover would have to have the potential to see or think differently, which, by the definition of pure actuality, he cannot. Bechler paraphrases Aristotle, saying, 'Pure actuality must be assumed as a pre-condition for the initiation of motion in the world' (Z. Bechler, *Aristotle's Theory of Actuality*, State University of New York Press, 1995, p. 209). Because of the notion of pure actuality (and, as a result of this, being incapable of change), the Prime Mover is at times referred to as the 'Unmoved Mover'.

As the Prime Mover is the ultimate cause of all things, it works as a Final Cause as opposed to an Efficient Cause. In other words, as opposed to causing the initial movement in the universe by giving it some kind of shove, or initiating the process of creation by pushing the first star into the sky, it is the purpose (*telos*) of all subsequent motion. This notion is an important factor in Aristotle's work, for if the Prime Mover were an Efficient Cause (i.e. giving the universe a push start), then it would be affected by this movement itself and would change – which, given the fact that the Prime Mover has to have fulfilled all potential to change as it is pure actuality, is impossible.

The key idea when considering Aristotle's view on motion is 'change'. Motion is more than the simple movement from the lounge to the bedroom. Motion is far more complex. It can be the change from a chrysalis to a butterfly; an ice cube melting in a cold drink; water turning into steam under intense heat pressure. All of these examples indicate signs of motion in Aristotle's thinking. Given that the Prime Mover is pure actuality and incapable of change or movement, how can it be that it is the cause of the first motion in the universe? For Aristotle, the Prime Mover causes movement by attraction. To illustrate this, let us consider a saucer of milk. If I were to place a saucer of milk on my kitchen floor, then, even though this milk would not move in any way, shape or form, it would cause my cat to move as the cat is drawn to the milk. Even though the milk attracts the cat and causes motion, the milk is not affected or changed in any way. As Sir Isaac Newton explained it, 'action and reaction are equal and opposite'. The Unmoved Mover causes *movement by attraction*.

For Aristotle, if the Prime Mover were to be moved or affected in any way, then the whole process would fall apart. The Prime Mover must be unmoved, unaffected, pure actuality. The Final Cause is an object of desire and draws things to itself whilst remaining unchanged. Aristotle argues that the Prime Mover must have *necessary existence* (cannot be thought not to exist). This is due to the fact that, in being pure actuality, the Prime Mover is not able to depend on anything to bring about its existence (as this would involve a 'Pre' Prime Mover, which would be impossible). Also, it cannot be thought to ever be removed from existence as, if this were the case, once again it would have to have the potential to be changed by an outside force (which is, again, incompatible with the concept of pure actuality).

Again, as a result of the Prime Mover being pure actuality, Aristotle reaches the conclusion that the Prime Mover is Immaterial, as material has the potential to be acted upon and is therefore subject to change. This poses the question: with no physical body, what does the Prime Mover do? What does he think about? Aristotle sees the actions of the Prime Mover as purely spiritual and intellectual. So, in response to the question 'What does the Prime Mover do?', the answer is 'He thinks.' What does he think about? As he is pure actuality and incapable of *any* form of change, he thinks only about himself.

It is worthy of note that Aristotle's concept of the Prime Mover must not be confused with that of Aquinas, who also coins the phrase 'Prime Mover' to describe something that consciously and deliberately creates the world *ex nihilo* (from nothing).

Ex nihilo:
'*Ex nihilo nihil fit*' – 'Nothing comes from nothing.'

Similarities between Aristotle's Prime Mover and Plato's Form of the Good

Although, as we have seen, much of Aristotle's work was inspired by his teacher, Plato, Aristotle did not agree with everything Plato had argued for. This is particularly true with his emphasis on **Empiricism**. There are, however, some similarities that can be drawn between Aristotle's concept of the Prime Mover and Plato's Form of the Good. It may be argued that both of these concepts are seen to exist merely as an explanation

Empiricism:
The theory that all our knowledge of the world is based on sense experience. It is particularly associated with Bishop George Berkeley and David Hume.

of why things are the way they are. Both Plato and Aristotle continue along the lines of pre-Socratic thinkers in their concern with *change*. Plato was concerned with the discomfort and uncertainty of change, where Aristotle's concerns lay more with how to *explain* the reasons why change occurs. Perhaps Plato and Aristotle were both seeking to look for some sort of certainty in an uncertain and changing world.

Another similarity between the two philosophers is the fact that neither the Form of the Good nor the Prime Mover is responsible for the creation of the world, and neither sustain it. There is no personal relationship between humankind and the Form of the Good or the Prime Mover. It does not affect humanity, nor does humanity affect it.

Although both ideas attempt to provide a theory of the world, or 'fill a gap' in our understanding of the ever-changing world, neither offers any firm or direct proof that their theory is indeed the correct solution.

> **Exercise**
>
> Do you think Plato is more successful than Aristotle in building a theory of the world? Do you agree that the unifying feature they both share is 'change'? If not, is there another theme that links them?

Evaluating Aristotle's Prime Mover

Whilst Aristotle does link his concept of the Prime Mover with God, it does not interact in any way within the universe and is wholly transcendent. This raises questions for religious believers as it would question the purpose of prayer. If prayer is an invocation or act that seeks to activate a rapport with an object of worship (God) through deliberate communication, then, if the Prime Mover can only think on its own wondrous self, does prayer have no purpose? In that case, do religious believers waste their faith and hope in having an immanent, omnibenevolent God watching over them who is concerned for their wellbeing?

Again, if the Prime Mover (God) is unable to interact within the world, then how does one account for the many religious experiences documented throughout time?

There is some confusion raised over the fact that, as a philosopher who holds an empirical view of the world, Aristotle can justify that a Prime Mover (pure thought and immaterial) causes movement in the physical universe? Surely this is contradictory to the empirical view of the universe he holds?

However, Aristotle's argument for the Four Causes and the Prime Mover has been hugely influential with such philosophers as St Thomas Aquinas and the Cosmological argument (see chapter 4). His ideas coincide with the Christian view that God is omnipotent and eternal. However, if there is to be an argument that the universe must have had a cause, then it can be argued that the cause is the Prime Mover – removed and disassociated from the universe and playing no part in it beyond causing the first movement by attraction. This may go some way to explaining the existence of evil and suffering in the world – the Prime Mover is incapable of changing or affecting what is happening in the world. Therefore, 'God' can exist at the same time as evil and suffering without the issue of the inconsistent triad being raised.

Also, for Christianity it could be seen that Aristotle is providing empirical evidence for the existence of God. The laws of cause and effect are (arguably) unquestionable. Therefore, there must have been a starting point because infinite regression is impossible. This must be a necessary being (for it to exist prior to anything). Therefore, God exists. A huge leap in assumptions for some, but for others this is a valid argument.

Strengths of Aristotle's theories

Accessibility

In a scientific age of 'proof and probability', Aristotle's empirical view of the world is accessible to all. How and why things come to be are questions asked by most from a young age (those with younger siblings may recognize the constant question 'Why?' ringing in their ears!). Aristotle begins his argument with empirical evidence, suggesting that a thing's form belongs in the realm of our senses rather than in an entirely separate, non-physical Realm of the Forms as in Plato's thinking.

Purpose

As you can see from the task below, as we look around at everyday objects we can see that everything has a function to fulfil – a purpose. The pen you are using has the purpose of writing. The bag you are holding has the purpose of transporting your belongings. The shoes you are wearing have the purpose of keeping your feet covered, comfortable and well supported (supposedly. . .). Each thing you are using is fulfilling the purpose for which it was made, making the correct use of materials in order to fulfil this purpose.

> **Exercise**
> List five objects in the room you are in and explain the purpose they fulfil.

Science

As scientists seek to understand more and more about the world, it would appear Aristotle has understood the concept of motion and change correctly. In his book, *Scientific Materialism*, Mario Bunge states: 'Science denies the thesis that matter is inert and supports instead the philosophical generalization that all matter is continually in some process of change or another' (Springer, 2013, p. 5). Here, we can note the scientific support of Aristotle's theory that all matter is in a process of continual change from potentiality to actuality, and taking on characteristics of new form.

Weaknesses of Aristotle's Theories

The fallacy of composition

> **Fallacy of composition:** The mistaken assumption that the whole must share the same properties as its parts.

In the book, *Macroeconomic Methodology*, Jesper Jespersen identifies the **fallacy of composition** as occurring when 'One incorrectly attempts to generalize from a relationship that is true for each individual, but is not true for the whole' (Edward Elgar Publishing, 2011, p. 180). Therefore, the fallacy of composition is an error in reasoning. When Aristotle states that, because each part of the body has a purpose, then the body as a whole has a purpose, he is partaking in the fallacy of composition – just because each body part has a purpose does not necessarily mean that the body as a whole has a purpose.

Indeed, one may reject the original statement that each part of the body has a purpose. Take the appendix, for example – many people live very happy and fulfilled lives having had it removed as it is a superfluous organ. It is entirely unnecessary for the continued existence of mankind. Another example would be that of the male nipple – utterly redundant for the continuation of the species. So, it can be argued that the fallacy of composition weakens Aristotle's theories.

Purpose

Questions may also be raised about Aristotle's use of the term 'purpose'. One can argue that people can have purpose – they can decide what it is they want to achieve and then work towards that point in order to fulfil the purpose they have set for themselves (for example, working hard at a summer job and taking extra shifts in order to save money for the purpose of travelling the world). However, humanity places these purposes onto themselves. These purposes are not innate. When I was born, I was not informed that the purpose of my life would be to become a teacher – I found my purpose through my experiences as a child and later as a student. I felt I had a purpose because I placed the ideal onto myself and worked to achieve my goal.

Can the same be said about inanimate objects? In my kitchen, I have a wooden bowl that has a purpose – it holds fruit. I could use it for other purposes, such as holding nuts or eggs or coins or paper clips, but the bowl, in itself, is just a bowl, and it is difficult to place innate purpose on a natural thing.

Efficient Cause

For Aristotle, the efficient cause of an object is the manner in which it was brought about. However, these assumptions made by Aristotle can be questioned. He *names* the process, but goes no further in *explaining* it. Something brings about a change in materials and we refer to this as the *efficient cause* – however, other than the name of the cause, we know little else.

This notion goes no further into explaining what *has* happened – rather, it only tells us that *something* has happened. Given that change in the universe involves chemical, physical, biological, man-made (etc.) changes, it would appear that the concept of an Efficient Cause is too broad and vague to be informative in any useful way.

The universe

When considering the concept of 'purpose' in more depth, it becomes difficult to argue that the universe has a purpose. In his 1948 radio debate with F. C. Copleston, Bertrand Russell famously stated 'I should say the universe is just there, and that is all.' This view suggests that Aristotle is looking to place purpose and value onto the universe when it is not there. The universe just 'is'.

In his book, *Darwin and the Theory of Evolution*, Robert Greenberger states:

> As much as man has looked up at the sky and wondered what is out there amongst the stars, he has also looked at the world in which he lives, and asked, 'How did I get here?' Man looked for ways to explain things that seemed unexplainable. Different populations around the world believed in a variety of gods, which helped explain how . . . the world was formed and why. . . . Yet as man learned more about the world through observation and scientific study, it became apparent that the myths believed by people of the past did not always support the evidence that the scientists discovered. By the nineteenth century, an entire branch of science grew around the idea that mankind evolved, or gradually changed, in response to its environment.

(Rosen Publishing Group, 2005, p. 4)

Arguably, it is a natural state to ponder our existence and the existence of the universe. It may be a terrifying realization that the only reason we are here is by complete random chance and survival of the fittest. Our universe is filled with vast expanses of nothingness and random lumps of rock and gas that serve no apparent end – how can it be suggested that there is a purpose in this? Could we argue that the only purpose in the universe is the purpose humanity places upon itself – the rest of the universe just 'exists'.

One Prime Mover

Aristotle jumps from the notion that all motion is subject to change (concept of cause and effect). If we look at the world around us, there are a number of examples of motion:

- The trees outside my window are blowing as a result of the wind.
- The child's bike wheels are turning as a result of the force of the child pushing on the pedals.
- The paint is moving from the tin to the fence as a result of the motion of the painter and brush strokes.

Looking at these examples, it is clear to see that, although Aristotle was correct in his assessment that the world was in constant flux, he may be incorrect to assume there is one single Prime Mover that started all of the motion.

All of the motion discussed above was caused by a different force, or action. Could the same not be said for the Prime Mover? If there are many possible causes of change, is it correct to jump from 'many possible causes' to 'single cause' (Prime Mover)?

Religion

Aristotle's idea of God is far removed from the God of the Abrahamic religions. Aristotle's God is not concerned with creation in any way – he simply caused the first movement (by attraction) and has been distant and apart from creation ever since.

For the Abrahamic religions, God is immanent. He cares for his creation: he suffered on earth through Jesus – which, from a Christian perspective, illustrates how directly involved God is with creation. The Bible reveals God's plan to deliver his creation from pain, sin and suffering. This idea of God is far removed from the impersonal, distant God of Aristotle.

There would be no point in praying to Aristotle's God, and one may question whether an indifferent and ineffective God would be worthy of any form of reverence or worship.

FURTHER READING

Aristotle, *The Metaphysics*. Penguin, 1998

Jonathan Barnes, *Aristotle: A Very Short Introduction*. Oxford University Press, 2000

D. Bradshaw, *Aristotle: East and West. Metaphysics and the Division of Christendom*. Cambridge University Press, 2004

H. Lang, *Aristotle's Physics and its Medieval Varieties*. State University of New York Press, 1992

J. Lear, *Aristotle: The Desire to Understand*. Cambridge University Press, 2011

Stanford Encyclopedia of Philosophy (2006, rev. 2012), 'Aristotle's Natural Philosophy', https://plato.stanford.edu/entries/aristotle-natphil.

A.E. Taylor, *Aristotle*. Dover Publications, 2003

Thought Points

1. Summarize the differences between Aristotle's and Plato's philosophy

2. Explain Aristotle's idea of the Four Causes, using your own examples.

3. Explain Aristotle's idea of the Prime Mover.

4. 'Aristotle's view of how the world works is more successful than that of Plato.' Discuss.

5. 'Aristotle's idea of the Prime Mover doesn't really fit into the rest of his theory.' To what extent do you agree with this statement?

6. 'The idea of the Prime Mover is of no value, as it is completely transcendent and therefore unknowable.' How far do you agree with this statement?

CHAPTER 3

Soul, Mind and Body

LEARNING OUTCOMES

In this chapter, you will be learning about:

- the philosophical language of soul, mind and body – the thinking of Plato and Aristotle
- the metaphysics of consciousness, including substance Dualism and materialism
- Plato's view of the soul as the essential and immaterial part of a human, temporarily united with the body
- Aristotle's view of the soul as the Form of the body; the way the body behaves and lives; something that cannot be separated from the body
- the idea that mind and body are distinct substances
- Descartes's proposal of material and spiritual substances as a solution to the mind/soul and body problem
- the idea that mind and consciousness can be fully explained by physical or material interaction
- the rejection of a soul as a spiritual substance

What is a human being?

The influential German philosopher, **Friedrich Nietzsche (1844–1900)** asked the fundamental question of what it is to be 'human'. In his widely read and influential book *Thus Spoke Zarathustra*, he says:

> 'I am body and soul' – so speaks the child. And why should one not speak like children? But the awakened, the enlightened man says: I am body entirely and nothing beside; and soul is only a word for something in the body. The body is a great intelligence, a multiplicity with one sense, a war and a peace, a herd and a herdsman. Your little intelligence, my brother, which you call 'spirit', is also an instrument of your body, a little instrument and toy of your great intelligence. You say 'I' and are proud of this word. But

greater than this – although you will not believe it – is your body and its great intelligence, which does not say 'I' but performs 'I'.

(Nietzsche, *Thus Spoke Zarathustra*, trans. R. J. Hollingsworth, Penguin Books, 1969 [1883], pp. 61f.)

The question he raises here is what it is to be a human being. This question has been discussed by philosophers and religious believers since ancient times.

In this section of the chapter, we will be discussing what it is that makes up a human being, whether humans are more than their body and, if so, whether the 'mind' or 'soul' is immortal.

> **Exercise**
> What do you think are the similarities and differences between the following definitions of 'human'? How would you define 'human'?
>
> - a member of the genus *Homo* and especially of the species *Homo sapiens*
> - a person
> - having or showing those positive aspects of nature and character regarded as distinguishing humans from other animals
> - having the form of a human
> - a thinking, intelligent being that has reason and reflection and can consider itself the same thinking being in different times and places

The self / personal identity

For many religious believers, the focus of their beliefs is on having a personal relationship with God. This idea permeates all aspects of their lives, including their moral beliefs and practices, their attitudes to life generally and their relationships with other people. Underlying all of this is the question of what it is that makes a person who they are. 'Who am I?' is a fundamental question that each individual person, whether religious or not, must contemplate at some point if they are to make sense of themselves and the kind of life they lead. For some, this will involve profound philosophical questions about whether humans are just physical entities, or whether they have a 'mind' or 'soul' as well and, if so, what the relationship is between these. In philosophical terms, this discussion has been framed in terms of the '**Mind–Body Problem**' or the difference between a 'Dualist' view and a 'Monist' or 'Materialist' one. The answer to this problem will determine many important decisions concerning how an individual lives their life and their attitude to the nature of God. These questions are the subject of this chapter.

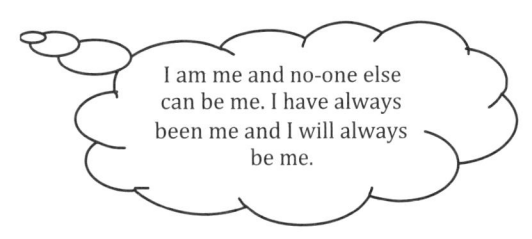

I am me and no-one else can be me. I have always been me and I will always be me.

Mind–Body Problem: The question of how the mind, a non-physical property, can interact with the body, a physical property.

Concepts of the self

Monism

> **Monism**: The view that humans are made up of only a single (material) substance.

One position to take on this problem is called **Monism** or, as it is now generally called, **Materialism**. This is the view that humans are made up of only a single (material) substance.

One of the very earliest types of Monism was practised by the Eleatic school of Greek philosophy. They based their views on the idea of the *monad* – the Greek word for 'single' or 'without division'. Several of the Greek Pre-Socratic philosophers described reality as Monistic and explained this by taking one aspect of the world as the single thing that unified everything – so, for example, Thales chose water, Anaximenes chose air, Heraclitus chose fire, and Parmenides chose the One (a perfect, unchanging and undivided sphere).

There are two main types of Monism: **Idealistic Monism** and **Materialistic Monism**.

> **Idealistic Monism**: Only the mind exists and consequently the external, physical world is an illusion created by the mind.

Idealistic Monism argues that only the mind exists, and consequently that the external, physical world is an illusion created by the mind. This view has been quite popular in western philosophy and is seen in the work of Gottfried Leibniz and George Berkeley, and in G. W. F. Hegel's Idealism.

> **Materialistic Monism**: The single reality is matter, made up either only of atoms or of some world-forming substance. The essential view is that all states may be reduced to the physical.

Materialistic Monism, on the other hand, argues that the single reality is matter, made up either only of atoms or of some world-forming substance. The essential view is that all states may be reduced to the physical. 'Emotion' (anger, love, happiness, etc.) is a physical state and does not exist outside physical reactions. The philosophers Thomas Hobbes and Bertrand Russell were supporters of this view.

In the twentieth and twenty-first centuries, the type of Materialistic Monism known as **Behaviourism** has been popular among many philosophers. Behaviourism holds that all mental states are simply descriptions of behaviour that can be observed. Mental thoughts and emotions are processes of the body and we have no mind or soul. Monism has not been a widely held view in the history of philosophy, particularly in the West. Since the eighteenth century, however, it has grown somewhat more popular. **Christian von Wolff (1679–1754)**, for instance, was the first to use the term 'Monism' and attempted to categorize all the different types of philosophy into one and have a single guiding principle for everything.

> **Behaviourism**: All mental states are simply descriptions of behaviour that can be observed.

More recently, Canadian analytic philosopher **Paul Churchland (1942–present)** has argued that there is no convincing evidence to refute the contention that human beings are anything more than the physical matter that they are made up of. He summarizes this idea by stating:

> The important point about the standard evolutionary story is that the human species and all of its features are the wholly physical outcome of a purely physical process. . . . If this is the correct account of our origins, then there seems neither need, nor room, to fit any nonphysical substances or properties into our theoretical account of ourselves. We are creatures of matter. And we should learn to live with that fact.
>
> (Churchland, *Matter and Consciousness*, p. 25)

PHILOSOPHICAL LANGUAGE AND THOUGHT

Another view supporting Monism puts forward the claim that all mental properties are identical to the physical properties of the brain, i.e. that mind and brain are the same thing. What we call the mind is simply brain activity and there is no need to suggest some non-physical mind or soul. The existence of emotion, consciousness and freedom of the will can all be explained in terms of physical activity in the brain.

> **Exercise**
>
> From the information in the paragraphs above, write in the definition of the terms in the grid below:
>
> **Monism**
> **Materialism**
> **Idealistic Monism**
> **Materialistic Monism**
> **Behaviourism**

> **Exercise**
>
> Look up the Persinger's Helmet experiments, in which Dr Michael Persinger, an American neuroscientist, devised a helmet that seems to have produced experiences described as like 'mystical experiences and altered states' in some volunteers, but not in others.
>
> Do you think that the effects of the helmet count as evidence in favour of Monism or against it? Explain your reasons.

Dualism

Despite these more recent ideas and discussions on Monism, however, the prevalent view is that of Dualism. The most important proponents of Dualism have been Plato, Aristotle, Aquinas and Descartes.

Dualism is the idea that human beings are made up of two substances – a physical or material substance (the body) and a non-physical non-material substance, often called the soul or mind. The main problem with this view is how these two substances interact – how can a physical body relate to or be influenced by a non-physical soul? There certainly appears to be some interaction between the two as, for instance, when I think that I am hungry, my body moves to the fridge and picks out something to eat. Similarly, when I realize that I need to write my RS essay because it is due tomorrow, my hand picks up the pen and starts to write.

Dualism: The view that humans consist of two substances – body and mind/soul.

Plato's Dualism

As you have seen in chapter 1, Plato was one of the most important philosophers of the ancient world. One of the metaphysical questions he wanted to answer was how ordinary human life related to the eternal Forms. (See chapter 1, pp. xx–x). He was a Dualist, believing that humans were made up of two distinct substances, body

Soul, Mind and Body

and soul. His thoughts on this relationship and his arguments in favour of Dualism are found principally in the Theory of Forms and in his dialogue *Phaedo*. Plato uses Socrates to put forward his own views on the soul.

Phaedo is set on the final day of Socrates' life. Socrates had been sentenced to death by poisoning on the charge that he had corrupted the youth of Athens (by teaching them philosophy!). Socrates taught the friends who were to witness his death that the soul is trapped in the body, it is like a prisoner and restricted in what it can do. It can contemplate truths about the universe but can only do so imperfectly. It cannot grasp knowledge of the highest, eternal and unchanging knowledge of the Forms. The embodied soul is capable of perceiving certain truths about actions that are just, for instance, but cannot perceive the Form of Justice. This is the reason why Socrates was happy to die. He did not fear death because it would free his soul from the prison of the body and he would then gain full knowledge and understanding of the eternal Forms.

In *Phaedo*, Plato puts forward three main arguments in favour of his belief in Dualism, especially in the immortality of the soul:

(a) The argument from opposites (also known as the cyclical argument)
Plato says that everything comes into existence through its opposite:

> Well now, consider the matter, if you want to understand more readily, in connection not only with mankind, but with all animals and plants; and, in general, for all things subject to coming-to-be, let's see whether everything comes to be in this way; opposites come to be only from their opposites – in the case of all things that actually have an opposite – as, for example, the beautiful is opposite, of course, to the ugly, just to unjust, and so on in countless other cases.
>
> (Plato, *Phaedo*, reprinted in Brian Davies, *Philosophy of Religion*, Oxford University Press, 2000, pp. 707–8)

Plato says here that everything comes into existence from its opposite. For example, an educated person is someone who was previously uneducated, an adult was previously a child, an active volcano was previously inactive, and so on. Plato makes the important point that someone who is alive was previously dead because living is the opposite of death, just as death is the opposite of life. For Plato, this implies that here is a constant chain of birth, death and rebirth. The constant in this cycle is the immortal soul.

(b) The argument from recollection
Plato uses one of the characters (Cebes) in *Phaedo* to explain his view of how a person knows information that they should not be expected to:

> Cebes replied, 'there's also that theory you're always putting forward, that our learning is actually nothing but recollection; according to you too, if it's true, what we are reminded of we must have learned at some former time. But that would be impossible, unless our souls existed somewhere before being born in this human form; so in this way too, it appears that the soul is something immortal.'
>
> (Davies, *Philosophy of Religion*, p. 710)

In another dialogue, *Meno*, Plato questions an uneducated slave boy to elicit answers to some problems of geometry that he could not have known the answers to. This showed that the information must have been recollected or remembered from the boy's previous life and therefore that they came from the soul and that the soul must be immortal.

(c) The argument from affinity

In order to clarify that the soul must be immortal, Plato has to advance a technical argument that makes a clear distinction between the Forms and material things, such as humans and things in the world. If the soul is immortal, it must be constant and not capable of breaking apart, because, if this were the case, the soul could not carry anything from one life into the next. A soul cannot change in any way. This quality makes the soul different from other things. Everything in the world, on the other hand, is constantly changing, like human bodies ageing or trees growing or rivers changing their course over time, and so on. In addition, Plato points out that the Forms are invisible and can only be understood by the mind, whereas material things are understood by sense experience: 'Soul is most similar to what is divine, immortal, intelligible, uniform, indissoluble, unvarying and constant in relation to itself; whereas body, in its turn, is most similar to what is human, mortal, multiform, non-intelligible, dissoluble, and never constant in relation to itself' (Davies, *Philosophy of Religion*, p. 718).

Difficulties with Plato's Dualism

1. In his argument from opposites, Plato makes a subtle change in his description of opposites. In the first part, he gives examples like smaller and larger, slower and faster, which are comparative terms, so that, when you are an adult, you are taller than when you were a child. These are opposites, but in different degrees. In the second part of the argument, Plato shifts from comparative examples to what we might call 'absolute' opposites – he talks of the states of being 'dead' and 'alive', for instance. These are clearly not comparative terms – you cannot be 'aliv-er' or 'dead-er', you can only be 'alive' or 'dead'. Some philosophers think that this is a logical error by Plato and that the argument fails. It may be an example of the fallacy of equivocation, in which the meaning of a word is subtly changed during an argument, either deliberately or accidentally.
2. One of the main characters in *Phaedo*, Simmias, agreed with Socrates' argument, but criticized the argument from recollection because it did not prove that souls exist after death, but only before birth. Socrates does not really answer this criticism, suggesting only that, as the soul comes to life out of death (as he had shown in the argument from opposites), it must be the case that the soul must exist after death too.
3. In relation to the argument from affinity, Plato believed that there were a fixed number of souls in the world. Perhaps this is excusable given his historical context, in which most of the world outside Europe was undiscovered and he would have had no idea that there were millions of people spread throughout these parts of the world. Today, of course, there is an ever-increasing number of people in the world, so this raises the question of how Plato might account for the 'extra' souls.

Aristotle's Dualism

Aristotle's Dualism and view of the relationship between the body and soul was radically different from that of his former teacher, Plato. Whereas Plato believed that the soul was immortal and moved from body to body, Aristotle believed that the soul (*psyche*) was possessed by all living things, not just humans, and was not immortal. For Aristotle, the soul was a substance, the form or essence of each existing thing. The soul made the difference between a person/animal or vegetable being alive and being dead, so it can be thought of as the 'life-force' of all things that exist.

Aristotle spent much of his life investigating the natural world as a scientist, wishing to discover how things worked. He wrote a major treatise on the soul, called *On the Soul* (*Peri Psyches* (Greek), *De Anima* (Latin)). He thought that all living things had a soul and that the idea of a body without a soul was unintelligible. At the beginning of *De Anima*, Aristotle says that: 'The knowledge of the soul admittedly contributes greatly to the advance of truth in general, and, above all, to our understanding of Nature, for the soul is in some sense the principle of animal life.'

At the beginning of part 2 of *De Anima*, Aristotle writes that there are three kinds of substance:

- Matter (that has potentiality)
- Form (that has actuality)
- A compound of matter and form.

All things that are alive have souls, so even plants and animals have souls, and having a soul is what makes them alive. For instance, a cat has matter and a particular form – four legs, a swishy tail, whiskers, a loud miaow, and so on – but, if the cat were not alive, it would not have a soul (and it would not be a cat either – it would be a dead cat). Aristotle is only interested in things that are compounds of matter and form. The 'matter' of the cat is its potential to perform 'cat-like' activities, such as to eat, breathe, run around, curl up and sleep, grow, excrete, etc. Anything that can perform these kinds of actions is alive. For Aristotle, the capacities of a thing (the cat) to do so constitute its soul. The soul is what is causally responsible for the activities of a living thing.

Aristotle believed that there were three different kinds of soul, each of which had different capacities:

- the nutritive soul (in plants) had the capacity to take in nutrition so they could grow and reproduce
- the sensitive soul (in animals) had the capacities of the nutritive soul plus being able to move and perceive the world around them and react to stimuli
- the rational soul (in humans) had the capacities of the other two types of soul plus the ability to think and make qualitative moral judgements.

A key question for Aristotle was whether the soul could exist without the body. As we saw above, Plato had believed in the immortality of the soul and therefore the independence of the soul from the body. For him, when the body died, the soul lived on. Aristotle's views were very different. He says: 'the soul neither exists without a body nor is a body of some sort. For it is not a body, but it belongs to a body, and for

> Nutritive soul – all living things, including trees, plants, animals and humans have the capacity to grow and reproduce

> Sensitive soul – animals and humans have the ability to move and perceive the world.

> Rational soul – only humans have the ability to think and make moral juddgements

this reason is present in a body, and in a body of such-and-such a sort' (*De Anima*, 414a20ff.).

In Aristotle's view, then, although the soul is not a material substance, it cannot be separated from the physical body. The soul is not a substance that exists independently from the body. Nor is it a substance that 'sits inside' the body, observing what the body does. It has a more direct link to the body: the soul is the 'form' of the body, not a separate substance inside another substance (the body) of a different kind. The soul, for Aristotle, is a *capacity*, rather than the thing that has the capacity.

This means that the soul is not capable of being separated from the body. Just as the form of one human being is essentially the same as the form of any other human being, so the soul of one human being is essentially the same as that of any other human being. For Aristotle, then, there are no individual souls, there is only 'soul'. Different individual people are made up of different compounds of form and matter and are made alive by the same set of capacities, i.e. the same kind of soul.

> **Exercise**
> Organize a class debate on the motion 'This house believes that Aristotle's view of the soul is superior to that of Plato because it is based on sense experience.'

Difficulties with Aristotle's Dualism

Aristotle was too quick to dismiss the importance of Plato's theory of the Forms. He claimed that there was no clear evidence in their favour. He chose to promote sense experience, as, in his view, there *is* very clear evidence in its favour as a reliable source of knowledge and authority. Many philosophers and religious scholars, however, would argue that there are other reliable sources for knowing the world that are just as important as – or even more important than – experience. For example, religious believers would propose religious experiences such as that of Bernadette at Lourdes, or their own faith in God and God's revelations to individuals, as well as knowledge of God and the world gained through studying the Bible.

Aristotle lays a great deal of importance on causality, the idea that everything must have a cause. He uses this idea to argue that everything must have a Final Cause that gives purpose to everything in the world. Scientists would disagree with this view based on their studies of the universe. Many would say that the only purpose the universe may have is simply to exist, and this is not sufficient reason to posit the idea that everything in the universe has an individual purpose.

Aristotle contradicts himself when he says that, although everything in the universe is caused to come into existence, there is one thing – the Unmoved Mover – that is not caused to come into existence. Since Aristotle's whole argument for causation depends entirely on the Unmoved Mover, this logical contradiction shows that it fails as a convincing argument.

Aquinas and the soul

Aquinas was heavily influenced by the philosophy of Aristotle. Aquinas immersed himself in Aristotelian philosophy and used it in his own works, including what he wrote on the soul.

For Aquinas, the soul is 'the first principle of life in living things'. By this, he means that the soul is the opposite of the body. The body is material, the soul is immaterial; the body is corruptible, the soul is incorruptible. He says that the soul can exist apart from the body after the body's death because of its incorruptibility. The soul, he argues, is incorporeal so does not cease to exist when the body dies: 'Therefore, the intellectual principle, which we call the mind or the intellect, has an operation in which the body does not share. Now only that which subsists in itself can have an operation in itself. . . . We must conclude, therefore, that the human soul, which is called intellect or mind, is something incorporeal and subsistent' (*Summa Theologica*, 75, 2).

Aquinas's conclusion here causes a problem for him. On one hand, he believed that the soul is the form of the body, the principle by which bodily functions, like movement and sensation, take place. Such activities imply that humans are composed of both body and soul. On the other hand, Aquinas believed that the ability of humans to use their intellect and reason comes from the soul, not the body. He believed that the soul exists separate from the human body. The problem he has is that all other souls that are in a body, e.g. those of animals, cannot exist without their body, but those of humans can. His answer to this is that the soul can exist independently of the body, but that, in doing so, it is not a complete substance (*Summa Contra Gentiles*, II, 68). So, the disembodied soul cannot do what is natural for it to do, such as using its powers of intellect and reason. It then needs God to reunite it with its body.

Aquinas became the foremost Christian theologian and the ultimate authority on almost every aspect of theology for several hundred years. His views on the soul, heavily influenced by Aristotle, went virtually unchallenged until the seventeenth century, when René Descartes put forward his radical views.

Descartes and Substance Dualism

> **René Descartes (1596-1650)** was a French philosopher and mathematician who lived at a time of radical change, when the old medieval ideas about the world were being rejected in favour of a new, mechanistic, understanding of how things worked. Descartes was a highly influential figure in the Scientific Revolution, whose followers asserted a materialistic universe where everything was explicable by scientific 'truths' and where God was no longer necessary. Although Descartes was accused of being a materialist, he rejected this in favour of a Dualistic philosophy that argued for the existence of both material and non-material substances, such as God and human souls. His form of Dualism became the basis on which many religious believers were able to justify their theistic beliefs despite living in a materialistic world. One of the most important contributions Descartes made to this debate was the Ontological argument for God's existence. (See chapter 5 p. 89.) His form of Dualism came to be known as 'Substance Dualism'.

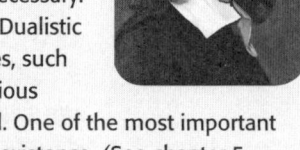

Descartes began by asking whether there was any knowledge that could be known with such certainty that no-one could doubt it. His background in Mathematics (you will probably have heard of or studied Cartesian geometry) made him determined to find a philosophical equivalent to mathematical certainty. He gives examples of how people can be mistaken about the evidence they perceive through sense experience. For example, putting a straight stick into water makes it look bent, or students may mistakenly think they have heard the bell for the end of the lesson. He even wonders whether there may be an evil demon deliberately misleading people about what they think they know from their senses.

If this idea is taken to its extreme, we would have no way of knowing *anything* about the world, and everything could conceivably be a dream or an illusion. He believes that there is only one piece of absolutely certain knowledge – this is his most famous quote: '**Cogito ergo sum**', 'I think, therefore I exist.' By this, he meant that he could not doubt the fact that he was thinking. It was impossible to doubt his own existence because he had to exist as a thinker in order to have the thought that he was thinking! He could not yet be certain that he had a physical body, however, because that could have been implanted in his mind by an evil demon. For Descartes, the inescapable conclusion from this observation was that body and mind must be separate from one another and were therefore distinct substances. The mind could not be doubted, but the body could. He argues that

> There is a very great difference between a mind and a body, because a body is by nature divisible, but the mind is not. Clearly, when I think about the mind, that is, of myself as far as I am a thing that thinks, I am not aware of any parts in me – that is, I understand myself to be one whole person. Although the whole mind seems united to the whole body, if a foot, or an arm, or another limb were amputated from my body, nothing would be taken from my mind. Mental faculties, such as 'willing', 'sensing', 'understanding' cannot be called its 'parts', because it is always the same mind that wills, senses or understands. But any corporeal or physically extended thing I can think of, I can easily think of as divided

---

'Cogito ergo sum': 'Cogito ergo sum' is the famous Latin version of Descartes's French phrase 'je pense, donc je suis', which is usually translated into English as 'I think, therefore I exist.' By this, Descartes meant that thinking about anything must necessitate our existence.

It is also known as 'the cogito'.

into parts . . . . This reasoning alone would be enough to teach me that the mind is wholly different from the body.

(Descartes, *Meditations on First Philosophy*, VI, in *René Descartes Discourse on Method and Meditations*, trans. Elizabeth S. Haldane and G. R. T. Ross, Dover Philosophical Classics, 2003)

This view caused a problem for Descartes, just as it had for Aquinas. If body and mind were necessarily separate, how could they interact with each other? For example, if my mind makes a decision, say, to read my RS textbook, then exactly how does it communicate this decision to my body to walk to where the book is, pick it up and start reading it? For a non-physical 'force' (the mind) to affect a physical body goes against all the known laws of physical science. This is, in fact, a problem that Descartes was never able to solve satisfactorily.

Descartes did make an attempt to solve this difficulty by trying to locate how the mind could communicate with the body. First, he describes the body as being like a machine and compares it to the workings of a clock:

> And as a clock composed of wheels and counter-weights no less exactly observes the laws of nature when it is badly made, and does not show the time properly, than when it entirely satisfies the wishes of its maker, and as, if I consider the body of a man as being a sort of machine so built up and composed of nerves, muscles, veins, blood and skin, that though there were no mind in it at all, it would not cease to have the same motions as at present.
>
> (*Meditations*, VI)

In his work *The Passions of the Soul*, published in 1649, he puts forward the idea that the pineal gland in the brain is 'where the soul exercises its functions more particularly than in the other parts of the body'. Just before making this statement, Descartes stresses that the soul is joined to the whole physical body, not just any individual part of the body. Body and soul are an indivisible unity. Nevertheless, he says, the pineal gland is where the soul is more highly concentrated, as this gland is 'the innermost part of the brain'. He describes exactly where the pineal gland is located, between the two lobes, in 'the middle of the brain's substance and suspended above the passage through which the spirits in the brain's anterior cavities communicate with those in its posterior cavities' ('René Descartes: The Passions of the Soul', ed. and trans. Elizabeth S. Haldane and G. R. T. Ross, *Descartes Key Philosophical Writings*, Wordsworth Classics, 1997, p. 372). Descartes was here using the medical knowledge of the time to attempt a location of the soul/mind. He had observed that the pineal gland was a single body part, which made it different from many others – there were two lobes of the brain, two eyes, two ears. This difference made him think that the pineal gland contained 'animal spirits' that controlled sense-perception, imagination and memory (Descartes, 'Letter to Father Mersennes 1 April, 1640', in A. Kenny (ed.), *Descartes: Philosophical Letters*, Clarendon Press, 1970, p. 137).

This interesting suggestion is more ingenuous than ingenious. It may have come up with a possible location for the intersection of body and mind, because no-one at the time knew what the function of the pineal gland was. However, Descartes is still unable to explain *how* the link between body and mind was made. Another difficulty with Descartes's views is that of what is meant by 'willing'.

50 PHILOSOPHICAL LANGUAGE AND THOUGHT

> **Exercise**
> Find out what the function of the pineal gland is. Do you think that Descartes's view of the soul depends on his attempt to 'locate' it in the body?

Gilbert Ryle and the 'ghost in the machine'

British philosopher **Gilbert Ryle (1900–76)** argued against what he called 'the doctrine of body–mind dualism', which saw the mind and body as distinct entities. Instead, he saw them as being intrinsically linked. *The Concept of Mind* is a sustained and powerful criticism of Descartes's substance Dualism. He ridicules Descartes's concept by calling it 'the ghost in the machine', meaning that Descartes had completely failed to explain the relationship between the body and the mind. Ryle calls this a '**Category Error**'. Descartes had made an error, not just in a detail of the theory, but in fundamental principle. In Ryle's opinion, Descartes had confused things from different categories, when he compared a mind, which is a non-material substance, with a body, which is a material substance. To describe the mind as an 'immaterial object' was a 'Category Error'. He says:

> I hope to prove that it is entirely false, and false not in detail but in principle. It is not merely an assemblage of particular mistakes. It is one big mistake and a mistake of a special kind. It is, namely, a category-mistake. It represents the facts of mental life as if they belonged to one logical type or category (or range of types or categories), when they actually belong to another.
>
> (Ryle, *The Concept of Mind*, p. 16)

Analytical school of philosophy:
This was a development in early twentieth-century European philosophy that focused on attempting to make language as precise and clear as possible. In addition to Gilbert Ryle, central figures include Bertrand Russell, Ludwig Wittgenstein, G. E. Moore and the Logical Positivists.

Category Error:
To confuse items or ideas from different categories.

To help explain what he means, Ryle cites several examples of Category Error:

1. Someone visits Oxford or Cambridge for the first time. They are shown a number of colleges, libraries, playing fields, scientific departments, museums, and so on. At the end of the tour, the visitor says that they have seen where the people work, where the students live and everything else, and then says 'But where is the University?' This a Category Error because the visitor has assumed that 'the university' must be a separate institution, different from everything he has seen, whereas in reality the university is simply the way that all the colleges and other buildings that have been seen are organized. He was mistakenly allocating 'the university' to the same category that other institutions belong to.
2. A child watched a military march-past of a division. All the battalions, batteries and squadrons are pointed out to him. When they have all disappeared, he asks

when the Division is going to march past. He was assuming that the Division was something different from all the other sections he had already seen, whereas, in fact, it was the collective term for all of the groups.
3. Someone watches his first game of cricket and is told what the functions of the bowlers, batsmen, fielders, umpires and scorers are. He then asks whose role it is to exercise 'team spirit'. This is a Category Error because 'team spirit' is not another piece of equipment or team member – it is the enthusiasm shown by everyone on the team to do their best to win the game.

Ryle continues by saying that there is a common feature of all these examples of Category Errors – 'The mistakes were made by people who do not know how to wield the concepts *university*, *division* and *team-spirit*. Their puzzles arose from inability to use certain items in the English vocabulary' (*The Concept of Mind*, p. 17).

Ryle's point here is that Descartes is guilty of a Category Error because he makes the assumption that mental events and physical events were the same kind of thing, whereas, according to Ryle, they are not. Ryle did not deny that people have minds or mental events, but he dismissed the idea that these were a separate part of a human being. In the same way as the university is not an addition to the colleges and other buildings, so the mind was not an addition to the physical aspects of a person. The two things are parts of the same person. So, for instance, when I think I will go on holiday to France, it is not a case of my 'mind' as a separate thing telling my body to do this, it is just *me* making the decision.

> **Exercise**
>
> Do you think that Ryle's concept of Category Errors is convincing? If so, what are the implications for religious belief?

Materialism

Materialism as a philosophical position may be traced back thousands of years to at least the ancient Indian Carvaka school of thought around 600 BCE. It rejected any suggestion of the supernatural, of an immaterial soul or god, or of life after death. The only aim that individuals ought to pursue was pleasure.

In the fifth century BCE, the Greek philosopher Leucippus and his student Democritus developed the theory of Atomism, arguing that the world was made up of atoms, which were uniform, homogeneous, colourless, tasteless and indivisible. Each atom has several 'primary qualities': size, shape, weight and movement. Atoms do not have 'secondary qualities', such as smell, taste or colour. From this, they conclude that the only things that exist are atoms and, as such, there can be nothing that exists other than (physical) atoms – no soul, no mind, no immaterial substance. These views held until the classic statement of materialist philosophy in 50 BCE when the Greek writer Lucretius wrote *De Rerum Natura* (*On the Nature of Things*).

With the development of Christianity, materialist ideas almost disappeared until the seventeenth and eighteenth centuries, particularly with the work of **Baron**

d'Holbach who published anonymously *La Système de nature* (*The System of Nature*) in 1770. This and the advancement of scientific (anti-religious) ideas and theories – including Darwinian evolution, neuroscience and computer technology – saw the re-emergence of materialism in European thought.

Richard Dawkins

Richard Dawkins (1941–present) is a biological materialist who believes that human beings are only made up of physical attributes:

> There is no spirit-driven life force, no throbbing, heaving, pullulating, protoplasmic, mystic jelly. Life is just bytes and bytes of digital information.
> (Richard Dawkins, *River out of Eden: A Darwinian View of Life*, Basic Books, 1995, p. 18)

> We are survival machines – robot vehicles blindly programmed to preserve the selfish molecules known as genes.
> (Dawkins, *The Selfish Gene*, Flamingo, 1978 p. 2)

Dawkins has two views of what the soul is. As an evolutionary biologist, he seeks to find an all-encompassing physical explanation for the world. He uses definitions of 'soul' from the *Oxford English Dictionary* (*OED*) (a strange decision, as there are several other more technical dictionaries which he could have used instead) to begin his discussion and critique. He describes 'soul one' as the 'non-physical vital principle, animated by some anima. Vitalised by a vital force. Energised by some mysterious energy. Spiritualised by some mysterious spirit'. Dawkins argues that science has either destroyed the soul or is in the process of doing so. In Dawkins's view, this argument is circular and therefore useless.

To explain 'soul two', Dawkins uses another *OED* definition: 'Intellectual/ spiritual power. High development of mental faculties'. This is the definition that the poet Keats suggested Newton had used to destroy 'all the poetry of the rainbow when he unwove it' with his mechanical view of the universe. Dawkins argues that 'soul two' is what he refers to as an 'awakening imagination' of the human spirit, a 'spirit' which all humans have, just because they are human.

Dawkins's views on 'soul one' and 'soul two' may be compared to Ryle's materialist views. For Dawkins, 'Soul one' would be like Ryle's 'category error', a sort of grammatical error that makes something that does not really exist into a concrete substance. 'Soul two' is rather like the idea of '**qualia**', which is a term used in the philosophy of mind and refers to the individual, subjective experiences that people have. In religious terms, things such as religious experiences could be counted as 'qualia'. In non-religious terms, an example might be having a very vivid dream, or feeling energized after a vigorous workout at the gym.

Several criticisms may be made of Dawkins's ideas about the soul. First of all, as mentioned above, he uses a non-technical definition of 'soul'. He does not provide a reason for doing this. This can be seen as undermining his credibility. More importantly, he starts the discussion from a 'closed' viewpoint – he will not accept

Qualia: Qualia is the name given to individual, subjective experiences that people have.

that the universe is anything other than being totally physical and explicable by scientific methods. Anything that is not explicable by science must, a priori, be false. From the start, he is biased and prejudiced against religious views of the world, and nothing can change his mind on this. 'Soul one' is therefore dismissed out of hand as being meaningless. The language he uses to describe 'soul one' – 'energised energy', 'animated anima', 'spiritualised spirit' and 'conscious consciousness' are meaningless.

Dawkins appears to be ambiguous about whether science has killed religion. He says that science is killing or has killed religion. Only one of these statements can be true. He does not explain this statement, nor does he justify it with evidence. This does not seem to be a scientific approach! This criticism also applies to Dawkins's view on 'soul two'. Dawkins has said that humans are just 'bytes and bytes of . . . information', nothing more and nothing less. If this is true, what he describes as 'soul two' must have been an anomaly in evolution. His idea of the mind would appear to be caused by electro-chemical changes in the brain. But if, for Dawkins, everything – including the mind – is physical, then how can consciousness happen, how can humans make real choices and have individual emotions? Dawkins suggests that science will explain these issues one day. Again, however, Dawkins has no sound evidence to support this view, so, in one way, his argument seems as tenuous as those of religious believers.

Exercise

1. Explain Dawkins's view of the soul to a classmate.
2. Do you agree with Dawkins's idea of 'soul one' and 'soul two'? Give reasons for your answer.

FURTHER READING

Susan Blackmore, *Consciousness: An Introduction*. Routledge, 2010

Paul M. Churchland, *Matter and Consciousness*, 3rd edn. MIT Press, 2013

R. Dawkins, *The God Delusion*, 10th Anniversary edn. Black Swan, 2016

Unweaving the Rainbow: Science, Delusion and the Appetite for Wonder. Penguin, 2006

N. Humphrey, *How to Solve the Mind–Body Problem*. Imprint Academic, 2000

J. Kim, *Mind in a Physical World: an Essay on the Mind–Body Problem and Mental Causation*. MIT Press, 2000

G. Ryle, *The Concept of Mind*. Penguin, 1949

R. Swinburne, *The Evolution of the Soul*, Oxford University Press, 1997

J. Westphal, *The Mind–Body Problem*. MIT Press, 2016

Thought Points

1. Summarize the main points of Plato's and Aristotle's Dualism.

2. To what extent do you agree that Descartes's Dualism is more convincing than that of Aquinas?

3. Explain how Ryle's idea of 'Category Errors' relates to religious belief.

4. 'Dawkins's view that consciousness is nothing more than electro-chemical events in the brain is totally convincing.' Discuss the extent to which you agree with this statement.

5. 'Substance Dualism is not convincing as a solution to the problem of body and soul.' Discuss.

6. 'Dawkins's ideas on the soul make no rational sense.' To what extent do you agree with this statement?

7. 'To be religious requires belief in a separate body and soul.' Discuss how far you agree with this statement.

SECTION II
THE EXISTENCE OF GOD

CHAPTER 4
Teleological and Cosmological Arguments

LEARNING OUTCOMES

In this chapter, you will be learning about:
- the meaning of the terms 'teleological' and 'cosmological' as applied to arguments for God's existence
- two Teleological arguments for God's existence based on observation of the world
  - Aquinas's Fifth Way
  - Paley
- Cosmological arguments for God's existence
  - Aquinas's first three ways
- criticisms of each of these arguments
  - Hume
  - evolution

Introduction

Attempting to establish the existence of God is the central question of the Philosophy of Religion. As we will see, there are several distinct and rational ways of making the attempt. The two ways we will discuss in this chapter are teleological and cosmological types of argument. They all share the basic idea that it is possible to determine whether or not God exists by using rational arguments and logic. For some religious believers, however, using reason is unnecessary and even counter-productive. These believers say that God's existence is simply a matter of faith – God may be found through religious experience, prayer, meditation or revelation. (See chapter 6).

The Teleological argument (or Design argument)

The phrase 'Teleological argument' refers to a number of arguments that aim to show the reasonableness of the existence of God. These arguments are based on human observation of features in the world that are claimed to show that the world is not random. Instead, things on both the micro-cosmic and macro-cosmic levels show evidence of purpose and design by some cosmic force or being that monotheists call 'God'.

A very brief history of Teleological arguments

The Teleological argument is probably the best-known argument for the existence of God. The first known version comes from the ancient Greek philosopher **Anaxagoras (*c.*500 BCE)**, who argued that there was an 'intelligence' or 'mind' (in Greek, *nous*) that gave the universe its natural order. Plato's teacher, Socrates, was probably the first philosopher to put forward a formal argument from Design for the existence of the gods. In a discussion with Protarchus, Socrates talks about the apparent order throughout nature, using as an example the way the parts of the human body seem to be adapted to each other, such as how the eyelids protect the eyeballs. According to Socrates, this could not have happened by chance, so must show wise planning of the universe by the gods.

Plato develops a Teleological argument in his famous work *Republic* (Book X) and in the *Timaeus*, where he argues that a cosmic creator, whom he calls the 'Demiurge', had supreme intelligence to design the world. The Demiurge did not have the power to create anything out of nothing (*ex nihilo*) but used the already-existing material in the universe to create an orderly and beautiful world. Later, Plato's pupil Aristotle developed the idea of a creator of the entire cosmos, which, in his book *Metaphysics*, he referred to as the 'Prime Mover'. The idea of the Prime Mover becomes very important later in Christian philosophy, when St Thomas Aquinas uses it to refer to how God created the universe. Aristotle argued that the whole of nature displays an inherent purpose and direction. Aquinas's arguments will be discussed below (see pp. 59–60). In the first century BCE, the Roman writer Cicero (106–43 BCE) also formulated a Teleological argument. In his work *De natura deorum* (*On the Nature of the Gods*), he maintained that a divine power may be found in the principle of reason that pervades the whole universe: 'When you see a sundial or a water-clock, you see that it tells the time by design and not by chance. How then can you imagine that the universe as a whole is devoid of purpose and intelligence, when it embraces everything, including these artifacts themselves and their artificers?' (*De natura deorum*, ii. 34).

Teleological arguments for God's existence have existed since the beginning of Christianity. St Paul says, in Romans 1:18–20:

> The wrath of God is being revealed from heaven against all the godlessness and wickedness of people, who suppress the truth by their wickedness, since what may be known about God is plain to them, because God has made it plain to them. For since the creation of the world God's invisible qualities – his eternal power and divine nature – have been clearly seen, being understood from what has been made, so that people are without excuse.

Paul argues here that God's power and nature make it obvious that the universe has been created so that even godless and evil people should be able to see that it has been designed.

The early Christian writer **Minucius Felix (late second century CE)** used an analogy to argue for the existence of God:

> Supposing you went into a house and found everything neat, orderly and well-kept, surely you would assume it had a master, and one much better than the good things, his belongings; so in this house of the universe, when throughout heaven and earth you see the marks of foresight, order and law, may you not assume that the lord and author of the universe is fairer than the stars themselves or than any portions of the entire world?
> (*The Octavius of Minucius Felix*, ch. 18)

Later, another very important and influential Christian thinker, **St Augustine (354–430 CE)**, put forward the view that the world's 'well-ordered changes and movements', together with 'the beautiful appearance of all visible things', provided strong evidence that it could only have been created by (the Christian) God.

Aquinas's Teleological argument

Aquinas developed several arguments (he called these 'ways') that he thought proved God's existence. His Teleological argument is generally called the 'Fifth Way'. He states it very briefly:

> The fifth way is taken from the governance of the world. We see that things that lack knowledge, such as natural objects, act for an end, and this is evident from their acting always, or nearly always, in the same way, so as to obtain the best result. Hence it is plain that they achieve their end by design and not by chance. It is clear that something that lacks knowledge cannot move towards an end unless it is directed towards that end by some being that has knowledge and intelligence, just as an arrow is fired towards its mark by the archer. Therefore, intelligent being exists which directs all things towards their end. This being we call God.
> (Aquinas, *Summa Theologica*, 1, 2, 3)

Design *qua* purpose: Aquinas's term for the way the parts of the universe fit together for a purpose.

Design *qua* regularity: Aquinas's term for the way that the order and regularity in the world are proof of a designer.

There are several important points that need to be explained in this argument. First, this is an a posteriori argument. This means that he uses things in the world that we can observe to argue for the existence of God. All versions of the Teleological argument are a posteriori arguments.

Aquinas's argument focuses on purpose (**design *qua* purpose**) as well as regularity (**design *qua* regularity**). This means that Aquinas teaches that it is an observable fact that things do not just behave randomly but act for a *telos* or purpose. So, for instance, a plant seed does not behave randomly but demonstrates its purpose by growing into a plant producing flowers or fruit as appropriate to its nature. Similarly, as a human body develops from its embryonic stage into a new-born child and then into adult life, the body's cells change into liver or kidney or heart or brain cells, each with its own function and purpose. For Aquinas, the purpose of every living thing is almost always the 'best result' and is achieved in nature by things behaving in a highly *regular* way. For instance, kidney cells will act in the same way in all human beings, rather than acting differently in different individuals. Aquinas also argues that things like cells act towards their proper purpose instinctively, without knowledge or intelligence. They do not have the ability to decide what kind of cell they become, nor do they have any knowledge of how to achieve their purpose. Aquinas says that things without knowledge cannot act towards their ends unless they are aided by something that *does* have knowledge and intelligence. He explains this by using Zeno's analogy of the archer and the arrow: the arrow cannot move itself (because it does not have 'knowledge' or 'intelligence') and can only move towards its target (i.e. its '*telos*') when directed by the archer (who does have knowledge and intelligence). This leads Aquinas to conclude that there must be some intelligent being who directs all natural things to their allotted and appropriate *telos*. For Aquinas, this 'intelligent being' is God.

> **Exercise**
>
> Research the ancient Greek philosopher Zeno of Elea (c.490–430 BCE) and consider his examples of analogies.

William Paley's Teleological argument

> **William Paley (1743–1805)** was an Anglican theologian, who studied Philosophy at Cambridge, where he became a Fellow of Christ's College. He had a successful academic career there, teaching Ethics, Metaphysics and New Testament Studies, before being ordained in 1767. He served in various parishes in the north of England before becoming Prebend in 1780, then Archdeacon in 1782, of Carlisle cathedral. He wrote several books using philosophical arguments in defence of the Christian faith, and won much credit for his first book *The Principles of Moral and Political Philosophy*, which put forward utilitarian ideas as they related to ethics and politics. He is now best known for two books: *A View of the Evidences of Christianity* (1794) and *Natural Theology, or Evidences of the Existence and Attributes of the Deity, Collected from the Appearances of Nature* (1802), in which he amasses hundreds of examples of apparent design in nature.

His classic Teleological argument is explained fully in his *Natural Theology*. It is in two sections, the first of which is:

> In crossing a heath, suppose I pitched my foot against a *stone*, and were asked how the stone came to be there, I might possibly answer, that, for anything I knew to the contrary, it had lain there for ever: nor would it perhaps be very easy to show the absurdity of this answer. But suppose I had found a *watch* upon the ground, and it should be enquired how

Teleological and Cosmological Arguments

the watch happened to be in that place, I should hardly think of the answer which I had before given, that, for any thing I knew, the watch might have always been there. Yet why should not this serve for the watch, as well as for the stone? Why is it not as admissible in the second case as in the first? For this reason, and no other, viz., that, when we come to inspect the watch, we perceive (what we could not discover in the stone) that its several parts are framed and put together for a purpose, e.g. that they are so formed and adjusted as to produce motion, and that motion so regulated as to point out the hour of the day; that, if the different parts had been differently shaped from what they are, if a different size from what they are, or placed after any other manner, or any other order than that in which they are placed, either no motion at all would have been carried on in the machine, or none which would have answered the use that is now served by it.

(William Paley, *Natural Theology* (1802), ch. 1, quoted in John Hick, *The Existence of God*, MacMillan, 1964, pp. 99–100)

Natural Theology: The attempt to use rational, scientific evidence about the world to argue for the existence of God.

Many theologians and philosophers from the Enlightenment period up to the early twentieth century, including Paley himself, had been trained in the natural sciences. The term **Natural Theology** came to be used to describe some of the methods theologians used to argue for the existence of God. They used reason and our experience of how nature works to look for evidence of design and purpose in the world that would point to the existence of God. Natural Theology pre-dates Christianity, with Plato giving the first written account in his *Timaeus* and in the *Laws*. It is also seen in Roman philosophy in Marcus Terentius Varro (116–27 BCE), then in Islamic philosophy, particularly that of **Al-Kindi (*c*.801–*c*.873 CE)** and Averroes (1126–98 CE). Aquinas was influenced by the arguments put forward by this Natural Theology tradition and, as we have already seen, put forward his own version in the Teleological argument. The other main way of viewing the world and its relationship to God is known as **Revealed Theology.** This is the idea that humans know what God is like only because he 'reveals' himself to them, especially through sacred texts such as the Bible in Christianity or the Qur'an in Islam.

Revealed Theology: In contrast to Natural Theology, this is the belief that God is known through the sacred texts of a religion.

The first part of Paley's argument is rather like a puzzle. He poses a contrast between two examples. In the first, it seems self-evident that the stone has just been there for a very long time and has no purpose. In the second, no sensible person would deny that the watch does have a very specific purpose – to tell the time. It is important to note here that the kind of watch Paley was familiar with was not electronic or digital! Watches were made from a complex arrangement of cogs, springs, levers, dial and glass, amongst other parts. He asks what it is that makes the difference between the two examples. His answer is that we can intuit or infer from the watch something that we cannot do from the rock – the existence of apparent order and purpose. Paley then argues that the parts of the watch are placed in a particular way for a specific purpose – to 'produce motion' that enables us to tell the time. Telling the time is the purpose of the watch. He then states that, if the parts had been organized in any other way, either the watch would not work or it would function in a different way. Although Paley does not explicitly say at this point, he implies that anything that shows evidence of order and purpose can only be the result of an intelligent agency, meaning that there must be a designer. He equates this designer with God.

Paley is here arguing from analogy, saying that the order and purpose found in the watch *are like* the order and purpose that can also be found in the world. This was a common feature of many eighteenth- and nineteenth-century arguments for the existence of God. For Paley, the watch, with its mechanisms and its purpose of telling the time, is like the mechanisms that we observe in the world. Paley spends most of *Natural Theology* discussing examples from the natural world that illustrate the central features of order and purpose, thus supporting his argument that there must be an intelligent designer, not just of the watch, but also of the entire world. He argues from inference, on the basis of 'similar effects having similar causes'. So, just as the mechanism of the watch shows purpose and design, so many features of the natural world show evidence of order and purpose, and these lead inescapably to the existence of the intelligent designer, God. Additionally, the analogy shows that the watch's designer – the watchmaker – is similar in kind to the world's designer – God – but dissimilar in degree. God is hugely more powerful than the watchmaker because God has designed and brought the entire world into existence.

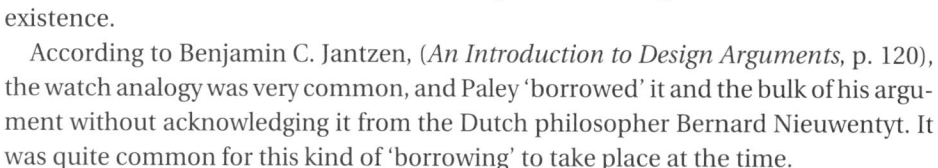

A mechanical watch, showing design, complexity and purpose

According to Benjamin C. Jantzen, (*An Introduction to Design Arguments*, p. 120), the watch analogy was very common, and Paley 'borrowed' it and the bulk of his argument without acknowledging it from the Dutch philosopher Bernard Nieuwentyt. It was quite common for this kind of 'borrowing' to take place at the time.

Paley pointed out the complexity of nature and how this complexity is far greater than any human being or other mechanism could bring about. Probably the most famous example from nature used by Paley is that of the human eye.

He observes that the many parts of the eye are intricately formed in order to see, and goes into great detail about how they fit together to provide sight. Paley uses this detailed evidence to argue that the eye, like the watch, contains many parts that are clearly arranged for a particular purpose. He concludes that the eye must have a designer, and that designer, by necessity, is God.

Paley uses the evidence from all the examples he discusses to conclude that there is a great deal of fine-tuning in the world that helps to preserve life. This includes the correct amounts of water, heat, light, balance of gases, and so on. He also anticipates some potential criticisms of his argument. He lists a number of factors which may be raised as objections, but which he thinks do not shake or weaken the fundamental conclusion that the watch (and, by analogy, nature) has a designer. Paley includes these at this point in an attempt to respond to some criticisms that had been raised to the Teleological argument.

1. It does not matter, Paley says, if we are ignorant of watchmakers and watchmaking. Our ignorance would only increase our awe at the designer's skill – it does not make us question the existence of the designer. I may never have seen a watch made, or known any watchmakers, but do not conclude from this that watches are unmade and that there are no such things as watchmakers. Likewise, just because we have not seen the manufacture of the universe, or encountered its designer, this does not mean we can question that such a designer exists.
2. Imperfections in the watch. If the second hand on the watch occasionally froze for a second or two, this would not lead us to the conclusion that the watch had

no designer after all. Likewise, just because there are apparent flaws in nature this does not mean we can deny the existence of the designer of nature.
3. Ignorance of some of the functions of some elements of the watch, or the apparent superfluous nature of some of the parts. Just because some parts seem superfluous or we cannot explain the functions of some of the parts, this does not give us reason to suggest the watch did not have a designer. Likewise, we may not understand the purpose of everything in nature, and there may seem to be superfluous parts, but this does not mean that we can deny the existence of the great Designer.
4. The criticism that the composition of the watch was simply one of the billions of possible combinations of the constituent parts. Here Paley is warding off the claim that as things must be composed in *some* way, the formation of any particular object is not evidence of design – it is simply a matter of a *chance* coming-together of things.
5. The claim that a pre-existing and impersonal 'principle of order' disposed the parts of the watch into their present form. Paley claims that to say that such a principle of order led to the composition of the watch makes no sense. He thinks it makes no sense to talk about a principle of order distinct from the intelligence of the watchmaker. Perhaps here he is suggesting that we cannot account for the regularity and purpose in nature by pointing to forces like gravity, as these 'principles' come from the designer (God): they are his inventions and his tools.
6. The claim that the mechanism of a watch is not proof of design, but simply a motive to induce the mind to think there is design. Perhaps Paley here is considering the claim that, because the mind naturally wants to give order and purpose to its environment, it will impose structure on it.
7. The claim that the watch may be derived from the 'law of metallic nature'. Here Paley is anticipating the claim that there could be some natural laws that force the development of certain regular, purposive objects. For instance, perhaps there is a law of vegetable nature that causes vegetables to develop in a certain way. Here Paley argues that a law *presupposes* an agent. Laws that cause things to act towards an end are precisely the sort of things that we need an intelligent mind to account for.
8. The claim that Paley is ignorant. If the thinker understands that the watch has a useful purpose, to which the parts of the watch are clearly adapted, then he understands enough to claim there is a designer. Similarly, ignorance about a great deal of the universe does not prevent us from seeing regularity and purpose, and these are all we need to posit a designer.

Paley also goes on to consider some further points:

- If the watch could reproduce itself, this would increase our admiration for the designer (not make us believe he did not exist). Paley also argues that we could not regard the watch itself as the designer of the next watch. We still need the original designer to (a) create the first watch, and (b) account for the fact that the watch can reproduce itself.

- No matter how far back the chain of reproducing watches went, we would still stand in need of an intelligent mind to account for the design existing at all.
- Hence, it does not matter that plant and animal species reproduce, they still stand in need of a designer – their reproduction depends on a designed system. Also, the way in which life reproduces life (for instance, the 'miracle' of conception) should increase our awe of God the Designer.
- In these points, Paley is anticipating the counter-argument posed by evolutionary theory, and sowing the seeds of a reply.

> **Exercise**
> Create a mind map or other diagram to summarize Paley's argument.

Criticisms of the Teleological argument

David Hume

> **David Hume (1711–76)** is arguably the greatest philosopher that Britain has ever produced. He was born and brought up in Edinburgh, studying law at the university. He never practised the law, as he found it dull and preferred 'the pursuits of philosophy and general learning' (Hume, *My Own Life*, Cosimo Classics, 2015 [1777], p. 3). Apart from philosophy, he won international fame for his literary works, especially his multi-volume *History of England* (1754–62). Because he was perceived as a radical, he was turned down for professorships in Philosophy at both Edinburgh and Glasgow universities and had to make a living from tutoring and being a librarian. He is the key figure in the Scottish Enlightenment and a defining thinker in the empirical tradition, seeking to show how the mind is entirely furnished with its ideas from experience and sense impressions. He made significant inroads into the philosophical problem of induction. His *Dialogues Concerning Natural Religion* was written before 1752, but not published until 1779, three years after his death, for fear of prosecution.

At this point, we need to explain that, before Paley's version of the argument, there had been many other versions, including some that Hume had seen and discussed. Hume was not criticizing Paley's version of the argument. His criticisms were published twenty-three years before Paley put his Teleological argument forward. There is no evidence that Paley had actually seen Hume's criticisms. Although it sounds strange to us in the twenty-first century, with our very swift means of disseminating information, it is likely that Hume's views on the Teleological argument were not widely known. He was more famous for his historical writings than his philosophical ones, so Paley probably never saw them.

We have seen above that Paley tried to anticipate some of the criticisms that might be made against his argument. There were a number of philosophers, however, who criticized it forcefully and drew out its essential weaknesses. Hume actually put forward his own version of the Teleological argument before setting about demolishing it. His argument is as follows:

> Look around the world: contemplate the whole and every part of it. You will find it to be nothing but one great machine, subdivided into an infinite number of lesser machines, which again submit of subdivisions, to a degree beyond what human senses and faculties can trace and explain. All these various machines, and their minute parts are adjusted to each other with an accuracy, which ravishes into admiration all men, who have ever contemplated them. The curious adapting of means to ends, throughout nature, resembles exactly, though it much exceeds, the production of human contrivance; of human design, thought wisdom and intelligence. Since therefore the effects resemble one another, we are led to infer, from all the rules of analogy, that the causes also resemble; and that the Author of nature is somewhat similar to the mind of man; though possessed of much larger faculties, proportioned to the grandeur of the work, which he has executed. By this argument, a posteriori, and by this argument alone, do we prove at once the existence of a Deity, and his similarity to human mind and intelligence.
> (David Hume, *Dialogues Concerning Natural Religion*, ed. Norman Kemp Smith, Thomas Nelson, 1947 [1779], p. 143)

Hume's argument has an immediate appeal. It is stated simply and its logic is clear. If anyone were to look around them and observe how nature works (for example, the changing of the seasons; the necessity of water, nutrients and heat for plants to grow; the way that human bodies operate), it seems self-evident that there are order and purpose in the world. This seems to be true, not just at the macro-cosmic level, but also at the micro-cosmic level (e.g. the intricacies of the human eye, as Paley was to discuss). As Jantzen (*An Introduction*) notes, however, Hume devastated the argument from analogy and 'unmasked the design argument as a hopeless failure' (p. 99).

Hume begins by saying that, even if the Teleological argument works philosophically, we could only prove that a design-producing entity existed. It would not prove the existence of the God of classical theism. The Teleological argument depends on the resemblance between a mechanism that we know has been designed and something that bears certain resemblances to that. Hume argues that the difference in scale between a human mechanism and the universe makes it highly implausible that the resemblance is true. Further, because God (the supposed designer) and the universe (the supposed effect) are unique by definition, there is no real analogy and the argument is false. Or, to put it another way, we already know that a watch has been designed because we are familiar with the processes involved in watchmaking. We can have no experience of the processes of world-making, however, because the universe is unique and therefore the supposed analogy breaks down.

Another of Hume's criticisms is that, if a divine mind created the universe, this mind must itself show order and purpose. In this case, we would need to ask what was the cause of the design in this mind. This would lead to an infinite regression of causes and therefore the argument fails to convince. This is a strong objection and the only response to it can be that the explanation must come to an end at some point and be accepted as a 'brute fact'. Even scientists do this with the infinite space-time singularity. The question is, what is it more acceptable to take as brute fact – scientific phenomena (which should always, in principle, be open to scientific enquiry), or the supernatural (which, by its very nature, may be beyond the scope of investigation)?

Another strong objection from Hume concerns the similarity between a watch and the universe. If the supposed similarity leads us to the conclusion that the causes of design in both must be similar, then this must lead to **anthropomorphism**. God must resemble the human designer – but how could this be so? Does God have a gender or body? Is God limited and mortal? The better the analogy between watch and universe, the more anthropomorphic must be our conclusion. However, the weaker the analogy, the weaker our argument must be for the existence of God. Hume is saying here that the design argument would only work if there is a close analogy between mechanisms and natural objects. If there is a very close analogy, however, then the causes must be closely similar.

> **Anthropomorphism:** The idea that God may be understood by attributing human characteristics to him.

Hume's next criticism is to ask why there must be only *one* designer God. Designing and producing the universe, which would be a huge undertaking, would require a whole team of designers and this implies not just one God, but several.

Another argument discussed by Hume concerns the amount of suffering and evil in the world. If God were an omnipotent, **omniscient** and benevolent creator, why would there be so much evidence of bad design? Natural disasters, such as earthquakes that cause the death of thousands of people, must lead, he says, to the conclusion that God is either a bad designer, or is not all-powerful, all-knowing or benevolent. If this is the case, why would any human want to worship this kind of God? Any supposed design in the world is at best only partial. He says:

> **Omniscient:** All-knowing

> This world is very faulty and imperfect, and was only the first rude essay of some infant deity who afterwards abandoned it, ashamed of his lame performance; it is the work only of some inferior deity and is the object of derision to his superiors; it is the production of old age in some superannuated deity, and ever since his death has run on from the first impulse and active force which he gave it.
>
> (*Dialogues Concerning Natural Religion*, pt V)

In fact, Paley pointed out that evidence of imperfection in the world would not of itself deny the existence of a designer, but it does cast significant doubt on the nature of such a designer, in particular questioning whether he can be both omnipotent and benevolent.

> **Exercise**
> Which of Hume's criticisms do you think is most powerful? Explain your reasons.

Kant and apparent design

Immanuel Kant (1724–1804) believed that, in experience, we are simply presented with raw sense-data – we do not experience things-in-themselves, as they are in the external world. Our *mind* then orders such sense-data into space and time. We impose regularity and purpose on to the raw data of experience, and so cannot use such regularity and purpose as any kind of objective proof for God's existence.

John Stuart Mill

Mill (1806–73), widely known for his development of Utilitarianism (see Mark Coffey and Dennis Brown, *Religion and Ethics for OCR*, Polity, 2016, pp. 62–8), expressed strong objections to the Design argument in his book *Nature and Religion* (1874). He picked up on Hume's criticism concerning the imperfections in the world. Mill discusses the Problem of Evil as a major argument against the existence of a benevolent designer. He focuses on natural evil, whereby there are many aspects of the natural world that do not function as if they have been correctly designed. He gives many examples, including 'death by a hurricane and a pestilence'. He thinks it is plain for any intelligent person to see that, if the world had been designed, it had not been done well. The result of this bad or non-existent design was that human beings suffered. Many things in nature appear to be random and destructive, thus demonstrating convincingly that humans do not live in a good world that has been designed by a benevolent God. He makes an analogy with humans who do evil things to others: we expect them to be punished for their actions. The same treatment, he says, should be meted out to God.

Darwin and evolution

Charles Darwin (1809–82) was one of the most important scientists and thinkers of the nineteenth century. In his world-shattering book *On the Origin of Species* (1859), he developed one of the most significant theories in the history of thought. He proposed, in his **Theory of Evolution**, that living organisms developed from simpler to more complex forms gradually over time and through the purely natural processes of random variation, natural selection and the survival of the fittest.

At first sight, it looks as if the Theory of Evolution has successfully explained how everything in the world has developed, apparently without any need for God. Paley's Design argument would seem to be unnecessary. There is no need to posit a cosmically powerful Designer of the world. Neal Gillespie takes this view in his book *Charles Darwin and the Problem of Creation*:

> It has been generally agreed (then and since) that Darwin's doctrine of natural selection effectively demolished William Paley's classical design argument for the existence of God. By showing how blind and gradual adaptation could counterfeit the apparently purposeful design that Paley . . . and others had seen in the contrivances of nature, Darwin deprived their argument of the analogical inference that the evident purpose to be seen in the contrivances by which means and ends were related in nature was necessarily a function of the mind
>
> (Gillespie, *Charles Darwin and the Problem of Creation*, University of Chicago Press, 2001, pp. 83–4)

Despite the apparently crushing effect the Theory of Evolution had on the Design argument, Darwin himself seemed to believe that the two theories were not incompatible. A year after the publication of *On the Origin of Species*, he wrote to the Harvard biologist Asa Gray:

> I am inclined to look at everything as resulting from designed laws, with the details, whether good or bad, left to the working out of what we may call chance. . . . I cannot think

---

Theory of Evolution: Living organisms developed from simpler to more complex form gradually over time and through the purely natural processes of random variation, natural selection and the survival of the fittest.

that the world as we see it is the result of chance; yet I cannot look at each separate thing as the result of Design.

(Charles Darwin, letters to Asa Gray (22 May and 26 Nov. 1769), as quoted in Meister, *Introducing Philosophy of Religion*, p. 96)

Darwin's view of the relationship between evolutionary theory and the Design argument seems to have been ambiguous. In his early life, he had been a practising Anglican but, following his travels and meeting people of other religions, he became more sceptical concerning Christianity and more agnostic about God's existence. After formulating his evolutionary theory and convinced by the overwhelming scientific evidence in its favour, God's importance receded in Darwin's mind, though it never quite disappeared.

Richard Dawkins

In *The Blind Watchmaker* (W. W. Norton, 1986), Dawkins argues that the complexity of nature needs to be explained, but that this explanation is found in the 'blind' process of evolution. Evolution is a race in which only the winners are seen, and the winner looks as though it was designed for the race. There is no God, but only 'the blind, unconscious, automatic process' that Darwin discovered.

Modern restatements of the Design argument

Frederick R. Tennant

Tennant (1866–1957) taught at Cambridge University and wrote the influential two-volume *Philosophical Theology* (Cambridge University Press, vol. I, 1928; vol. II, 1930), in which he wrote an extended defence of Natural Theology. He argued that the reality of God could be established by using philosophical reasoning and the evidence from nature. Importantly, he thought that it was impossible to come to a definitive proof of God's existence, and that we live our lives on the basis of probabilities. His arguments on God's existence were therefore based on the probability of their being persuasive, rather than conclusive. He tried to establish what he called the 'theistic hypothesis' as the most probable explanation for the world, including the existence of human beings. Further than this, he argues that all the elements of the natural world interact with each other in order to support human life. This fine-tuning could only have been brought about by God.

There are six strands to Tennant's argument, which has come to be known as the **Anthropic Principle**. The name was first coined by the Australian theoretical physicist Brandon Carter (1948–).

First, nature and knowledge are mutually adapted to each other. He argues that the world is more or less intelligible to humans. It is a coherent universe, whereas, if the elements of the universe had been even very slightly different, it would have been chaos.

Second, Tennant accepts Darwin's evolutionary ideas and says that it is not the mechanism of how evolution happened that is most important, but the fact of the whole process being successful that points to the existence of God (the 'theistic hypothesis').

> **Anthropic Principle:** The idea that the universe is fine-tuned so that humans can live in it.

Third, the fitness of the physical world and its ability to continue to sustain life is consistent with a formative principle. For Tennant, this is God. He says:

> The fitness of our world to be the home of living beings depends upon certain primary conditions, astronomical, thermal, chemical, etc., and on the coincidence of qualities apparently not causally connected with one another, the number of which would doubtless surprise anyone wholly unlearned in the sciences. Unique assemblages of unique properties on so vast a scale being thus essential to the maintenance of life, their forthcomingness makes the inorganic world seem in some respects comparable with an organism. It is suggestive of a formative principle.
>
> (Tennant, *Philosophical Theology*, vol. II, p. 86)

Fourth, Tennant notes that the world is essentially beautiful. Everything in nature exhibits aesthetic qualities, and these are in tune with its intelligibility. He thinks that this strengthens the case for God's existence.

Fifth, human beings are part of the natural world, but transcend it by being rational and moral creatures. This point must be explained, says Tennant, in any reasonable explanation of the world.

Finally, Tennant argues that his previous five points reinforce each other and have a cumulative effect. When all five are seen together as aspects of a complex universe that is ordered to produce a consistent and inter-connected whole, culminating in human intelligence, the theistic hypothesis becomes inescapable. Tennant concludes that the existence of God is the best reason, not only for the existence and continuance of the world, but more importantly for it being fine-tuned for human beings to live in it.

Developments in Tennant's Anthropic Principle

Since Tennant's formulation of the argument, the Anthropic Principle has been discussed by theologians, philosophers and scientists. One development was that two forms of the theory came into being: the 'Weak' and the 'Strong'.

- The Weak version argued that, if the world had been different, human beings would not and could not exist. This does not really cause any difficulties as it merely states that the world exists as it does.
- The Strong version, however, is more controversial. It argues that the world *must* be the way it is, so that human beings can exist in it. The way the world developed made it inevitable that humans would exist. This is a more controversial statement and has led to a great deal of discussion and debate amongst both philosophers and scientists.

Criticisms of Tennant

Several criticisms have been made of Tennant's theory, including the following:

1. It is possible that an infinite number of universes exist and do so in parallel. We do not have access to any of these alternate universes. In an infinite number of universes and infinite possibilities, it would not be surprising that

one universe – ours – was suitable for life to emerge. In this scenario, there is no need for a designing 'creator'.
2. It is illogical to argue that the universe is structured specifically in order to allow human beings to exist. The theory suggests awarding humans a special and central position in the universe, but, if the structure of the universe were even slightly different, any other creature – cats, sparrows, maggots, for instance – could have been dominant and it would be possible to argue that any of these creatures were the reason for the 'design' of the universe. There is therefore no logical reason to suggest that humans should take centre place.
3. Given that there may be an infinite number of universes and an infinite number of possibilities for life in each of these, the probability of any single event taking place is highly unlikely. So, the possibility of the universe being 'designed' for humans is just as unlikely as any other event taking place. For example, the possibility of my being involved in a car crash while driving on a deserted straight road where there is excellent visibility is highly unlikely. I could have chosen not to drive on that day, to take a different route, take a break on the way, visit a friend and so on. My having a car crash would just have been one among many possibilities. There would not have been any 'design' in it. As people sometimes say when something unusual happens, it was just a coincidence. It was a random event and does not prove the existence of God.

> **Exercise**
> Write a dialogue between Tennant and an atheist on the Anthropic Principle, explaining arguments on both sides about whether there actually is design in the world.

Richard Swinburne on design

Swinburne (1934–present) is a renowned English philosopher of religion and was the Nolloth Professor of the Philosophy of the Christian Religion at the University of Oxford. Swinburne argues that the laws of the universe act according to very simple principles, are regular and observable, and can be understood by using scientific methods. He says:

> not only are there enormous numbers of things, but they all behave in exactly the same way. The same laws of nature govern the most distant galaxies we can observe through our telescopes as operate on earth, and the same laws govern the earliest events in time to which we can infer as operate today. Or, as I prefer to put it, every object, however distant in time and space from ourselves, has the same powers and the same liabilities to exercise those powers as do the electrons and protons from which our own bodies are made. If there is no cause of this, it would be a most extraordinary coincidence – too extraordinary for any rational person to believe.
>
> (Swinburne, *Is There a God?* p. 54)

Swinburne argues that it would be unbelievable if the regularity of the laws of the universe were merely a coincidence. He believes that there must be a logical reason for their regularity. He invokes **Ockham's Razor** to conclude that it is much more

Ockham's Razor: English philosopher William of Ockham (c.1285–1347) developed the logical principle that 'entities should not be multiplied beyond necessity', i.e. that the explanation with fewer assumptions is the correct one.

Teleological and Cosmological Arguments

likely and believable that there was a designer of the laws of the universe than that they occurred due to random chance.

For Swinburne, it is not only the regularity of the laws that is impressive, but also that they are easily observable by humans. For these reasons, he believes that the existence of God is the logical conclusion to be made from the scientific evidence:

> The great simplicity of a wide hypothesis outweighs by far its wideness of scope in determining intrinsic probability. Perhaps it seems *a priori* vastly improbable, if one thinks about it, that there should exist anything at all logically contingent. But, given that there does exist something, the simple is more likely to exist than the complex. . . . The intrinsic probability of theism is, relative to other hypotheses about what there is, very high, because of the great simplicity of the hypothesis of theism.
>
> (Swinburne, *The Existence of God*, Oxford University Press, 1979, p. 106)

Here, Swinburne comes to the conclusion that belief in God is an extremely 'simple' proposition. He says that the simplicity of God is much more likely than all the characteristics of the universe that demand further explanation. This latter possibility is far less likely because it leaves too many important questions unanswered. The fact that the universe exists makes it more likely that God created it than that it came into existence by chance.

Swinburne's argument has been severely criticized:

1. Writers such as Michael Palmer raise the question of whether theism as a concept is, in fact, simple, as Swinburne supposes. Palmer says:

   > For while the *definition* of the divine attributes may seem straightforward enough, its implications may be much less so. Let us take just one: omniscience. What is the relation between omniscience and divine providence? Does omniscience impugn the concept of free will? Does omniscience require a knowledge of the evil that is to occur and thus either a malevolent desire that it should occur or an impotent inability to prevent it occurring?
   >
   > (Palmer, *The Question of God*, p. 140)

   The point here is that humans cannot know what is in God's mind, so we cannot say that positing God's existence is a simple explanation.

2. Swinburne used Ockham's Razor to argue that it is more likely than not that there was a designer of how the world is. However, it is not necessarily correct that what appears to be the simplest solution (God) is, in fact, the correct or only one. It might be that a combination of factors is more likely to be the most satisfactory solution.

3. As both Hume and Mill said, the existence of evil in the world is a major objection to having God as the ultimate explanation. Swinburne does not answer this successfully. If the existence of evil in the world were to be understood as part of the 'simple' explanation, many people, both religious and non-religious, would find this to be unsatisfactory.

> **Exercise**
>
> Summarize Swinburne's arguments on design and compare them with those of Hume.

The Cosmological argument

A brief history of Cosmological arguments

Another example of a Natural Theology approach to establishing the existence of God is the Cosmological argument, which is more accurately described as a series of linked arguments. These arguments are formulated with the aim of inducing or inferring the existence of God from facts about the world, such as causation, change, motion and contingency. This type of argument goes back at least to Aristotle and was used by early Christians. It also developed in Islamic theology, following the re-discovery of Aristotelian philosophy, when scholars such as Al-Kindi and **Al-Ghazali (1058–1111 CE)** advanced strong versions of the argument, including the Kalam argument. Aquinas discovered the argument through studying translations of these Islamic authors and created his own formulations that make up the first three of his 'Five Ways'. The argument has continued to find support since the Middle Ages. **Gottfried Leibniz (1646–1716)** made an important contribution in his '**Principle of Sufficient Reason**', and recent defenders of the Cosmological argument, including **William Lane Craig (1949–present)** and **William L. Rowe (1931–2015)**, have continued to debate the issues.

> **Cosmological:** A type of argument that looks at the world (cosmos), searching for evidence of God's existence.

> **Principle of Sufficient Reason:** Based on the premise that there must be an explanation (rather than a cause) for the existence of the universe and every thing in it. Argues towards there being sufficient reason for the universe.

Aquinas's Cosmological arguments

Aquinas published his three Cosmological arguments in his major work, the *Summa Theologica*. The arguments are known as the first three of his Five Ways. The first 'Way' is from motion, the second from causation, and the third from contingency.

The First Way (Motion and First Mover)

> The first and more manifest way is the argument from motion. It is certain and evident to our senses that in the world, some things are in motion. Now whatever is in motion is put into motion by another, for nothing can be in motion unless it is in potentiality to that towards which it is moved; whereas a thing moves insofar as it is in act. For motion is nothing else than the reduction of something from potentiality to actuality. Nothing can be reduced from potentiality to actuality except by something in a state of actuality. So that which is actually hot, like fire, makes wood, which is potentially hot, to be actually hot, and thereby moves and changes it. Now it is not possible for the same thing to be both in actuality and potentiality in the same respect, but only in different respects. What is actually hot cannot simultaneously be potentially hot, it is simultaneously potentially cold. It is therefore impossible that in the same respect and in the same way, a thing should be both mover and moved i.e. that it should move itself. Therefore whatever is moved must be moved by another. If that by which it is moved is itself moved, then this must also be moved by another, and that by another again. But this cannot go on to infinity, because then there would be no first mover, and, consequently, no other mover, since subsequent movers only move because they are moved by the first mover, just as the staff moves only because it is moved by the hand. Therefore it is necessary to arrive at a first mover, moved by no-one else. This, everyone understands to be God.
>
> (Aquinas, *Summa Theologica*, 1, 2, 3)

Teleological and Cosmological Arguments

The First and Second Ways are known as *chain of causes* arguments, and the Third Way is a version of the argument from contingency. The First Way argues from the existence of motion to the existence of God. The traditional reading of this argument is simply stated as follows:

We see from observation (i.e. a posteriori) that objects are in motion, but they cannot cause their own motion. A child's roundabout, for example, cannot move itself and will be brought into motion by someone pushing it. Before they move, these objects have the *potential* to move, but are not *actually* in motion. Only other objects that are already in motion (in a state of actuality) can cause their motion. No object can simultaneously be in a state of both potentiality and actuality, and no object can cause itself to change its state. So some *other* object in a state of actuality (i.e. actually in motion) must cause the motion of the potentially moving object. But the motion of this other object cannot have been caused by itself, so a chain of objects in motion is needed stretching backwards, each accounting for the motion of the next. Crucially, Aquinas argues that infinite regress is impossible. Therefore, there must have been a Prime Mover that is unmoved by anything else (that is, something which depends on nothing else for its motion, and accounts therefore for the motion of all moving things). For Aquinas, this Unmoved Mover is God.

When Aquinas refers to 'motion' he does not necessarily mean things that are physically moving. Rather, he means anything going from a state of potentiality to actuality. Aquinas uses an example to illustrate his point. Wood, he says, is something that has the potential to become hot. Only something actually hot (such as fire) can cause wood (which is potentially hot) to become actually hot. The wood itself could not cause its own hotness, as to do so it would have to first be actually hot, which it cannot be if it is potentially hot. (When it is actually hot, it is potentially cold, not potentially hot).

Criticisms of the First Way

1. Against the claim that nothing causes its own motion, it has been argued that animals cause their own motion. Also, philosopher Anthony Kenny has claimed that Aquinas contradicts Newton's first law of motion: 'at any given time the rectilinear uniform motion of a body can be explained by the principle of inertia in terms of the body's own previous motion without appeal to any other agent' (*The Five Ways: St. Thomas Aquinas' Proofs of God's Existence*, Routledge, 1969, p. 28).
2. Aquinas's claim that something can be made F only by something that is actually F is clearly false. Take Aquinas's own example of wood becoming hot. There need be no actually hot thing (like fire) to make wood hot, as wood can be made hot by rubbing two sticks together. Also, as Kenny points out, 'a king-maker need not himself be king, and it is not dead men who commit murder' (ibid., p. 21).
3. **Brian Davies (1951–)** has attempted to answer these critical points. He claims that the fact that an aspect of the animal which is not in motion causes the 'in motion' aspect of the animal, shows that it is still true that nothing moves or changes itself (the walking part of the dog is not the cause of its walking). He also feels that Newton's law has been misapplied. True, the *continuous* rectilinear

motion of *x* need have no cause other than *x*, but this continuous motion is not change as conceived by Aquinas. Change, in this case, would be slowing, accelerating or deviating – none of which could be caused by *x*.

4. Finally, Davies claims that Aquinas only believed that something which actually *has the power* to make something F can make something F – not that the thing had to be F itself. He thinks that a thinker such as Aquinas could not have made the elementary mistake he is accused of. However, we could ask whether Davies's reading is consistent with the text, and, if it is, may it not prevent a chain of causes argument – with one moving thing causing another moving thing – from working? If we say that *x* causes the movement of *y* because it *actually has the power to do so*, even though it is not actually moving itself, then there is no further movement to be accounted for and no chain to culminate in God.
5. This argument proceeds from out-dated Aristotelian thought. His teleological view of nature, and distinction between actuality and potentiality, are simply no longer relevant.

The Second Way (causation and First Cause)

> The second way is from the nature of efficient cause. In the world of sense we find there is an order of efficient causes. There is no case known (neither is it, indeed, possible) in which a thing is found to be the efficient cause of itself; for so it would be prior to itself, which is impossible. Now in efficient causes it is not possible to go on to infinity, because in all efficient causes following in order, the first is the cause of the intermediate cause, and the intermediate is the cause of the ultimate cause, whether the intermediate cause be several, or only one. Now to take away the cause is to take away the effect. Therefore, if there be no first cause among efficient causes, there will be no ultimate, nor any intermediate cause. But if in efficient causes it is possible to go on to infinity, there will be no first efficient cause, neither will there be an ultimate effect, nor any intermediate efficient causes; all of which is plainly false. Therefore it is necessary to admit a first efficient cause, to which everyone gives the name of God.
>
> (Aquinas, *Summa Theologica*, 1, 2, 3)

The traditional understanding of Aquinas's Second Way – from Cause – is as follows:

Everything has an efficient cause and this cause also has a cause of its existence. Nothing can be the efficient cause of itself as causes are prior to effects and nothing can be prior to itself. An infinite regress is impossible, as, if there were no first cause, there would be no subsequent causes and hence no effects in the present. This is contrary to our experience of the world. So the series of 'caused causes' implies an uncaused cause, i.e. something that is not caused by anything else. There must, therefore, be a first Uncaused Cause and Aquinas thinks of this as God.

As mentioned above, Aquinas was heavily influenced by the philosophy of Aristotle, and his ideas on cause and effect in the Second Way are an important case in point. Aristotle had posited four kinds of cause – material, formal, efficient and Final. The first two (material and formal) are the substance of a thing and its description. The efficient and Final causes are how the object is made – or what Aristotle calls the prior conditions or events that have caused the object to come about – whereas the Final Cause is what specific event causes the thing to come into existence. (See the discussion of Aristotle's Four Causes in chapter 3.) These may be explained best by using Aristotle's favourite example, a marble statue:

> ***Material cause***: the marble from which the statue is to be made. Within this block of marble is its inherent potential to become a statue.
> ***Formal cause***: this is where the sculptor studies and recognizes how best to make the marble into a statue. It is a formal idea that explains how to move from the material to the efficient cause.
> ***Efficient cause***: this is where the sculptor actually chisels the block of marble into a statue.
> ***Final Cause***: this is where all can recognize the marble as being a particular thing, that is, the finished statue.

These categories help to explain how Aristotle and Aquinas can move from the 'potential' of something to its 'actuality'. The block of marble has the potential to become a statue, but there has to be something (or someone, the sculptor) that brings to fruition the change from potential to actuality (the statue).

These Aristotelian categories remained important in western philosophy until the seventeenth-century scientific revolution. They were finally disposed of when philosophers such as Spinoza and Descartes argued that efficient causes are all that are necessary to explain how the world works.

Some modern examples to help explain Aquinas's understanding of the relationship between cause and effect / potentiality and actuality are suggested below:

(a) Dominos – you have a domino rally set up. Imagine you see the end of the rally with the last domino being toppled by the previous and you decide to follow the chain back to the first domino.

After several miles of walking, you are still following the trail. There is no end in sight, so would you simply conclude that there was no first domino? Of course not, according to Aquinas's reasoning, for then the domino rally could never have reached the final domino. We need a starting point for forward movement to occur, leading to the most recent event in the chain.

(b) Train carriages – Suppose you are stopped at a level crossing and see a train carriage being shunted up the track. This carriage is being shunted by the next, and the next one by the one before and so on for as far as you can see. Would you accept that this chain could be endless and that there is no engine somewhere down the track providing the impetus for the movement? Again, you would not accept this conclusion and would reason that there must be an engine even though you cannot see it.

Criticisms of the Second Way

The Second Way seems far more persuasive than the First. To dismiss the argument, a number of avenues are open:

1. The argument is based on the claim that everything that happens has a cause. If successfully denied, the argument could be rejected.

2. The above claim is heavily supported by Leibniz's Principle of Sufficient Reason, which will be examined below. Rejecting this principle would remove support for the claim that everything has a cause.

Criticisms relevant to both the First and Second Ways

1. *God may be dead.* Perhaps there was once an Unmoved Mover or an Uncaused Cause, but there are no guarantees that this entity still exists. As a proof of the current existence of God, the Cosmological argument seems a non-starter. Aquinas has assumed God's continued existence, not argued for it.
2. *The arguments are self-contradictory.* The First Way asserts that every moving thing depends on another moving thing for its motion and then concludes there is an Unmoved Mover – a moving thing which depends on no other moving thing for its motion. The Second Way asserts that nothing happens without an efficient cause and concludes that there is an Uncaused Cause – something without an efficient cause. These claims are simply and obviously self-contradictory and cannot be taken seriously.

Stretch and challenge: is there a solution to the First and Second Ways?

In response to the problems associated with thinking of God as the First Cause *in time*, a new understanding of Aquinas's First and Second Ways has been developed, especially by the Jesuit scholar **F. C. Copleston (1907–94)**, and for the sake of clarity will be applied here to the Second Way. Copleston argues that 'First Cause' could be understood in two ways: as the *temporally* First Cause, or as the *ontologically* 'ultimate' cause. Copleston believes that Aquinas is arguing *not* that God is the temporally first cause at the beginning in time of a long sequence of causes, but rather that he is the ontologically ultimate cause. To understand this better we must understand the difference between ***in fieri*** and ***in esse*** causes.

A cause *in fieri* is one that causes an effect to become what it is, whereas causes *in esse* are causes that sustain the being or existence of the effect. So, for example, my mother is one of the causes of my existence *in fieri*, but she is not my cause *in esse*. Oxygen, on the other hand, is one of the causes of my existence *in esse*.

If this reading is legitimate, Aquinas is not interested in a temporal, linear chain of *in fieri* causes with God at its start, but with an ontological, 'vertical' chain of *in esse* causes with God at the top. He is the ultimate *in esse* cause without whom the other *in esse* causes would cease to exist. God is therefore rather like the electricity that keeps light bulbs alight. Once the electricity is switched off, the light ceases.

Michael Palmer explains the significance of Copleston's point:

> This distinction clarifies Aquinas's argument. He is not concerned with causes *in fieri* but with causes *in esse* – not with a lineal or horizontal series but with a vertical hierarchy – and an infinite regression of these causes is impossible. For without the first member, a mover

Ontology: The study of 'being' – that is, the nature of the properties of something.

Cause *in fieri*: A cause that causes something to become what it is.

Cause *in esse*: A cause that sustains the being or existence of an effect.

which is not itself moved or a cause that does not itself depend on the causal activity of a higher cause, it is impossible to explain why there is motion or change *here and now* amongst the lower members. Self-evidently, a thing cannot cause itself. Thus, if it is not uncaused or its own cause, its present existence must be caused by another, whose own existence sustains it. Since, therefore, no member of any causal series can exist except through the present operation of a first cause, no dependent causes could operate without this superior cause. Thus we are led to conclude that there must be a first efficient and completely non-dependent cause, an actual cause now operating to preserve the being of all existing things and without which the whole universe would cease to be.

(Palmer, *The Question of God*, pp. 54–5)

Aquinas's Third Way (from possibility and necessity)

The Third Way is taken from possibility and necessity, and runs thus. We find in nature things that are possible to be and not to be, since they are found to be generated, and to corrupt, and consequently, they are possible to be and not to be. But it is impossible for these always to exist, for that which is possible not to be at some time is not. Therefore, if everything is possible not to be, then at one time there could have been nothing in existence. Now if this were true, even now there would be nothing in existence, because that which does not exist only begins to exist by something already existing. Therefore, if at one time nothing was in existence, it would have been impossible for anything to have begun to exist; and thus even now nothing would be in existence – which is absurd. Therefore, not all beings are merely possible, but there must exist something the existence of which is necessary. But every necessary thing either has its necessity caused by another, or not. Now it is impossible to go on to infinity in necessary things which have their necessity caused by another, as has been already proved in regard to efficient causes. Therefore we cannot but admit the existence of some being having of itself its own necessity, and not receiving it from another, but rather causing in others their necessity. This all men speak of as God.

(Aquinas, *Summa Theologica*, 1, 2, 3)

According to Aquinas, it is an a posteriori fact that things not only exist but exist contingently – that is, they have the possibility of either existing or not existing. Anything that is capable of not existing at some time does not exist. So, at some point in time, *each* contingent thing did not exist. Over a huge amount of time, there must be some point at which *every* contingent thing does not exist at the same time. But if that were the case, then nothing could exist now, as nothing can happen without a cause. Things do exist now, therefore, there must exist a necessary being (one which is incapable of not existing) that explains the existence of contingent things now. This necessary being is God.

Criticisms of Aquinas's Third Way

1. Is it true to say that, given an infinite amount of time, every single contingent thing will actualize its potential not to exist at the same time? Aquinas seems to be moving from the claim that every contingent thing will cease to exist at some time (plural), to the claim that there is some time (singular) when every contingent thing will cease to exist. This is logically inconsistent and therefore fails as an argument.

2. As Aquinas seems to have done in the first two ways, he appears to be making another self-contradictory argument here. He begins with the premise that everything is capable of not existing, and concludes that there IS something (God) that is not capable of not being. As a counter-argument to this criticism, however, Aquinas may be defended by refining his statement to say that all *observable* things are contingent, and proving from this that there must be at least one non-observable, necessary being.

Leibniz - argument from contingency (Principle of Sufficient Reason)

In the seventeenth century, German philosopher and mathematician Gottfried Wilhelm Leibniz took the Cosmological argument in a new direction. Instead of focusing on the idea of contingency, it is based on the premise that there must be an explanation (rather than a cause) for the existence of the universe and every thing in it. It argues towards there being sufficient reason for the universe.

In simple terms, Leibniz argues that everything in the universe needs an explanation for why it exists. Nothing in the world provides an explanation for itself, including the world as a whole. So the explanation must come from outside the universe, which is sufficient for this purpose. We call this explanation 'God'. American philosopher, **Chad Meister (1965–present)** provides a summary of the argument:

> 1. All things (beings) which exist must have a sufficient reason for their existence.
> 2. The sufficient reason for the existence of a thing must either lie in the thing itself or outside the thing.
> 3. All things in the universe are things the sufficient reasons of which lie outside themselves (i.e. nothing in the universe provides its own explanation for its existence).
> 4. The universe is nothing more than the collection of the things of which it consists.
> 5. Thus, there must be a sufficient reason for the universe as a whole which lies outside itself.
> 6. There cannot be an infinite regress of such sufficient reasons, for then there would be no final explanation of things.
> 7. Therefore, there must be a first explanatory thing (Being) whose sufficient reason for its existence lies in itself rather than outside itself (i.e. a Necessary Being whose non-existence is impossible).
>
> (Meister, *Introducing Philosophy of Religion*, p. 73)

Leibniz gives a famous example to illustrate his thoughts. Suppose, he says, that you possess a geometry book that has been meticulously copied from another, earlier copy, which has, in turn, been copied from another earlier copy, and so on. To explain the existence of your geometry book by saying it is the copy of another one explains nothing. Only asserting the existence of some original author will give a sufficient reason for the existence of your book. Likewise, it is no use appealing to a contingent thing, or series of contingent things, as an explanation of the universe. Only a necessary being can fill this role.

Criticisms of the Principle of Sufficient Reason

The Principle of Sufficient Reason – that nothing occurs without sufficient reason for why it is and not otherwise – underpins most versions of the Cosmological argument (even though its name was coined by Leibniz). However, this principle has been widely criticized, and if these criticisms are successful, this would strike at the heart of the Cosmological argument.

Sufficient reason is not a logical requirement

The requirement to find an explanation of the world is not a logical one. It may be a fact of our rationality that we constantly seek explanations, and it may be an empirical fact that these explanations are normally found, but it is not a matter of logical *necessity* that such explanations will be found, or even that they exist.

According to Oxford philosopher **James Mackie (1917–81)**, we feel obliged to assume there is a reason for the universe in order to conclude that the world is not pointless, but to conclude that the world is pointless is not self-contradictory. These reflections are supported by Bertrand Russell who famously asserted that the universe is simply a *brute fact*: 'I should say that the universe is just there, and that is all' (BBC radio debate between Copleston and Russell, 1942, quoted in Hick, *The Existence of God*, p. 164).

The principle is established a posteriori, then treated as if it were a logical truth. It is the product of our observation of causation in the world and is useful in understanding our world of experience. However, when we apply the principle to the world of experience *as a whole* and claim that it must have a cause, we are moving *beyond* the realm in which there is any empirical observation – we are using the principle in a realm where we can have no idea whether or not it applies. To suggest that the principle applies here is to treat it as logical truth, not an a posteriori principle.

One reply to this criticism, however, is that the Cosmological argument is inductive. Even if the Principle of Sufficient Reason is not *logically* necessary, it is true of all our experience, and is a presupposition of our interaction with the world. Hence, it is highly probable, if not logically necessary.

The logic of the principle is not consistently applied

If our explanations must stop somewhere, then why not with the existence of the universe as a brute fact? If the universe demands an explanation, then why do we not demand the same of God? If we must ask what caused the universe, then surely we must ask what caused God. If it is replied that we do not demand the same of God because he is *necessary*, then this raises two further difficulties:

- how do we know the universe is not necessary? Just because things within it are contingent, doesn't mean the universe as a whole is contingent.
- why is it that a necessary being needs no sufficient reason? Why doesn't a necessary being depend for its existence on another necessary being (possibly leading to an infinite regress of gods)?

Fallacies of reasoning

1. The Cosmological argument commits the fallacy of composition. This is the mistaken assumption that the whole must share the same properties as its parts. It is erroneous to assume that just because every event in the universe has a cause, the *whole* universe has a cause. Bertrand Russell likened this to saying that because every human has a mother, the human race must have a mother.
2. The Cosmological argument commits the **quantifier shift fallacy**. Similarly, there seems to be an erroneous shift in the Cosmological argument between the claim that 'everything has a cause (plural)', to 'there is a cause (singular) of everything'. This is akin to saying 'Every nice girl loves a sailor (plural), therefore there is a sailor (singular) that every nice girl loves'.

> **Quantifier shift fallacy:**
> The mistaken assumption that because everything (plural) has a cause there is a cause for every thing (singular).

Objections to causation

At the heart of the Cosmological argument is the belief that there are causes and effects: that causation is an objective fact about the world. Suppose, however, that causation is not an objective fact about reality, but merely a product of the human mind. If this is the case, then the Cosmological argument is built on a non-existent platform. If there is no causality in the world, there can be no cosmological proof of God. This view is associated with Hume and Kant.

Hume argues that the ideas of cause and effect are entirely distinct – a so-called 'cause' and a so-called 'effect' can easily be conceived of as occurring one without the other. He concludes: 'Consequently the actual separation of these objects is so far possible that it implies no contradiction or absurdity.' Hume's view here seems to be supported by recent science. Quantum theory holds that tiny particles of matter *can* pop into existence from a vacuum without a cause. This seems to lend empirical weight to the claim that things could come into existence without a cause, albeit in very specific and particular circumstances.

Second, as a strict empiricist, Hume believes that we arrive at all knowledge through observation. He argues, however, that we simply cannot observe causation. We can only observe one event immediately followed by another. If we observe the same subsequent event following the same prior event on numerous occasions (what Hume refers to as 'constant conjunction'), a *habit of mind* leads us to think of one as a 'cause', the other as an 'effect', and to assume a causal relation between the two. If this is true, then causation is an idea formed by the human mind, and not an empirical fact about the world.

Third, an implication of Hume's theory of constant conjunction is that we have no grounds whatsoever to speculate about the cause of the universe. The habit of mind by which we identify 'cause' is stronger the more past observations of constant conjunction we have had. The more frequently we observe y preceded by x, the more we are entitled to think of x as the 'cause' of y. However, as we have experience of only one universe and have *never* experienced its beginning, we have no constant conjunction by which we could identify a 'cause'.

Replies to Hume

1. Copleston argues that being able to *imagine x* occurring without a cause does not demonstrate that *x could actually happen* without a cause – 'even if one can imagine first a blank, as it were, and then x existing, it by no means follows necessarily that x can begin to exist without an extrinsic cause'.

    Quantum theory is just a theory. Even if such spontaneous generation of matter does occur, the weight of experience demonstrates that in all but the most unusual of circumstances everything has a cause. However, the quantum physicist has an obvious reply here. The very rare circumstances in which he claims things can come into being without a cause are precisely those circumstances which pertain to the origins of the whole universe, which is the issue at hand here.

2. Causation is *obviously* an empirical fact about the world – all science and human interaction with the world seems to be premised on this notion. It seems almost a self-evident truth. The ordered, predictable nature of our world bears out the fact that not only are all events caused, but they are caused in consistent, predictable ways. For instance, much of medicine is occupied with the interrogation of causes. A doctor may accept that a certain rare disease she is treating may have an unknown cause, but not *no cause at all.*

    In addition, it should be noted that Hume, in his later work, claimed he had been misunderstood on this issue: 'Allow me to tell you that I never asserted so absurd a proposition as *that anything may arise without a cause.*'

3. This criticism of the Cosmological argument holds only if Hume is correct in his overall epistemology – only if he is correct that our idea of cause is gleaned from a habit of mind.

Theological objections

1. **Not the God of classical theism**. Many theists believe that only a threadbare concept of God is supported by the Cosmological argument. It tells us nothing about God's nature, such as God's omnipotence or omniscience, and therefore it is not satisfactory for theists in any meaningful way.
2. **Deism**. Many theologians have objected to the cosmological proof as it seems to lead to a deist concept of God as having set the world off in the beginning, but having no influence upon it now. This in turn leaves open the possibility that such a God has ceased to exist.

A new view of the universe

British physicist and cosmologist Stephen Hawking (1942–present) has speculated that the universe is a four-dimensional entity with a finite surface which has no beginning or end (perhaps somewhat like a sphere). In other words, he is postulating space/time curvature. The attractiveness of this position is that it offers a third alternative:

1. Alternative 1: The universe had a beginning – this needs to be explained and leaves room for a creator God
2. Alternative 2: The universe is linear with a past stretching backwards infinitely – this is subject to all the problems of actual infinities and infinite regress which seem insurmountable
3. *Alternative 3: This avoids both of the above problems.* In Hawking's words: 'If the universe really is self-contained, having no boundary or edge, it would have neither beginning nor end. What place then for a creator?' (*A Brief History of Time*, Bantam Press, 2011, p. 127).

FURTHER READING

B. Clack and B. Clack, *The Philosophy of Religion: A Critical Introduction*. 2nd edition. Polity, 2008

M. A. Corey, *God and the New Cosmology: The Anthropic Design Argument*. Rowman & Littlefield, 1993

John Cottingham, *Philosophy of Religion: Towards a More Humane Approach*. Cambridge University Press, 2014

William L. Craig, *The Cosmological Argument from Plato to Leibniz*. Wipf & Stock, 2001

B. C. Jantzen, *An Introduction to Design Arguments*. Cambridge University Press, 2014

J. L. Mackie, *The Miracle of Theism: Arguments For and Against the Existence of God*. Clarendon Press, 1982

Chad Meister, *Introducing Philosophy of Religion*. Routledge, 2009

Michael Palmer, *The Question of God*. Routledge, 2001

William L. Rowe, *The Cosmological Argument*. Fordham University Press, 1998

Richard Swinburne, *Is There a God?* 2nd edition. Oxford University Press, 2010

Thought Points

1. In your opinion, do the strengths of the Teleological argument outweigh its weaknesses?

2. To what extent do you agree that there is not enough evidence to prove that God exists?

3. Explain what is meant by 'proof' in the context of the arguments for God's existence.

4. 'The Problem of Evil proves that there is no benevolent design in the world.' Discuss this statement.

5. 'The design argument for God's existence is of no value in the twenty-first century.' To what extent do you agree with this statement?

6. 'The Design argument for God's existence is more convincing than the Cosmological argument.' Discuss.

7. 'The universe is just a brute fact – it has no cause.' How far do you agree with this statement?

8. Explain each of Aquinas's Cosmological arguments to someone who has never heard about them.

9. 'Aquinas's Cosmological arguments make no sense in the twenty-first century.' Do you agree? Give reasons for your answer.

10. 'The Cosmological argument has no serious flaws.' To what extent do you agree with this statement?

CHAPTER 5
The Ontological Argument

LEARNING OUTCOMES

In this chapter, you will be learning about:
- the Ontological argument (Anselm and Descartes)
- Gaunilo's criticisms
- Kant's criticisms
- whether a priori argument is a persuasive style of argument
  - can existence be treated as a predicate?
  - does the Ontological argument justify belief?
  - are there logical fallacies in this argument that cannot be overcome?

The Ontological argument

Sir **Richard Southern (1912–2001)** says of the Ontological argument: 'The ontological argument for the existence of God has fascinated philosophers ever since it was formulated by St. Anselm of Canterbury (1033–1109). It is doubtful, I think, that any person was ever brought to a belief in God by this argument, and unlikely that it has played the sort of role in strengthening and confirming religious belief that, for example, the teleological argument has played' (R. W. Southern, *Saint Anselm and His Biographer: A Study of Monastic Life and Thought 1059–c.1130*, Cambridge University Press, 1963, pp. 57–8).

In his biographical study of **Anselm**, Southern summarizes a remarkable fact about the Ontological argument for God's existence. It has fascinated many philosophers, both religious and atheist. It is an entirely different kind of argument from the Design or Cosmological arguments. These are inductive arguments based on (alleged) evidence in the world, while the Ontological argument is based not on empirical evidence, but on pure logic. In this emphasis on logic, it is unique among all the arguments for God's existence.

Southern attempts to find the explanation for the continual fascination with the Ontological argument. He offers two reasons for its special status. The first is that it 'offers an enormous return on a pretty slim investment', by which Southern means that the argument is very compact, consisting of a definition of God, an unlikely connection between 'existence' and 'greatness', and a conclusion. Such apparent simplicity masks the complex logic of the argument. The second reason offered by Southern is that, although this simple argument seems in some ways to be logically unsound, it is very difficult indeed to see exactly what is wrong with it.

Although Anselm is universally acknowledged to be the first to formulate the Ontological argument, some scholars think that a form of it goes back to St Augustine in his fifth-century work *De Libero Arbitrio* (*On Free Will*), in which he uses the phrase 'the Fool who said "There is no God"' and the definition of God as that 'above which there is no superior'. It is likely that Anselm had read these phrases in Augustine and used them in his Ontological argument. The history of the Ontological argument begins with Anselm and stretches to the present day. There has been constant discussion of the argument and we will look at some of the most important of these debates.

St Anselm of Canterbury (1033–1109) was one of the foremost Christian theologians and philosophers of the Middle Ages. He was born in Aosta, northern Italy, and became a monk at the Benedictine monastery at Bec in Normandy, eventually becoming its abbot in 1078. Anselm was made Archbishop of Canterbury in 1089, but, because of a political quarrel, he did not take up this post until 1093. He died in Canterbury in 1109 and was canonized (made a saint) in 1163.

Central to Anselm's approach to theology and philosophy was his view that faith and reason went hand in hand. He believed that faith preceded reason, and used the phrase 'Credo ut intelligam' ('I believe in order to understand'). For Anselm, faith not only came from the authority of scripture and tradition, but could also be demonstrated by rational argument. To explain his general approach, Anselm used the phrase 'Fides quaerens intellectum' ('Faith seeking understanding').

Anselm's Ontological argument

Anselm states the argument in his work *Proslogion*. The argument is given in two parts, the first in chapter 2, the second in chapter 3. In this work, he wants to come up with 'a single argument which would require no other for its proof than itself alone; and alone would suffice to demonstrate that God truly exists, and that there is a supreme good requiring nothing else, which all other things require for their existence and well-being'.

And so, Lord, do thou, who dost give understanding to faith, give me, so far as thou knowest it to be profitable, to understand that thou art as we believe; and that thou art that which we believe. And indeed we believe that thou art a being than which nothing greater can be conceived. Or is there no such nature, since the fool has said in his heart, there is no God? (Psalm 14:1). But at any rate, this very fool, when he hears of this being of which I speak – a being than which nothing greater can be conceived – understands what he hears, and what he understands is in his understanding; although he does not understand it to exist.

For it is one thing for an object to be in the understanding, and another to understand that the object exists. When a painter first conceives of what he will afterwards perform, he has it in his understanding, but he does not yet understand it to be, because he has not yet performed it. But after he has made the painting, he both has it in his understanding, and he understands that it exists, because he has made it.

Hence, even the fool is convinced that something exists in the understanding, at least, than which nothing can be conceived. For, when he hears of this, he understands it. And whatever is understood, exists in the understanding. And assuredly that, than which nothing greater can be conceived, cannot exist in the understanding alone. For, suppose it exists in the understanding alone: then it can be conceived to exist in reality; which is greater.

Therefore, if that, than which nothing greater can be conceived, exists in the understanding alone, the very being, than which nothing greater can be conceived, is one, than which a greater can be conceived. But obviously this is impossible. Hence, there is no doubt that there exists a being, than which nothing greater can be conceived, and it exists both in the understanding and in reality.

(Anselm, *Proslogion*, ch. 2)

The first thing to say about Anselm's argument is that it is an a priori deductive proof for the existence of God. An a priori argument is not based on experience of the world, but solely on logic or reasoning. Anselm attempts to argue from the definition of God to the necessary existence of God – i.e., that God cannot not exist. Another way of putting this is to say that God's existence does not depend on anything else, such as time or circumstances.

Anselm's argument is in two stages.

Anselm's argument – Stage 1 (*Proslogion* 2)

Anselm begins with the definition of God: God is 'that than which nothing greater can be conceived' (in Latin: 'Deus est aliquid quo nihil maius cogitari possit'). Many writers on the Ontological argument translate the Latin as 'the greatest conceivable being', but this is incorrect, as Anselm wants to show that God is much 'greater' than anything humans can think of or understand. He uses the word 'greater' because he wants to avoid specific characteristics of God, e.g. being physically bigger, more knowledgeable, having better eyesight, etc.. For Anselm, God is greater in every respect than humans can understand.

Next, Anselm says that even an atheist must have some understanding of the idea of God because he needs this definition in order to deny God's existence. Anselm distinguishes between two kinds of existence – *in intellectu* ('in the mind') and *in re* ('in reality'). Something is 'greater' if it exists in reality than if it only exists in the mind or imagination. If God is 'that than which nothing greater can be conceived', he cannot only exist in the imagination (that is, only exist for a time and then cease to exist). God must exist necessarily (that is, exist always and never cease to exist). If God existed only in the mind or imagination, he would not be 'that than which nothing greater

The Ontological Argument

can be conceived', for we could conceive of something greater – a God who existed in reality as well. Therefore, God must exist in reality. Only a 'fool' would claim that there is no God because to make this claim would be a self-contradiction.

Gaunilo's rejection of the argument

On first reading, Anselm has produced a very strong argument, based on logic rather than experience. A contemporary of Anselm, Gaunilo, a fellow Benedictine monk at Marmoutier, near Tours in France, criticized the argument by using it in a different context to show that it is absurd. This was a *reductio ad absurdum* type of argument, a 'reduction to absurdity'. This was a common type of argument in the Middle Ages and Gaunilo uses it here to attempt to show that Anselm's logic leads to clearly false conclusions. By doing this, he hoped to reduce the argument to absurdity. Gaunilo asks us to imagine the greatest possible island. Once we have an idea of the greatest island, we can apply Anselm's logic. We can say that the island would be greater if it existed *in re* rather than just *in intellectu*. Hence, to deny that the greatest island exists would be a self-contradiction, and the island must indeed exist. The same logic could be applied to any conceivable object. Gaunilo believes that his counter-example demonstrates the absurd (and hence false) nature of Anselm's argument.

Gaunilo imagined a perfect island

Anselm's argument – Stage 2 (*Proslogion 3*)

> And it assuredly exists so truly, that it cannot be conceived not to exist. For, it is possible to conceive of a being which cannot be conceived not to exist. Hence, if that, than which nothing greater can be conceived, can be conceived not to exist, it is not that, than which nothing can be conceived. But this is an irreconcilable contradiction. There is, then, so truly a being than which nothing greater can be conceived to exist, that it cannot even be conceived not to exist; and this being thou art, O Lord our God.
>
> So truly dost thou exist, O Lord my God, that thou canst not be conceived not to exist; and rightly. For if a mind could conceive of a being better than thee, the creature would rise above the creator; and this is most absurd. And, indeed, whatever else there is, except thee alone, can be conceived not to exist. To thee alone, therefore, it belongs to exist more truly than all other beings, and hence in a higher degree than all others. For, whatever else exists does not exist so truly, and hence in a less degree it belongs to it to exist. Why, then, has the fool said in his heart, there is no God (Psalm 14:1), since it is so evident, to a rational mind, that thou dost exist in the highest degree of all? Why, except that he is dull and a fool?
>
> (Anselm, *Proslogion*, ch. 3)

Anselm believed that his argument was not defeated by Gaunilo's attack. He does this by reminding readers of the definition of God as 'that than which nothing greater can be conceived', and then identifies Gaunilo's mistake by identifying and focusing

THE EXISTENCE OF GOD

on two types of existence – contingent and necessary existence. **Contingent existence** means that something is capable of not existing, while **necessary existence** means that something is incapable of not existing.

Anselm's argument is that a being is 'greater' if it has necessary existence than if it has only contingent existence. For Anselm, God is 'something that can be thought of as existing but which cannot be thought of as not existing'. This means that everything in the world has only contingent existence and at some point will cease to exist. Only God has necessary existence, as God is 'that than which nothing greater may be conceived'. It is self-contradictory to say that God does not exist, because having necessary existence is part of the concept or definition of God. Gaunilo's 'perfect island' example fails because we can conceive of it not existing and therefore it has only contingent existence.

> **Contingent existence:** Something that is capable of not existing at some point.
>
> **Necessary existence:** Something that is not capable of not existing.

Exercise

1. Copy the grid and provide brief definitions of the following terms:

    A priori

    Necessary existence

    Contingent existence

    Ontology

2. Explain how Anselm used his definition to conclude that God exists.
3. Explain what Anselm meant by the term 'necessary existence'.
4. What did Anselm mean by the phrase 'faith seeking understanding'?

Other versions and responses

After Anselm's death, the Ontological argument became neglected for five centuries. This was probably because of the importance of St Thomas Aquinas, who, as we have seen in chapter 4, developed two different kinds of argument for God's existence: the Teleological and Cosmological arguments. In fact, Aquinas rejected the Ontological argument because he thought that human beings cannot know God's true nature. He says:

> A thing can be self-evident in two ways: on the one hand, self-evident in itself, though not to us; on the other, self-evident in itself and also to us. A proposition is self-evident because the predicate is included in the essence of the subject; e.g. Man is an animal, because 'animal' is contained in the essence of 'man' ... there are some to whom the essence of the predicate and the subject is unknown, but the proposition will be self-evident in itself, but not to those ignorant of the meaning of the subject and predicate of the proposition. Therefore, as Boethius says, there are some concepts that are common and self-evident only to the learned, e.g. ... incorporeal substances are not in space.
>
> Therefore, I say that the proposition God exists is in itself self-evident, because God is his own essence ... [But] because we do not know the essence of God, the proposition is not self-evident to us, but must be demonstrated by things that are more known to us, though less evident in themselves – namely, by his effects.
>
> (Aquinas, *Summa Theologica*, 1, 2, 1)

In the seventeenth century, however, the Ontological argument was revived by the French philosopher, **René Descartes (1596–1650)**.

Descartes's Ontological argument

Descartes's version of the argument appeared in the fifth of his *Meditations*. He states:

> If, from the mere fact that I can produce from my thought the idea of something entails that everything that I clearly and distinctly perceive to belong to that thing really does belong to it, is not this a possible basis for another argument to prove the existence of God? Certainly, the idea of God, or a supremely perfect being, is one that I find within me just as surely as the idea of any shape or number. And my understanding that it belongs to his nature that he always exists is no less clear and distinct than is the case when I prove of any shape or number that some property belongs to its nature.

Descartes begins with the idea of the *supremely perfect* being. God is the supremely perfect being and must therefore possess all perfections. Existence is a perfection, therefore God must exist. Descartes argues that clear and distinct ideas in the mind possess their own unchanging natures. Descartes was an important mathematician and uses the example of a triangle to illustrate his point. Triangles have certain necessary qualities – to have three sides and internal angles that add up to 180 degrees. Without these defining characteristics, a shape cannot be a triangle.

Descartes continues by stating, controversially, that 'existence is a certain perfection'. For him, this means that God is unchanging, has always existed and will always exist. God must exist necessarily, as, in Descartes's words, 'existence can no more be separated from the idea of God' than the idea of three internal angles equaling 180 degrees can be separated from the idea of a 'triangle'.

Scottish empiricist philosopher David Hume rejected the argument because it lacked evidence, and he rejected the claim that anything can exist by definition.

Immanuel Kant (1724–1804) was born in Königsberg, at that time the capital of the province of East Prussia. It was a busy industrial city with an important military base and a well-respected university. He was born into a working-class family; his father made saddles and harnesses and his mother was the daughter of a harness-maker. He attended a Pietist school that taught the importance of Christian piety, a strong moral conscience and control of the passions. His mother encouraged him to study hard, which he did, but he reacted against the strict piety of his youth in favour of living according to reason, independent of revelation or devotion. He attended the university in his home town and became fascinated by Philosophy. Kant grew up during the period called the European Enlightenment, sometimes called the 'Age of Reason'. He was to become one of the last and greatest thinkers of this period.

Kant's philosophy attempted to answer three questions: 'What can I know?', 'What should I do?' and 'What can I hope for?' His project was to synthesize Idealism and Empiricism, arguing that knowledge was restricted to the phenomenal world of appearance – that is, the world that we can see in time and space. He was very interested in religion, and wrote several books on it. Particularly interesting is *Religion Within the Limits of Reason Alone*, in which he develops parallels between revealed religion and philosophical theology. He concludes that everything that is essential in religion is morality. Religious beliefs must be put into practice because, otherwise, they mean nothing.

Kant's first objection – 'existence' is not a predicate

In his *Critique of Pure Reason* (1781), Immanuel Kant posed the most serious and lasting objection to the Ontological argument. Although he directed his thoughts against Descartes's version of the argument, they are thought to apply to Anselm's version as well.

Kant argues that *existence is not a predicate*. Descartes's and Anselm's arguments both assume that existence is a 'predicate' of God. A predicate is a property of something. For example, consider the statement 'Fizz is a cat.' The word 'cat' is a property of the subject of the sentence, Fizz. He would not be Fizz if he were not a cat. His 'catness' is an essential 'predicate' or property of Fizz.

Fizz the Cat

> **Predicate:** A predicate is a property or attribute of something

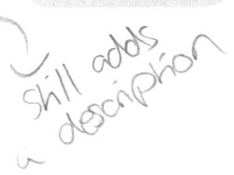

Immanuel Kant's criticisms were more sustained and detailed than most others. He focuses on the predicate 'existence' when it is applied to God. He argues that adding the predicate 'exists' adds nothing to the description of God.

Now, says Kant, it would be easy to assume that existence is indeed a predicate. Take the sentence 'The ball exists.'. Grammatically speaking, it appears that the ball is the subject, and existence is the predicate or object. However, claims Kant, existence is not a genuine predicate as it does not give us any further information about the nature of the subject – it does not 'enlarge our concept' of the subject. Rather than being a predicate or property of the subject, existence is the *precondition* of an object having any predicates or properties. In other words, unless the ball exists, it cannot have any other properties – any other genuine predicates like redness or its size. Another example (not given by Kant!) might be 'Shrek exists.' It would be possible to give a definition of Shrek – large, green, ugly creature who falls in love with Fiona . . . but simply providing a definition of something or someone does not necessitate their existence in the real world.

Descartes' Ontological argument fails if existence is not a perfection, and Anselm's fails if existence is not a property which adds to greatness. According to Kant's reasoning, then, both arguments fail.

Following on from this, Kant's most radical objection to the Ontological argument is that all existential propositions are synthetic. An existential proposition simply means any proposition that asserts the existence of something. Kant is pointing out here that we can know whether any proposition is true or false only by using our sense experience, not by defining it. Sometimes, it is easier to see the force of this point by putting it the other way round – because all existential propositions are synthetic, no existential proposition can be analytic. In fact, this is where we began the discussion of the Ontological argument. The Ontological argument wants to claim exactly this – that the phrase or proposition 'God exists' is an analytic statement. Kant claims that it is not and cannot ever be. For Kant, existence cannot be a legitimate predicate.

The Ontological Argument

Kant's first objection is also supported by more recent philosophers, who each make very similar points.

Bertrand Russell: 'existence' is not a real predicate

British philosopher Bertrand Russell, in his early philosophical life, accepted the Ontological argument, once exclaiming: 'Great God in Boots! – the ontological argument is sound!' He later criticized the argument, however, saying that 'the argument does not, to a modern mind, seem very convincing, but it is easier to feel convinced that it must be fallacious than it is to find out precisely where the fallacy lies' (*History of Western Philosophy* (Book 3, pt 1, section 11). He drew a distinction between existence and essence, arguing that the essence of a person can be described and their existence still remain in question.

Russell distinguishes between two different ways in which the word 'is' can be used. The first way is predicative. This is when the word 'is' ties a predicate to a subject. Hence, in the example 'The ball is red', 'is' is being used in the predicative manner. However, we can also use the word 'is' in the existential manner. So, if I say 'The ball is', I am not tying a predicate to the ball, I am instead making the claim that the ball exists.

Similarly, we can use the word 'is' in two ways when talking about God. If I say 'God is good', then I am using 'is' predicatively, but if I say 'God is' (or 'God exists'), I am using it existentially.

Crucially, Russell argues that supporters of the Ontological argument believe that, when they talk about God's existence, they are employing the predicative use of the word 'is'. That is, when they say God exists, they think they are giving some kind of property to God. But Russell argues that really they are using the word 'is' existentially, and under this usage the Ontological argument simply does not work.

Kant's second objection – the existence of God can be denied without logical contradiction

> The Ontological Argument is an *a priori* attempt to demonstrate the existence of God. Nothing is demonstrable *a priori* unless its contrary is a logical contradiction. Hence the statement that 'God exists' is only demonstrable *a priori* if the contrary – 'God does not exist' – is a logical contradiction. The Ontological Argument attempts to demonstrate in its various forms that 'God does not exist' is indeed a self-contradiction.

Both Anselm and Descartes had made the crucial claim that it is logically contradictory to deny the existence of God. For Anselm, denying the existence of God is akin to saying 'that than which nothing greater can be conceived is *not* that than which nothing greater can be conceived' – a clear logical contradiction. Similarly, Descartes claims that to deny God's existence is as much a logical error as it is to deny that triangles have three internal angles adding up to 180 degrees.

Kant attempts to show that there is actually no such contradiction involved in denying the existence of God. He argues as follows:

THE EXISTENCE OF GOD

In any statement, if the predicate appears in the definition, then it is logically contradictory to claim the opposite is true. The classic example of this is the statement 'A bachelor is an unmarried man.' The key terms in this statement are 'unmarried' and 'man'. These are contained in the subject of the statement, 'bachelor'. If we were to say 'a bachelor is a married man', this would clearly be contradictory to the meaning of 'bachelor' and the statement would be nonsense, as a bachelor cannot be married.

Anselm and Descartes believe that the predicate 'exists' is part of the definition of 'God', so to deny the predicate 'exists' is to deny the subject 'God'. For them, the existence of God is contained in the definition of 'God'. Critics of the argument, however, may take a different example and apply it to the Ontological argument. For example, a triangle is a three-sided figure with internal angles adding up to 180 degrees. If we say that there are no actual triangles in existence, the definition is correct, but the definition does not mean that there actually *are* any existing triangles. To claim that a triangle has three internal angles, does not tell us anything about whether there are any triangles in existence. It only tells us that, if there are any triangles, then they would have three internal angles. The criticism of the Ontological argument, then, is that adding 'existence' to the definition of God does not actually necessitate that God in fact exists.

Kant also attacks the second version of Descartes's argument: that God must exist necessarily. Kant replies that God can only exist necessarily if –and only if – it can be shown that God exists in the first place. If God exists, he must exist necessarily, so his non-existence would be impossible and self-contradictory. But Descartes or Anselm have not shown convincingly that God actually exists. As far as Kant is concerned, the Ontological argument fails. Adding existence to any statement adds nothing to the statement, because existence is not a proper predicate.

In the end, then, the Ontological argument fails to prove that God exists. Yet it remains the most intriguing and interesting philosophical attempt to prove that God exists.

> **Exercises**
> 1. Explain Descartes's definition of God as 'the supremely perfect being'. In what ways might this differ from Anselm's definition?
> 2. Explain Kant's phrase 'existence is not a predicate'.
> 3. In your opinion, does Russell's criticism 'existence is not a real predicate' add much to the discussion of the Ontological argument?
> 4. How far do you agree that 'everything that exists in the universe is contingent'?

Stretch and challenge: Norman Malcolm's Ontological argument

American philosopher **Norman Malcolm (1911–90)** produced an important new view of the Ontological argument in 1960, in which he discussed Anselm's concept of necessary being – the idea that God must exist and cannot not exist. He comments on this idea:

> What Anselm has proved is that the notion of contingent existence or of contingent non-existence cannot have any application to God. His existence must either be logically necessary or logically impossible. The only intelligible way of rejecting Anselm's claim that God's existence is necessary is to maintain that the concept of God, as a being a greater than which cannot be conceived, is self-contradictory or nonsensical. Supposing that this is false, Anselm is right to deduce God's necessary existence from his characterisation of Him as a being greater than which cannot be conceived.
> (Malcolm, 'Anselm's Ontological Argument', *Philosophical Review*, Jan. 1960, quoted in J. H. Hick, *Arguments for the Existence of God*, Macmillan, 1970, p. 91)

English philosopher Michael Lacewing summarizes Malcolm's argument:

1. God either exists or does not exist.
2. God can neither come into existence nor go out of existence.
3. If God exists, then He cannot cease to exist.
4. Therefore, if God exists, He exists necessarily.
5. If God does not exist, then He cannot come into existence.
6. Therefore, if God does not exist, His existence is impossible.
7. Therefore, God's existence is either necessary or impossible.
8. However, God's existence is only impossible if the concept of God is self-contradictory.
9. The concept of God is not self-contradictory.
10. Therefore, God's existence is not impossible.
11. Therefore, from 7 and 10, God's existence is necessary.

(Lacewing, *Philosophy for AS*, Routledge, 2014, p. 191)

On a surface reading, this argument appears to be logical and clear. Several philosophers disagree, however, arguing that Malcolm simply assumes that premise 9 (the concept of God is not self-contradictory) is logically sound. This would need an additional argument to show that it is correct. Another problem is that Malcolm ignores the circumstances of the argument's logical necessity. Premises 3 and 5, for instance, say that '*if* God exists' and '*if* God does not exist', but he assumes that these statements are logically correct. Again, he would have to argue for the truth of these assumptions. He fails to do this. All his argument shows is that *if* God exists, he must exist necessarily. Also, Malcolm does not decisively show that the concept of necessary existence is a perfection. So, if 'X necessarily exists' means 'X exists in all possible worlds', there is no logical reason why God's existence in all possible worlds would make God greater in the *actual* world. This is because, in *this* actual world, a God who exists necessarily is no greater than a God who exists contingently in this world. Malcolm's argument, then, ultimately fails to demonstrate definitively that the Ontological argument is correct.

> **Exercise**
> Do you agree that Malcolm's argument is flawed? Can you think of any ways to disagree with the criticisms made against Malcolm's argument?

THE EXISTENCE OF GOD

FURTHER READING

Daniel A. Dombrowski, *Rethinking the Ontological Argument: A Neo-Classical Theistic Response*. Cambridge University Press, 2011

Reto Gubelmann, *On Proving God's Existence by Reason Alone*. AV Akademikerverlag, 2014

John Hick, *The Many-Faced Argument: Studies on the Ontological Argument for the Existence of God*. Wipf & Stock, 2009

J. L. Mackie, 'Ontological Arguments', in Mackie, *The Miracle of Theism: Arguments For and Against the Existence of God*. Clarendon Press, 1982

Graham Oppy, *Ontological Arguments and Belief in God*. Cambridge University Press, 2008

Alvin Plantinga, *The Ontological Argument from St Anselm to Contemporary Philosophers*. Doubleday, 1965

Thought Points

1. Summarize Anselm's and Descartes's Ontological arguments. Note any similarities and differences between them.

2. Explain Gaunilo's criticism of Anselm's argument. Do you agree with it?

3. Make a summary of Kant's criticisms of Descartes's argument.

4. Research recent attempts to produce a convincing version of the Ontological argument, for instance by Alvin Plantinga.

5. 'The Ontological argument is a heroic failure.' Discuss.

6. 'The Ontological argument is only a play on words, it is not about the real world.' Discuss this statement.

7. 'The Ontological argument is successful in proving the existence of God.' Discuss how far you agree.

SECTION III
GOD AND THE WORLD

CHAPTER 6
Religious Experience

LEARNING OUTCOMES

In this chapter, you will be learning about:
- religious experience
  - what is religious experience?
  - different types of religious experience (mysticism, conversion)
  - different ways in which religious experience can be understood

Religious experience

What is religious experience?

> **Religious experience:** Any experience of the sacred in a religious context, including visions, and mystical and conversion experiences.

We live in a world obsessed by Empiricism, where the only things that are considered to be 'true' are those that can be 'proven' by concrete evidence. This is what makes any discussion of religious experience so difficult for 21st-century people. Religious experience, if it exists at all, is very often about how individuals 'feel', their personal reaction to stimuli that cannot be seen by anyone other than themselves, and they find great difficulty in trying to explain these to others.

Another difficulty with the discussion of religious experience is that the term is used in different ways. For some, having a religious experience might mean simply going to a regular service of worship, or living their everyday lives in the belief that God is looking after them. For others, however, a religious experience refers to a specific, life-altering event, such as conversion.

Religious experience can also be seen as an event or feeling that happens to individuals, while some religious experiences occur to groups of people, even thousands at a time. So, for example, religious practices such as prayer or the performance of a religious ritual may be a religious experience for one individual or for many people at the same time.

A further difficulty, found by many people who claim to have had such experiences, is in explaining them to others. Especially when the supposed religious experience is something out of the ordinary – a vision or near-death experience, for example – the individual who has it may have real difficulty in narrating what happened, their feelings about it and how and why they think that it is God-given.

Despite these difficulties of definition, some philosophers, such as Moojan Momen (*The Phenomenon of Religion: A Thematic Approach*, One World, 1999, p. 88), have found several general features that most kinds of religious experience have in common.

First, they are *universal*. Religious experiences occur around the world. Many studies and surveys show that a significant proportion of the world's population, both past and present, and including in highly secularized societies, has had religious experiences.

Second, they are *diverse*. There is a wide variety of religious experiences, and each experience is unique to the individual who has it. While there are some similarities among the religious experiences of believers in the different religious traditions, there are also differences. This diversity adds to the richness and variety of the experiences across the religious spectrum.

Third, religious experiences are *important* in fundamental ways, very often resulting in a transformed life for the people who have them, because they have to evaluate their lives. This often leads to a change in the way they view the world. In this sense, religious experiences are life-changing.

One question that arises from the difficulties associated with defining religious experience has to do with what makes an experience a 'religious' one? What is it that makes a religious experience different from an 'ordinary' experience? One philosopher who attempted to answer this question was **Friedrich Schleiermacher (1768–1834)**.

Schleiermacher was brought up in the Moravian community, a Protestant group that stressed the importance of individual faith and a personal response to God. For him, religious faith was not about assenting to a number of doctrines or set patterns of worship. His subjective approach led him to conclude that humans are intrinsically religious beings. Every experience a person has is therefore a religious experience, and these experiences provided each individual with a consciousness of the divine. The role of religion, in his view, was to foster an awareness, and to develop this consciousness, of the divine. He develops this idea in his most famous book, *On Religion: Speeches to its Cultured Despisers* (1799). The book, which had a major influence on Protestant thought in the nineteenth century, is split into five sections: the Defense, the Nature of Religion, the Cultivation of Religion, Association in Religion, and the Religions. The Defense is the most important section, as it explains his view that all religious experiences are 'self-authenticating'. By this, he means that religious experiences do not need any other authority or test to show that they are genuine. Here, he is criticizing established forms of Christianity, particularly the Catholic tradition in Germany, which emphasized the importance of reason. This tradition stated that individual religious experiences needed to be tested against established doctrines and the teaching of the Bible before they could be authenticated as genuine.

Schleiermacher stated that religious experiences should be accepted as genuine and be given priority over doctrine. The essence of religion lay in the 'consciousness of being absolutely dependent on, or, which is the same thing, of being in relation with God'. He believed that religion was 'a sense and taste for the infinite' or 'the feeling of absolute dependence' in each individual, where they were totally dependent upon God's will. This 'feeling' superseded any doctrine or statement from the Church. By 'sense', he means an emotionally coloured state of mind that carries with it some form of implicit understanding.

While Schleiermacher removes religion from the constraints of reason and finding evidence for belief, the obvious criticism of his view is that he puts too much emphasis on subjectivism. By moving in this direction, he unwittingly sacrificed Christianity's ability to communicate meaningfully with the non-religious world. Also, it would be open to the dangerous possibility of allowing *any* alleged religious experience as valid, even ones caused by drugs or hallucinations.

Another scholar who developed a theory about the nature and importance of religious experience was the German Protestant philosopher and theologian **Rudolf Otto**.

Rudolf Otto (1869–1937) was a German Protestant philosopher and theologian, educated at Erlangen and Göttingen. He taught Theology at the latter university, then at Breslau and Marburg. He is most famous for his influential book *The Idea of the Holy* (1923), in which he argues that 'the Holy' can be known through the idea of 'the **numinous**'. He argued that religion is essentially the apprehension of the numinous that people can understand. Otto's view of the world was of a mysterious place that could also be appreciated and understood with the aid of the 'non-rational' dimension that humans can access through the 'idea of the Holy'.

Otto became interested in, and influenced by, Eastern religions, after his visit to India in 1911 and his study of the Sanskrit language. He published *Mysticism East and West* in 1926, comparing a well-known medieval German mystic, Meister Eckhart, with a famous Hindu mystical philosopher, Adi Shankara. Otto's works influenced many of the most significant philosophers and psychologists of the twentieth century, including Karl Jung, **Karl Barth (1886–1968)** and **Paul Tillich**.

Numinous: Otto's term for an individual's encounter with 'the Holy', or God.

Mysterium tremendum et fascinans: For Otto, this was the effect that a religious experience had on an individual.

Otto was profoundly influenced by Kant and Schleiermacher. His main purpose in *The Idea of the Holy* was to analyse what it was that made the difference between an experience and a religious experience. His study of Schleiermacher convinced him of the priority of the non-rational emphasis in religion, as opposed to the rationalist approach of Kant. He believed that there was an element of religious belief that was irreducible, and he called this the experience of 'the Holy'. He was not particularly happy with this term, however, because it had become too much associated with the way Kant had used it in his ethical theory. He therefore coined the term '**numinous**' to describe what he meant. He thought that religious experience was like an encounter with something powerful, which could be strange, frightening, but also attractive, positive and fascinating. He calls this kind of numinous experience the '**mysterium tremendum et fascinans**'. It is non-rational and cannot therefore be described in ordinary language because it is a unique experience that comes from the Holy. He disagreed with Schleiermacher's definition of religious experience because Otto thought it was too subjective as it does not point clearly enough to the numinous object (God) as the source of the numinous (religious) experience. The experience of the mysterium describes the feeling of complete dependence on the source of the experience (God) – Otto calls this the 'wholly other'. This 'wholly other' being is both entirely unapproachable and awe-inspiring and overpowering (tremendum) for those who experience it, but also something that attracts the person like a magnet (fascinans) and is shown in concepts like love, mercy and goodness. Otto emphasizes, however, that while the numinous experience is the foundation of all religion, it also needs to have a rational framework in order for people to understand the experience, particularly its meaning and importance. For Otto, fitting numinous experiences into the scheme of a particular religion was both possible and essential. In his work, he studied several religions other than Christianity, and concluded that Christianity was the most appropriate religion in which to understand and experience the numinous.

Types of religious experience

'Religious experience', as we have seen, is used as a general term to describe how many people experience the world. They believe that there is more to the world than just its physical elements. There is something extra – something that is very difficult to quantify or describe. The term 'religious experience' can also be used in a more specific way to argue towards the existence of God. Two of the most important reasons for arguing in this way are mystical and conversion experiences.

1. Mystical experience

There are several central ideas in understanding what a mystical experience is. These include:

- **Mysticism** being described as the spiritual recognition of truths beyond normal understanding.
- It can also be thought of as a quest for the most direct experience of God (often bypassing ordinary understanding) or of the ultimate non-sensuous unity of all things.
- Mysticism can usefully be seen in contrast to the formalized religious rites, rituals and practices that characterize institutionalized religions. Mystics have often been dissatisfied with the limited experience of God provided by such practices, and have attempted to seek greater knowledge of and unity with the divine through their own meditation and mystical encounters.
- Mystics have often stemmed from religious traditions which emphasize a corporate act of worship above individual experience (e.g. Roman Catholicism), and their pursuit of mystical experience is seen by some as a reaction against this. German theologian Hans Kung put this view forward.
- Mysticism is a distinct type of religious experience – although it is often talked of as though it is identical to other forms of religious experience, such as visions or conversion experiences.

Mysticism: Mysticism is where a person feels that he/she is gaining spiritual truth beyond normal understanding as he/she is drawn into an ever-closer union with God.

- Mysticism differs from other types of religious experience, such as conversion. Each may have a mystical element, but the key aspect of each is not the mystical quality but other key components. There are, of course, overlaps in the types of experience, as we shall see.

How mysticism differs from Otto

It is useful to distinguish between a mystical experience and experience of the numinous as described by Otto. His notion of the numinous revolves around an awareness of (a) an absolute power, which is (b) wholly other. Mysticism differs from this view in two main ways. Firstly, the absolute power with which mystics claim to have engaged is not accurately described as wholly other. As we shall see, many mystics believe themselves to be united with this power. Other mystics, who disagree, still claim that this power is intimate and close. Secondly, mysticism has a number of other qualities and characteristics that are not referred to in Otto's account.

Characteristics of a mystical experience

The American philosopher and psychologist **William James** spent several years researching mystical experiences. He delivered the prestigious Gifford Lectures at Edinburgh in 1901–2 and he published his findings in his classic book, *The Varieties of Religious Experience*.

William James (1842–1910) was an American psychologist and Pragmatist philosopher, who published the classic book *The Varieties of Religious Experience*, based on his Gifford Lectures in Edinburgh, delivered in 1901–2. It is still a foundational study of religious experience and has been read widely since its publication in 1902. James studied Medicine at Harvard, but became more interested in philosophy and psychology. He taught the first university-level Psychology course in America.

James defines religion as 'the feelings, acts and experiences of individual men in their solitude, so far as they apprehend themselves to stand in relation to whatever they may consider the divine' (*Varieties*, Lecture 2).

James emphasizes the feelings that individuals experience when they encounter religion. For him, as for Schleiermacher, religious teachings and doctrines are of lesser importance, and he calls these 'second hand' religion. James had talked to numerous people from many different religious traditions and cultures and concluded that, although there was a great deal of variation in the accounts he heard, there were some identifiable common factors in their religious experiences. He identified three broad types of religious experience – the religion of healthy-mindedness, the sick soul and conversion, and the mystical. Here, we will focus on his views on mysticism.

He described a mystical experience as having the following four key characteristics that make any religious experience genuine.

Ineffability

According to James, this is the most easily identifiable characteristic of mystical experience. Mystical experiences are intensely private events and their content is often such that they cannot be described adequately to anyone else. For instance, the Spanish mystic St Teresa of Avila stated: 'I wish I could give a description of at least the smallest part of what I learned, but, when I try to discover a way of doing so, I find it impossible' (*The Life of the Holy Mother Teresa of Jesus*, Sheed & Ward, 1944, ch. 38). Often the descriptions given are so vague that they serve only to confuse the listener or to invite more questions than are answered. So, for example, if someone states that their experience is of the dissolution of the personal ego, it would be very difficult for someone who has not shared this experience to understand what it means.

Noetic quality

Noetic refers to the epistemological value of the experience. It is argued that no matter how ineffable the experiences are, they nevertheless do provide insights into normally unobtainable or inaccessible truths. Indeed, these truths are said not to be recognized by the intellect, and, as it is through the intellect that we form language, it could be argued that there is no tension between the noetic and ineffable properties. The knowledge gained is said to be acquired through some form of intuition or direct apprehension and awareness – not through the senses or the rational mind. In other words, the experience gives the mystic *direct* knowledge of God.

Transciency

Transciency refers to the contrast between the objective time of the experience and the apparent time taken up by the experience from the mystic's perspective. In other words, mystical experiences normally last between a few minutes and two hours, but they can seem much longer to the mystic. The significance and effects of the experience are certainly out of proportion to the time that the experience lasts for.

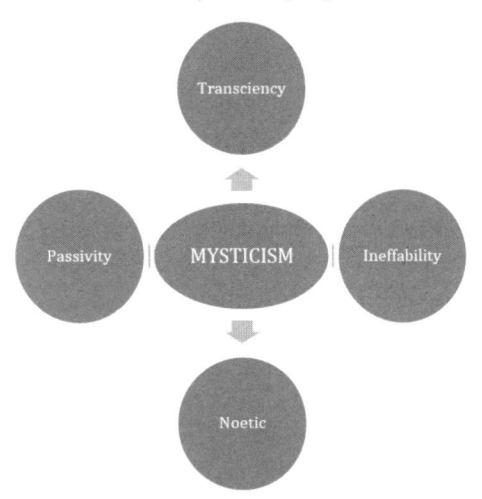

Passivity

Mystical episodes are often characterized by the loss of control experienced by the subject, and the feeling he or she has of being overwhelmed in one way or another by the greater power. The mystic does not initiate the experience, but feels like some benevolent 'force' takes them over and they can do nothing to resist it.

James makes it clear that not every mystical experience will include all four of these characteristics at the same time. He knew that the experiences were not physical, but were instead psychological states that could not be observed by anyone else. They seemed 'real' to the mystic, and James uses the term 'genuine'. This does not mean that the experiences are necessarily from God, only that they appear to be so to the mystic who has experienced them. They needed to be tested in order to verify whether they actually came from God.

Some philosophers and scholars have suggested amendments to James's list. For example, Canadian philosopher Ted Honderich has added *Altered States of Consciousness*. Honderich argues that mystical experiences are usually characterized by altered states of consciousness, such as trances, visions, suppression of cognitive contact with the ordinary world, loss of usual distinction between subject and object, and the weakening or loss of the sense of self.

Dualism versus Monism

Some mystics see their experiences as very much maintaining a distinction between themselves, the subject, and God, the object – even though the core of the experience might be some form of divine union between the two. This form of mysticism is more characteristic of the monotheistic religions.

Other mystics believe that they – the subject – and the divine reality are one and the same stuff: this is Monism. They believe that the distinction between self and the 'absolute' (usually God) is an illusion, and the mystical experience allows the subject to appreciate oneness with the divine. This view is more characteristic of mysticism within non-theistic religions or Eastern religions such as Hinduism.

Example 1 Dame Julian of Norwich

One example of a mystical experience is that of Dame Julian of Norwich.

Julian experienced both visions and 'shewings'. Her visions were mainly of the death of Christ. More unusual, however, were the mystical experiences that occurred in her shewings. It was these that set her apart from other mystics.

Dame Julian's shewings tended to occur in three parts:

1. Bodily sight
2. Words forming in her understanding
3. Ghostly sight.

Arguably, her most famous shewing was when God showed her a round ball the size of a hazelnut in the palm of her hand. This ball, she was informed, represented all that was made, which then led her to the understanding that we must believe that earthly things are meaningless if people wish to know and love God truly. In order to achieve this state, Julian emphasizes the need to deny the things of the world and lead a simple life.

Dame Julian of Norwich

> He shewed me a little thing, the quantity of a hazelnut, in the palm of my hand; and it was round as a ball. I looked, thereupon with the eye of my understanding, and thought: What may this be? And it was answered generally thus: It is all that is made. I marveled how it might last, for methought it might suddenly have fallen to nought for little. And I was

answered in my understanding: it lasteth, and ever shalt for that God loveth it. And so all thing hath the being by the love of God.

In this little thing I saw three properties. The first is that God made it, the second is that God loveth it, the third that God keepeth it.

(Julian of Norwich, *Revelations of Divine Love*, ch. 5)

Although Dame Julian had no formal education, she was led to consider other important doctrines through her mystical experiences, and wrote important things on the nature of the soul and its relation to God.

This example supports the argument that mystical experiences often occur to the formally *uneducated.* This is seen by supporters as evidence of divine involvement (e.g. the church doctrine espoused by the uneducated St Bernadette at Lourdes) and of God's love and goodness towards all people, regardless of social class or financial status. They also have an *effect on the lives of those who are witness to them.* Dame Julian is acknowledged by the Anglican and Lutheran Churches, but not by the Roman Catholic Church. The Catholic Church only acknowledges as authentic those visions which meet the following criteria: 'Faithfulness to the message of the Gospel, the authenticity of our life of witness, the results of holiness which flow out from it for the people of God are the criteria of an authentic Apparition in the Church.'

General and special revelation are often seen as working hand in hand towards the same goal. General revelation alerts mystics to the reality of God, whereas special revelation gives them a fuller understanding of God and his purposes.

The specific shewings are all examples of special revelation. Special revelation can be further subdivided, and revelation experiences fall into the Divine Speech category. Divine Speech is the verbal component of special revelation. God gives his messages through the voices of the prophets, and (from a Christian perspective) the message of his son Jesus Christ. Examples are the books of the Bible containing the words of the prophets, such as Isaiah or Jeremiah, or the writings of Paul (e.g. Galatians or Romans). The writer to the Hebrews states, 'In many and various ways God spoke of old to our fathers by the prophets, but in these last days he has spoken to us by his son.' Timothy states that 'All scripture is God breathed' (1 Tim. 3:16).

2. Conversion experience

A conversion experience is a specific type of religious experience in which there is a change or transformation in the subject's religious beliefs and lifestyle. This transformation may be from atheism to theism, or from one particular faith to another. In the former case, the atheist becomes assured of the truth and reality of the divine, whereas, in the latter, the religious believer becomes convinced of the truth of an alternative religious teaching. In both cases there is likely to be a significant sense of regeneration – of being 'made new'.

It is generally acknowledged that there two differing sorts of conversion experience:

Volitional
A volitional conversion is one in which the subject gradually develops new religious beliefs (as well as moral and spiritual practices) by exposing himself/ herself to, and

> **Conversion:**
> An experience that brings about a (usually) radical change in an individual, typically from atheism to theism.

reflecting on, the teaching of a particular religion. This can be seen as very much a rational, reflective and cerebral form of conversion.

Self-surrender

A self-surrender conversion tends to be one in which the subject becomes very suddenly, and in many cases involuntarily, convinced of the truth of the divine or the particular religious belief system to which he/she converts. This type of conversion often occurs *before* the subject has sufficient knowledge of the religion to which he is converting to make an informed and rational choice. These are called 'born again' conversions by some branches of the Christian Church.

In many self-surrender conversion experiences, there seems to be a common process involved for the individual:

- Before the conversion:
  The person's beliefs and lifestyle conflict with or oppose those that come about as the result of the conversion

- The actual conversion itself:
  'CRISIS': the person often feels overwhelmed by a sense of guilt and sin in the presence of a mighty God
  'REPENTANCE': the subject apologizes to God for his/her sinful nature and unworthiness to receive God's love
  'CATHARSIS': the subject is overwhelmed by a sense of forgiveness and love

- After the conversion:
  The subject has a sense of new purpose, and changes his/her lifestyle and beliefs
  The conversion often has a beneficial effect on others.

Example 1 – Nicky Cruz (from atheist to theist – self-surrender)

Nicky Cruz was born in 1938 on the island of Puerto Rico. As a child he was known to be violent, and because his parents were unable to control him he was sent to live with his brother in New York at the age of fifteen, in the hope that a change of surroundings might curb his violent tendencies and give him more hope of success in life. However, this plan did not prove to be successful and the move simply served to provide Cruz with greater opportunity to indulge his violent ways. At the time (late 1950s), the streets of New York were dominated by violent street gangs engaging in mass fights in disputes over territory, to settle grudges or simply to relieve boredom.

Cruz was eventually initiated into a gang called the 'Mau Maus'. The induction ceremony for the gang involved being kicked unconscious by other gang members. Nicky was embraced by his fellow Mau Maus and was quickly recognized as being the most violent and fearless member. He was involved in muggings, stabbings, gang rape, abduction and torture. He was eventually made gang leader, and under his presidency the Mau Maus became the most feared gang in New York City.

During the reign of Cruz, a young Pentecostal preacher called David Wilkerson believed that he had been called by God to take his word and the message of hope and salvation onto the streets of New York City. Wilkerson arranged a meeting at a local boxing arena and sent a bus around the streets of New York to pick up gang members and invite them there. Cruz and his gang decided to go, initially to cause trouble – however, when Cruz entered the boxing ring, he states he instantly 'felt guilty about all of the things he had done' and began to pray. After preaching, Wilkerson asked Cruz to organize the Mau Maus to sort a collection, which Cruz did, handing all the money collected to Wilkerson – against anything he would have done in the past.

Later in the service, Wilkerson gave an altar call and Cruz responded. Wilkerson prayed with Cruz, and during this time Cruz asked God to forgive him. After this event, Cruz and other gang members who had converted went to the local police station to hand in all of their weapons and drugs in order to start their new life.

Subsequent to his conversion, Cruz attended Bible college and became a preacher. He dedicated his life to preaching God's message to drug addicts, gang members, prostitutes and pimps. He founded an organization called 'Teen Challenge' which continues to see lives turned around in some of the toughest urban environments in the world.

Cruz's dramatic conversion not only radically altered his life, and the lives of those with whom he came into contact, but also provided a source of faith and inspiration for millions of other Christians across the world.

Example 2 – Conversion of Saul of Tarsus (from one religion to another)

> **Exercise**
>
> There are three versions of Saul's conversion: Acts 9:1–19, a retelling in Acts 22:6–21 and Acts 26:12–18 as Paul's testimony. There are some differences in the accounts that you should find and try to explain.

After the crucifixion and resurrection of Jesus, Saul of Tarsus swore to wipe out the new Christian Church. Acts 9:1 states him as: 'breathing out murderous threats against the Lord's disciples'. The High Priest provided Saul with letters to authorize the arrest of any followers of Jesus in the city of Damascus.

As they travelled to Damascus to arrest Jesus' followers, Saul and his companions were struck down by a blinding light and Saul heard a voice saying '"Saul, Saul, why do you persecute me?" (Acts 9:4); 'Saul was confused by the voice and when asked who it was speaking, the voice replied "I am Jesus, whom you are persecuting. Now get up and go into the city and you will be told what you must do"' (Acts 9:5–6).

Although the men travelling with Saul heard the sound, they did not see the blinding light that Saul did. Saul was blinded by this light for three days, leaving his companions to lead him towards Damascus to a man named Judas. For the three days Saul was blinded for, he did not eat or drink anything.

During this time, a disciple named Ananias experienced a vision of Jesus, who commanded him to go to Saul. This left Ananias afraid as he was aware of Saul's persecution of Christians and was reluctant to follow the command. However, Jesus repeated his command, informing Ananias that Saul was the chosen person to deliver his message of the Gospel to the Gentiles, the people of Israel and their kings.

Ananias travelled to the house of Judas and found Saul, praying for help. He informed Saul that Jesus had sent him to restore his sight and that he would be filled with the Holy Spirit. He laid his hands on Saul and something like scales fell from the eyes of Saul and he was able to see again. He arose and was baptized into the Christian faith.

Saul stayed with the disciples for three days, eating and drinking to restore his strength. After his conversion experience, Saul changed his name to Paul.

Saul on the Road to Damascus

Example 3 – Conversion of Malcolm Muggeridge (gradual conversion)

The conversion of Malcolm Muggeridge in 1982 made headline news in the media. He was a famous journalist, author and producer of some very well-known TV shows at that time.

His conversion was not a sudden 'awakening' as it was for Nicky Cruz and Saul of Tarsus. He spent a long time avoiding his conversion and he had been 'fighting against something he knew would ultimately capture him' (J. Pearce, *Literary Converts: Spiritual Inspiration in an Age of Unbelief*, Ignatius Press, 2006, p. 331).

Muggeridge was born in London in 1903. His father was an agnostic and religion had no place in their household, with the family taking the view that man was capable of building a socialist movement on earth – a peaceful, prosperous and just society – without the necessity of religion.

As a boy, he came across a copy of the Bible. He would study the Gospels intently, focusing on the areas which touched him the most – the passion and death of Christ. When he became an undergraduate at Selwyn College, Cambridge, Muggeridge continued to explore aspects of Christianity and prayed for a sign, to no avail. He wanted to understand faith and sought to find it, but had no success due to the struggles he faced with this.

After his graduation, Muggeridge lost his faith altogether and moved to India to teach, focusing on science as opposed to religion. During his travels, his discovery of other religions such as Hinduism, Buddhism and Islam did not shake off his fondness for Christianity, and in a letter to his father in 1926 he wrote 'Christianity is to life what Shakespeare is to literature: it envisages the whole.' During this time, he was clearly still seeking for the answers to his questions regarding his faith and the Christian religion, but was placing all of his faith in the ideas of socialism.

When Muggeridge married his wife, Kitty, in 1927, they both embraced their socialist ideas and saw themselves as being free from any religious constraints. This ended up with them viewing their marriage as a secular partnership that could be broken at any time – leading to numerous infidelities. After each infidelity, Muggeridge was guilt-ridden. He would turn back to the Christian principle that happiness could only be found 'In the rejection of the ego, and not in succumbing to it, in turning away from fleshly lusts and not in gratifying them' (Muggeridge, *Conversion: The Spiritual Journey of a Twentieth Century Pilgrim*, Fount, 1988, p. 130). After much thought, and having written his essay on the sexual revolution, 'Down with Sex!', in which he reflected on the deprivation and pain caused by infidelity, he and his wife entered a period of happiness as a committed married couple.

Throughout his life, Muggeridge never gave up on the pursuit of truth – he longed to understand faith and God. He studied St Augustine and found support in his writings. A defining moment in Muggeridge's conversion was meeting Mother Teresa when making a documentary film on The Missionary Sisters of Charity. He was unable to ignore her total devotion to Christ and her view that one should live as Christ lived (helping the poor and needy). This led him to question his own conversion and come to the view that a conversion experience was a lot like falling in love – with no set rules and no fixed time. For thirteen years after this meeting, Muggeridge attempted to consider himself a Christian without any affiliation to any particular denomination.

It took many years of spiritual maturation before Muggeridge and his wife were received into the Roman Catholic Church on 27 November 1982. As Muggeridge states, his conversion came with 'A sense of homecoming, of picking up the threads of a lost life, of responding to a bell that had long been ringing, of taking a place at a table that had long been vacant' (Muggeridge, *Conversion*, p. 13).

Two years before his death, Muggeridge wrote: 'I have always felt myself to be a stranger here on earth, aware that our home is elsewhere. Now, nearing the end of my pilgrimage, I have found a resting place in the Catholic Church from where I can see the Heavenly gates built into Jerusalem's Wall more clearly than from anywhere else, albeit if only through a glass darkly' (ibid., p. 134).

> **Exercise**
> Make a list of the similarities and differences between the three different types of conversion. What conclusions (if any) do you come to from this exercise?

The evidential value of religious experience

We have seen that religious experiences can take various forms, but a crucial question remains: are such experiences convincing evidence for the existence of God? This final section will consider the extent to which experiences do act as evidence for God's existence, and the extent to which it is reasonable for (a) the subject, and (b) others, to believe in God on the basis of religious experiences.

Richard Swinburne on religious experience

Richard Swinburne has been an influential proponent of arguments for the existence of God. In his book *The Existence of God*, he discusses three distinct ideas on the subject of religious experiences:

1. The Nature of God – If God does exist, then it is reasonable to suppose that this God would want to interact with and engage with his creation
2. Principle of Credulity – 'If it seems to a subject that X is present, then probably X is present; what one seems to perceive is probably so'
3. Principle of Testimony – 'In the absence of *special considerations* the experiences of others are probably as they report them'

Under 'special considerations', Swinburne includes:

- we know that the object was not there
- the person reporting the experience is a known liar
- the person reporting was under psychological stress
- the person had consumed alcohol or drugs
- the person is prone to hallucination and mistaken perception

For Swinburne, in these circumstances we cannot accept reports as veridical religious experiences; however, we must accept the evidential value of other types.

Swinburne places a 'burden of proof' on those who doubt religious experiences. He argues we have to accept these experiences as true unless somebody can categorically prove otherwise. He argues that it is unjustifiable and a matter of philosophical prejudice if we judge reports of religious experiences by a different standard from non-religious experiences (i.e., why would one automatically assume a person is lying about a religious experience when in any other circumstance the assumption is of truth). This draws on William Alston's idea from his book *Perceiving God* that all beliefs based on perception are *prima facie* justified (or, in other words, innocent until proven guilty).

There is also the consideration of the Cumulative argument, which states that so many people have claimed to have a religious experience that, for Swinburne, the sheer weight of testimony counts as strong evidence for the existence of God. So many people have experienced events and described them in such detail that they cannot all be mistaken or making them up. The historical influence of these experiences has to be considered too. For example, the influence of the Prophet Muhammad (pbuh) receiving the Qur'an has changed so many people's lives that it could be argued that it must have been a genuine religious experience for it to have had such a huge effect on society and Islam as a whole. Also, the likes of Muhammad (pbuh) and St Paul had nothing to gain from sharing their religious experiences, but a lot to lose. This raises the question of why they would consider making such a thing up. Their experiences, therefore, were probably real.

Arguments against religious experience

As we have seen, there is much evidence in support of religious experiences – however, not all people are convinced that they are anything more than made up stories, or hallucinations. For some, the notion of God's existence is impossible, therefore it is impossible to have experienced that which cannot be there. Even if one is to conclude that the existence of God is *unlikely*, then this is still sufficient reason to adopt a sceptical view of religious experiences and not to assume that the burden of proof lay on the unbeliever. Under these circumstances, Swinburne's principles of Credulity and Testimony should not apply for the following reasons:

- Credulity: If a person believes that God does not exist (or is unlikely to exist), then they must question any experience claiming to be from God.
- Testimony: 'Ordinary' experiences can be validated by proof or strong evidence for them having occurred; however, we should not apply the same reasoning with religious experiences as they are 'out of the ordinary'. Rather, we should compare and validate such experiences in the same way we do with *unlikely* or *extraordinary* experiences, such as claims of UFO or ghost sightings.

Another point to consider is the fact that there is no agreed quantifier to test what is a religious experience and what is not. If we cannot validate these experiences of God and say categorically whether they are genuine or not, then can any such claim be truly meaningful? How is it possible to verify whether it was God being experienced in the same way that we could verify a person walking past us as truly happening? For more on this idea, see chapter 10, pp. 187–9 on the Verification Principle of **A. J. Ayer (1910–89)**, which may legitimately be applied to this point.

If we were to argue that religious experiences were in fact true, then how would we account for contradictory experiences in different religions? Which religion is having the true experience of God – or do they simply cancel one another out? Could it ever be possible to work out which set of experiences is 'correct/ valid'? On the flip side to this, does the fact that the religious experience always seems to stem from and support an underlying religious belief suggest that these experiences are emerging from the pre-existing beliefs of the subject rather than coming directly from God? Further to this point, how is one capable of recognizing God? In order for the subject to assert that they have experienced God, they must have to have some awareness of how to recognize him. However, how is it possible to recognize a non-spatial and non-physical being? How could our finite and mutable minds truly comprehend an experience of an omnipotent and omniscient God?

> **Exercise**
>
> With a classmate, discuss the difficulties associated with religious experiences and how you might answer them. Then present your answers to the rest of your group and discuss the issues.

Naturalistic accounts of religious experience

We will now look at three alternative – *naturalistic* – accounts of how religious experiences may be explained without there being any need for the supernatural or any reference point to God. If religious experiences can easily be explained away without any need for a God, then perhaps this destroys the evidential value of these experiences. Naturalistic accounts describe in purely natural terms how such beliefs and experiences can be generated in a fully godless universe.

Naturalistic account 1 – neuro-physiological – temporal lobe epilepsy

Mystics throughout history have claimed that visions and trance-like states have come directly from God. However, as science and our understanding of the brain have developed, so has our understanding of diseases such as epilepsy and the effect they have on people's minds. Normally, if a person is asked to describe an epileptic seizure, the general response is 'somebody convulsing and losing consciousness'. As further studies have been conducted, however, scientists are now aware that there is an entire category of seizures which can cause a number of different symptoms. These range from experiencing déjà vu to hallucinations to intense feelings of depression or euphoria. Russian novelist Dostoyevsky describes the moments before his seizures as a 'happiness unthinkable in the normal state and unimaginable for anyone who has never experienced it . . . I am then in perfect harmony with myself and the entire universe' (Jacques Catteau, *Dostoyevsky and the Process of Literary Creation*, Cambridge University Press, 1989, p. 114).

It can be argued that these experiences are entirely subjective – through the eyes of a religious believer, this experience could be interpreted as an experience with the divine. A medical professional, however, may explain the feelings away in terms of it being a neurological disorder which causes sudden sensory disturbance as a result of abnormal electrical activity in the brain. The interpretation may therefore be entirely subjective.

Naturalistic account 2 – Feuerbach: psychological projection

The idea that religion is a man-made entity may be traced back to Ancient Greece; however, it was Feuerbach who determined academically that a non-theistic life was entirely possible, as opposed to the previous speculation of non-believers. For Feuerbach, the appeal of religion is the concept of immortality – the eschatological aim of survival beyond bodily death. Because Christianity offers the promise of life beyond death, if someone is willing to buy into the concept and accept Christ as their saviour, then they are able to escape their fear of death and live a life where they believe they will become immortal. Here, religion is seen to be a fundamental expression of human beings' deepest wishes and feelings – 'religion is the dream of the human mind'.

Religion is explained in sociological, cultural and psychological terms. For Feuerbach, 'theology is anthropology'. Feuerbach explains that humans feel helpless in an alien world and need to invent a God to comfort them. Human beings are fallible and limited, and there are questions to which they will never know the answer. As a result of this, Feuerbach argues that they 'project' their lack of wisdom onto an Omniscient God and therefore can rest easy in the knowledge that even though humankind do not have all of the answers, there is an entity that does. The same applies to the concept of love – people struggle with the fact they can be hurt and upset by the people they love, again because humans are fallible and mutably good. In turn, they project this dissatisfaction onto a God who is immutably good and omnibenevolent and then rest in the comfort that there is a Being who will always love and comfort them (as seen in the diagram below)

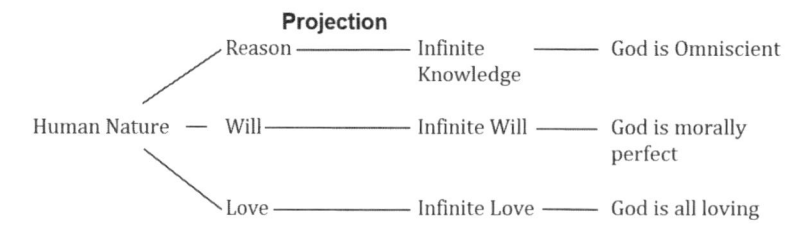

```
                              Projection
               Reason ————— Infinite ————— God is Omniscient
                             Knowledge
Human Nature — Will ——————— Infinite Will ——— God is morally
                                               perfect
               Love ——————— Infinite Love ——— God is all loving
```

The key for Feuerbach is projection. The qualities that humans have are projected in super-enhanced form onto a mythical being (God), which then provides support, comfort and a crutch in a frightening and alien world. Feuerbach's views had a significant influence on Marx, Freud and others.

Naturalistic account 3 – Freud: wish fulfilment

According to Sigmund Freud (1856–1939), religion is an illusion based on human wishes. He explains this point at length in his influential book, *The Future of an Illusion* (Hogarth Press, 1928 [1927]). The book explores Freud's views on the origins, development, psychology and future of religion and religious belief. He sees all religious beliefs as based on illusions. These illusions are created by the mind to overcome various psychological states.

According to Freud, religion is a form of neurotic illness. This stems from the subconscious mind and is the result of memories that have been incompletely repressed by an individual. These memories are repressed because they are very traumatic. The trauma is usually of a sexual nature. For Freud, religious belief stems ultimately from traumatic sexual experiences. These occurred when we were very young. As infants, individuals had ambivalent feelings towards the father figure, of both admiration and fear. These early feelings are projected onto belief in God and this phenomenon may be seen in every religious tradition. People need God because they feel vulnerable and helpless in the face of nature. Freud says: 'Thus [man's] longing for a father is a motive identical with his need for protection against the consequences of his human weakness' (p. 204).

Humans may console themselves in the face of the trauma of nature by creating gods. Originally, there were many gods, each of which had a distinct function. When formal religion developed further, a single God (who represented the father figure) took control of nature. This meant that humans 'could recover the intimacy and intensity of the child's relation to his father' (p. 199).

For Freud, all religious teachings are 'illusions, fulfilments of the oldest, strongest and most urgent wishes of mankind. The secret of their strength lies in the strength of those wishes' (p. 212). All religious experiences are caused by the primal need and desire for personal security in the face of stress caused by lack of knowledge about the way the world works. Religious structures provide security and meaning for individuals. Ultimately, for Freud, all religious experiences are illusions and hallucinations. There is no reality behind religious structures as 'God' is merely a social and psychological construct that provides security and meaning in life.

FURTHER READING

William Alston, *Perceiving God: The Epistemology of Religious Experience*. Cornell University Press, 1993

Peter Cole, *Access to Religious Studies: Religious Experience*. Hodder Education, 2005

William James, *The Varieties of Religious Experience*. CreateSpace Independent Publishing Platform, 2016

John R. Mabry, *Growing into God: A Beginner's Guide to Christian Mysticism*. Quest Books US, 2013

Bernard McGinn, *Essential Writings of Christian Mysticism*. Modern Library Inc., 2006

Ninian Smart, *The Religious Experience of Mankind*. Fount, 1971

Dimensions of the Sacred. Harper Collins, 1996

Thought Points

1. Summarize William James's ideas on mysticism.

2. Explain the weaknesses of James's views.

3. Explain Schleiermacher's views on religious experience.

4. Explain what Otto meant by 'mysterium tremendum et fascinans'.

5. Explain the importance for Swinburne of the Principle of Credulity and the Principle of Testimony.

6. 'Conversion experiences are more likely than mystical experiences to convince people that God exists.' To what extent do you agree with this statement?

7. 'All religious experiences are caused by the primal need and desire for personal security in the face of stress caused by lack of knowledge about the way the world works' (Freud). To what extent do you agree with this statement?

CHAPTER 7
The Problem of Evil

LEARNING OUTCOMES
In this chapter, you will be learning about:
- the Problem of Evil and suffering
  - natural evil
  - moral evil
- theodicies that propose explanations for why God would allow evil to exist
  - Augustine
  - Hick's re-working of Irenaeus' theodicy

You will also have the opportunity to discuss issues that arise from the existence of evil, such as
- whether God can be spared from blame in allowing evil
- which aspects of the Problem of Evil pose the greatest challenge to belief

The nature of evil and the origin of the Problem of Evil

The Problem of Evil is one of the most difficult problems for theists because it attacks the heart of the nature of God. It is difficult for two reasons: firstly, because religious believers must reconcile their belief in God with the existence of evil in the world, as seen in the pain and suffering of many people. Secondly, it is difficult because evidence of evil is often cited as an argument to deny the existence of God. The Problem of Evil comes about because, as individuals live their lives, they see examples of evil in the world almost every day. For theists and non-theists alike, the existence of evil in the world is not just an intellectual activity, it is one that affects very many people around the world. It is therefore very important to know what evil is and what its relation is to the nature of God and theistic belief.

GOD AND THE WORLD

What is evil? St Augustine defined it as 'that which we fear, or the act of fearing itself' (*Confessions*, book 7, ch. 5). This very brief definition, however, is not of much help. A somewhat more helpful one comes from American theologian John K. Roth:

> The word often functions as a noun, suggesting that evil is an entity. In fact evil is activity, sometimes inactivity, and thus it is a manifestation of power. Evil power displays are those that waste. That is, evil happens whenever power ruins or squanders, or whenever it fails to forestall those results. Evil comes in many shapes and sizes. The kind that concerns us here ignores and violates the sanctity of individual persons. Everyone inflicts that sort of pain and yet some individuals and societies are far more perverse than others. The measure is taken by the degree to which one's actions waste human life.
>
> (Quoted in Davis, ed., *Encountering Evil*, p. 8)

According to Roth, evil is fundamentally damaging to human beings. If this is correct, then it opens up a huge problem for theists, because God is believed to be the creator of everything in the universe. If evil may be called a 'thing', God must be responsible for the existence of evil. The definition of 'evil' leads us straight into the 'problem' of evil. The Problem of Evil is not just a game about the meaning of words, it is a real life-and-death issue for many people around the world and has led to powerful and emotive responses. It is the one issue that has led to more loss of faith and to more entrenched atheism than any other issue in the philosophy of religion, and one that needs sensitive treatment. Almost all discussion of evil focuses on two different but related aspects – the 'logical' problem and the 'evidential' problem, and this is how we shall approach it in what follows.

The logical Problem of Evil

There are many ways of stating the logical Problem of Evil, but the simplest one is usually called the 'inconsistent triad', which can be put in the following way:

1. God is perfectly good
2. God is all-powerful
3. God is all-knowing
4. Evil and suffering exist.

The problem is that, if God is all-knowing, God must know that evil exists and know how to eradicate it. Similarly, if God is all-powerful, God must be powerful enough to eradicate all the evil in the world. It is clear, however, that evil does exist. The inevitable and logical conclusion, then, must be either that God does not exist, or that God is not all-powerful, so does not have the power to get rid of evil, or God is not all-knowing, so does not know how to get rid of evil. For monotheists in the Christian, Islamic or Judaic traditions, this causes a huge problem, as God is understood as immanent and therefore personally involved with and concerned for his creatures. Various kinds of response have attempted to solve the logical Problem of Evil. We will focus here on Christian responses.

First is the idea that evil is inherent in human beings because they have fallen from God's grace. This view is particularly associated with St Augustine and John Calvin, as we will see later. Genesis ch. 2 in the Bible tells the mythical story of Adam and Eve, the first two humans created by God in the Garden of Eden. Adam and Eve were created with the possibility of not sinning, but they chose to go against God's will by disobeying his command not to eat the fruit of the tree of the knowledge of good and evil:

> 15 The Lord God took the man and put him in the Garden of Eden to work it and take care of it. 16 And the Lord God commanded the man, 'You are free to eat from any tree in the garden; 17 but you must not eat from the tree of the knowledge of good and evil, for when you eat from it you will certainly die.'
>
> (Genesis 2:15–17, New International Version (NIV))

As Adam and Eve were created with free will, they chose to sin and, as a direct result, were exiled from the Garden. In Christian belief, this first sin affected all subsequent humans to the extent that they no longer have the possibility of not sinning, and are in a state where human nature is inherently flawed and leads to evil. Evil, therefore, is not God's fault: it comes about because of human failure. God can still be seen as all-knowing and all-powerful.

> 14 So the Lord God said to the serpent, 'Because you have done this, Cursed are you above all livestock and all wild animals! You will crawl on your belly and you will eat dust all the days of your life. 15 And I will put enmity between you and the woman, and between your offspring and hers; he will crush your head, and you will strike his heel.' 16 To the woman he said, 'I will make your pains in childbearing very severe; with painful labour you will give birth to children. Your desire will be for your husband, and he will rule over you.' 17 To Adam he said, 'Because you listened to your wife and ate fruit from the tree about which I commanded you, "You must not eat from it", Cursed is the ground because of you; through painful toil you will eat food from it all the days of your life. 18 It will produce thorns and thistles for you, and you will eat the plants of the field. 19 By the sweat of your brow you will eat your food until you return to the ground, since from it you were taken; for dust you are and to dust you will return.'
>
> (Genesis 3:14–19 NIV)

Another response to the problem is that evil does not exist. This idea can be traced back to the neo-Platonic philosopher Plotinus (205–70 CE). He argued that the universe as a whole is good and perfect. Perfection in this sense means that every level of being must come into existence. Because there are different levels of being, there must be different levels of goodness. Some things will be at a lower level of goodness than other things and so will be less good. But because the existence of these less good things is necessary for existence as a whole to be perfect, they are part of the greater good. This means, for Plotinus, that evil does not exist.

This view was adopted by St Augustine, who, as we will see, used it in his **theodicy**. As a way of absolving God from allowing evil to exist, he advanced the argument that nothing is created evil by nature. Such evil as there is comes about from humans, not God, and God allows it to continue to exist so that there may be greater good. If the continuance of evil were not allowed, there could be no good in the world either. This is also the view of a modern pseudo-Christian sect known as Christian Science, according to its founder Mary Baker Eddy: 'Sin, disease, whatever seems real to material sense, is unreal . . . All in harmony of mortal mind or body is illusion, possessing neither reality nor identity though seeming to be real' (Mary Baker-Eddy, *Science and Health*, CreateSpace Independent Publishing Platform, 2016, ch. 14, 'Recapitulation').

> **Theodicy:**
> The idea that God allows evil to occur because he has a just reason for it.

Jewish philosopher Baruch Spinoza (1632–77) claimed that evil is an illusion which arises as the result of a subjective contemplation of reality. If something is not useful to us, we may label it 'suffering' or 'evil'. However, from an objective standpoint, we would realize that everything has its value, and is necessary in the overview of existence. Hence, 'all things are necessarily what they are, and in Nature there is no good and evil' (Spinoza, *Ethics*, Penguin, 1996, p. 10).

A third response was developed by Gottfried Leibniz. This is called the Best of all Possible Worlds argument. He argued that God could have created many universes. Because God is good, the universe he created must necessarily be the best of all possible worlds. Evil only exists because some evil is necessary for there to be good. Of all the worlds that God might have created, this one contains the least amount of evil and therefore the greatest amount of good possible for humans. This theory could be used to justify things like torture and rape, on the grounds that a world without them is inferior to a world with them. For example, the greatest thing that a human can do is to give up his life for another. If the 'evil' of death were not possible, people could not show their love for others by self-sacrifice. A world without the horrors of torture or terrorism would be inferior to a world with them because with them we are able to understand why people are important to each other. Leibniz argued that the imperfection and evil in the world predisposes people to do evil things through exercising their free will. Free will is necessary in Leibniz's argument because genuine freedom is needed so that a maximal variety of goods and evils to which humans can respond is generated.

A fourth response argues that evil is the result of God's nature and God's will. This view is associated with the idea that, because God is the creator of everything that exists, God 'determines' how everything will exist. Determinism is a strong belief in many Christian denominations, particularly Calvinism. It argues that all events are predetermined by God and are therefore God's will. Such groups argue that all events, both good and evil (either natural or moral), are determined by God. God is fully responsible for every single thing that takes place and every event must be accepted as the will of God, without question. All events, both good and evil, must be seen in this light.

The evidential Problem of Evil

Events that affect many thousands of people, killing, maiming or causing very significant hurt and damage to them, appear to occur with sickening regularity. For instance, during the first three months of 2017, the following 'evil' events took place in different parts of the world:

- Heavy rainfall across southern Africa affected several countries, including Mozambique, where at least 44 people died and 79,000 lost their homes and livelihood.
- In Afghanistan, heavy snowfall and freezing weather killed 27 children in the north of the country. A large number of avalanches and rain-related disasters caused 194 deaths and affected 7,600 people because of significant damage to homes. In addition, 20,000 hectares of arable land were submerged under flood water.

- In Algeria, an unusually cold season cut off numerous communities and caused hardship for over 27,000 people, with loss to livelihoods because of isolation, power cuts and material damages to the residents of these areas.
- Over 63,000 people were displaced as a result of flash floods in the Philippines. At least 48,000 inhabitants had to be housed in evacuation centres for several months.
- In Zambia, over 130,000 hectares of maize, the main food crop in the country, were destroyed by a severe infestation by the Fall Armyworm. The destruction of much of the crop caused hardship to many thousands of people.
- A tropical cyclone in Madagascar caused significant damage to housing and agriculture.
- A 6.7-magnitude earthquake caused loss of life and damage to housing in the Philippines.
- In Guinea, the Ebola Virus disease almost overwhelmed the health services, to the extent that a subsequent measles epidemic was declared in one-third of the country.

These serious recent events pale into insignificance against the backdrop of evils such as Hitler's death camps and the Holocaust, Chairman Mao's murder of *c.*100 million Chinese, or Pol Pot's 'reforms' in Kampuchea, claiming the lives of 2 million innocent people. In addition, there are enough weapons of mass destruction to destroy the world at least twenty times, and terrorism is a daily occurrence, claiming the lives of many individuals and diminishing the lives of the families of the victims.

All the examples above are the kinds of events that lead many people to formulate the 'evidential Problem of Evil'. The accompanying argument seeks to demonstrate that the many examples of 'bad things happening to good people' raises the question of why God would allow such a lot of suffering to occur and why God apparently does nothing to lessen the pain of those who are affected.

In the discussion of the evidential Problem of Evil, a distinction is made between moral evil and non-moral or natural evil. Moral evil is what occurs when human beings commit acts of cruelty and injustice to humans or other creatures. It may seem rather odd to call it 'moral' evil, but it deals with the kinds of actions the humans do as the result of choices they make, such as committing a murder. When a murderer makes the decision to end someone else's life, he is making a decision that concerns the difference between 'right' and 'wrong' – a moral decision. The decision is a moral one, but the resulting action is 'immoral'. 'Natural evil' refers to natural disasters, disease and the pain and suffering that occur to people and animals that is not caused by humans, such as that due to earthquakes or tsunamis.

Christian responses to evil

Several Christian theologians have attempted to explain the Problem of Evil, taking into account the difficulties posed by the fact that evil exists despite God being loving and all-powerful (the inconsistent triad). These responses are known as 'theodicies'.

The word 'theodicy' comes from two Greek words, *theos* meaning 'God', and *diké* meaning 'justice', so a theodicy attempts to show how God has good or just reasons for allowing evil to continue to exist in the world.

Evil does not, therefore, contradict God's characteristics of omnipotence, omniscience or omnibenevolence. The term 'theodicy' was first used by the German philosopher Gottfried Leibniz in his book *Theodicy*, published in 1710, though various responses to the Problem of Evil had been put forward long before then.

There have been two major theodicies in the Christian tradition: one by St Augustine and the other by St Irenaeus. Both are important, as each focuses on a different aspect of the problem. There is a third response to evil, which puts the responsibility for evil on humans – this is called the Free Will Defence.

The Augustinian theodicy

> **St Augustine of Hippo (354–430)** was born in Thagaste in Roman North Africa (modern Morocco) at a time when the Roman army was struggling to control several dissident barbarian groups who were invading various North African provinces. He was educated in Carthage and later in Milan, where he became Christian at the age of 33, via Manicheism and Platonism. Augustine was heavily influenced by the ideas of Plato and this may be seen in many of his writings. His *Confessions* offer a spiritual autobiography of striking insight and honesty. After living a life of worldly pleasure in his 20s, he lived with a woman with whom he had a son, and admits to God that 'I delayed from day to day the conversion to you ... even while I sought for it. I thought that I would be miserable if I were kept from a woman's arms.' This relationship did not lead to marriage, but may have been with a freed slave. In this case, the law would have forbidden him to marry her, as he was a Roman citizen. Augustine saw God as the source of all goodness and no evil, but that human nature, like the natural world, had a tendency to fall away from its eternal creator. Such is the corruption of the human will to obey divine commands that, without the assistance of God's grace, humans would be powerless to fulfill them. After he had been ordained priest, then Bishop, at Hippo, Augustine wrote a wide range of books, including polemics against heretical groups such as the Pelagians and Donatists, and theological and philosophical writings that have had a huge influence on the development of Christian thought.

Augustine developed four themes in his discussion of the Problem of Evil.

1 The privation of good

Augustine argued, from studying the Bible, that God was totally good. In Genesis 1, God is described as having created a world that was perfect in every respect; it was therefore free from any defective things, such as suffering and evil: 'God saw all that he had made and it was very good' (1:31).

Importantly for Augustine, 'evil' is not a substance or a thing, so God did not create it; evil occurs when something goes wrong with something good. An example he uses is of blindness. Blindness happens when the eye stops working correctly, where there is an absence of sight. Augustine used the term 'privation' to describe this state (a privation of something is an absence or lack of that thing). For example, 'evil' is an absence of 'good', so the blind eye is failing in its proper function of seeing. Blindness is not an evil in itself; it is simply the loss of function of the eye. Darkness is not a real thing in itself; it is simply the absence of light.

Augustine says, in the *Enchiridion*:

> What, after all, is what we call evil except the privation of good? In animal bodies, for instance, sickness and wounds are nothing but the privation of health. When a cure is effected, the evils that were present (i.e. the sickness and the wounds) do not retreat and go elsewhere. Rather they simply do not exist any more. As God made only things that exist, and because 'evil' is not an existing thing, so God cannot be responsible for any evil or suffering in the world.
> (Augustine, *Enchiridion*, 11)

2 The Free Will Defence

Augustine says that evil came not from God but from entities that have free will. God created all humans with free will. The story of 'the Fall' of Adam and Eve in Genesis 3 is key to understanding what Augustine means about free will. In his book *The City of God*, he discusses this story at length. Adam and Eve (who represent all humans) are tempted by the serpent (not an evil character) to eat the fruit of the tree of the knowledge of good and evil (which Adam and Eve want). They choose to ignore what God has said about this fruit and freely decide to eat it. The result is their shame and corruption and, through them, those of all human beings.

Augustine says that God foresaw that this misuse of free will would happen, because God is omniscient and planned to redeem humans by sending Christ, who would die and rise again for their sakes. He argued that some people will still go to hell, but this will be because of their abuse of their free will. Others will repent by using their free will, will turn to Christ and so will be saved. For Augustine, this shows clearly that God has a positive purpose in allowing evil to happen.

3 The principle of plenitude

The term 'plenitude' means 'fullness', 'abundance' or 'completeness'. The term is not Augustine's but was coined by the American philosopher and historian of ideas Arthur Lovejoy, in his book *The Great Chain of Being* (1936). The principle is traced back to Plato in the *Timaeus*.

Augustine argued that the best type of world is one that contains every possible variety of creature and not one that consists only of the highest kind of being. It is a universe where all possibilities of existence are realized. Some creatures are, therefore, imperfect. This results in a principle of variety, so that some creatures are stronger, some are more beautiful, some are more intelligent than others. Variety therefore entails inequality and, it could be argued, injustice. So, if we ask 'Why don't butterflies live as long as elephants?' or 'Why aren't elephants as beautiful as butterflies?', the answer is simple: if they were, they would not be butterflies and elephants. Why did God create such an imperfect creature as humans and not just angelic beings? The answer is that, if he had, it would not be a world but, rather, the highest heaven. For

Augustine, this principle of plenitude explains the problem of why God would have created such seemingly horrible, useless and destructive creatures as slugs, or such natural events as earthquakes or tsunamis.

4 The aesthetic theme

When British philosopher of religion **John Hick (1922–2012)** refers to Augustine's 'aesthetic theme', he has in mind the latter's belief that the universe is entirely good when seen in its totality, from God's perspective. He argues that humans see only part of the picture. Only God sees the total view. In one of his works, Augustine points out that such 'evils' as a substance that poisons, the fire that burns, and the water that drowns are evil only in a relative sense. So, for instance, if a famous art gallery burns down, it may be seen as a great tragedy by art lovers but not by many other people who do not like or appreciate art. Poisons are not 'evil' in themselves but are harmful only when brought into conjunction with other substances with which they react. A tidal wave is not 'evil' in itself but is 'evil' only when it damages buildings or kills humans. Augustine acknowledged that good things can come from evil actions. For instance, although a powerful cyclone may destroy a city, the city will be rebuilt with stronger houses that do not collapse in the future, meaning that the people who live in them will be safer.

The aesthetic theme is also an idea influenced by neo-Platonism, particularly in the works of Plotinus, who writes: 'We are like people ignorant of painting who complain that the colours are not beautiful everywhere in the picture: but the Artist has laid on the appropriate tint to every spot.' Augustine himself writes:

> All have their offices and limits laid down so as to ensure the beauty of the universe. That which we abhor in any part of it gives us the greatest pleasure when we consider the universe as a whole . . . The very reason why some things are inferior is that, although the parts may be imperfect, the whole is perfect . . . the black colour in a picture may very well be beautiful if you take the picture as a whole.
>
> (Augustine, *On True Religion*, xl, 76)

There is some similarity between certain aspects of Augustine's aesthetic theme and 'contrast theory', which states that the concept of goodness only makes sense in contrast to evil. Without the concept of evil, we would have no way of quantifying what goodness is.

> **Exercises**
> 1. Summarize each of the four justifications Augustine provides.
> 2. Do you think that any of them are persuasive on their own? Would they be more persuasive if they are all understood cumulatively? Explain your reasons.
> 3. Explain how Augustine justifies God's role in the existence of evil.

Strengths of the Augustinian theodicy

An important strength of Augustine's theodicy is that it takes the responsibility for evil away from God and lays it at the feet of humans.

The fact that humans have free will means that God is not responsible for evil.

This is especially relevant for moral evil, although, given that nature descended into chaos during the Fall, it is argued that all evil – including natural evil – is the responsibility of mankind. As Evans states:

> For Augustine, 'natural evils' are a question of very subordinate interest. He would not attribute them to God, but to man. For him, there is no such thing as a 'natural evil' (for that would either be a God-made evil or a manichee, alien power coequal with the good – by far the more acceptable option to fifth century thinkers). All evil arises in the will of man.
>
> (Evans, *Augustine on Evil*, pp. 97–8)

In addition to this, Augustine states that angels have free will as well as humans, and some angels decided to go against God's will. This resulted in such things as earthquakes, tornadoes and disease that bring death and suffering to humans. God is not responsible for natural evil.

Although God created everything, Augustine says that evil is not a substance but a privation. Just as blindness is not an entity in itself but is the lack of sight, and darkness is not a 'thing' but the absence of light, it is argued that evil is simply the lack of good. Therefore, if it is not a created substance and merely the lack of good, then God did not create it, which again leads to the conclusion that God is not responsible for evil in the world.

The aesthetic theme and the principle of plenitude show that human sin is a by-product of God's creation. Humans use it to do evil, but God reworks it for good, like an artist who uses shadows to illuminate the beauty and colour in their work. Augustine uses the existence of evil to emphasize his views about salvation. Human evil meant that God had to send Jesus to absorb the sins of the world on the cross so that humans could be brought back to God. This creates a greater world. For Augustine, complete happiness is not the point of this lifetime. Life is really a test for souls whereby their destiny in the next life will be decided. The existence of and hope for life after death are crucial for Augustine.

Weaknesses of the Augustinian theodicy

Many people do not accept that Augustine's argument takes the responsibility for evil away from God, because it seems that God created the enabling conditions in which evil could thrive.

Augustine says that God created a world that was perfect, but the existence of evil shows that the world is not perfect. This is a contradiction in his argument. Evil cannot have created itself from a perfect world, so God must have created it. If this is true, either God must be less than perfect or he intentionally created evil. This would mean that God was not omnibenevolent.

The argument that evil is not an entity in itself, merely a 'privation', strikes a chord with many. To deny the existence of evil is to render the suffering of many into nothingness. In the words of Charles T. Mathewes, 'Augustine's account essentially denies the reality of evil – it is a denial carried through only by reasoning captivated within a dubious theological ideology. Critics charge that Augustinian theory renders evil invisible, and Augustinians insensible to the tragic realities of injustice and suffering' (Mathewes, *Evil and the Augustinian Tradition*, p. 93).

The scientific theory of evolution shows that the world was not created perfect. Instead, it has been evolving and changing for many millions of years. Evolutionary theory shows that every living thing has a selfish desire for survival, and this does not fit with the biblical account of the Fall in Genesis chs. 2 and 3. Also, the idea that all humans inherit from Adam 'original sin' that predisposes them to do evil does not fit with modern scientific ideas about inheritance or the psychology of human behaviour. So, although this argument accords with the literal reading of Genesis, it stands at odds with current scientific theory and any non-literal interpretation of Genesis.

For Augustine, the afterlife would be a place of eternal punishment for those who had committed sin and evil. This raises a serious problem for believing that God is omnibenevolent. It seems to make a mockery of God sending Jesus to die on behalf of humans to take away their sins and bring them back to God. Augustine believed that hell was a necessary part of God's creation, but why would God do this if his creation was perfect? If God is omniscient, why would he create a world that was imperfect? Given that the suffering of those in hell would be infinite, it would seem to serve no purpose and it can be questioned whether indefinite punishment would seem an unfair response to any sin – especially from an omnibenevolent God.

Further to this point, Augustine's claim that God's foreknowledge does not limit human freedom is debatable. To argue that God's omniscience does not limit the free will of mankind, we may then have to change God's relationship with time in a manner that would be unacceptable to Augustine. However, if God's foreknowledge does rob humans of free will, then God is directly responsible for human sin.

Even if free will and God's omniscience are compatible, it can be argued that God still has to take *some* responsibility for the existence of evil in the world. God's foreknowledge indicates that he knew at the point of creation that he was creating a world that would generate a Hitler who would instigate a Holocaust and the mass murder of 6 million Jews, yet he did it anyway. If we *deny* God's foreknowledge, then we have to question the attributes of God, which would leave us with an arguably reckless God who would be culpable for the existence of evil regardless.

Exercise

Which of the criticisms above do you think are most convincing? Give reasons for your view. If you think none of them is convincing, say why.

> **St Irenaeus (c.130–202 CE)**
> Not a great deal is known about Irenaeus, but he was born in Smyrna and was probably a native of Asia Minor. He may have spent some time in Rome before he moved to Lyons in France, where he became the city's Bishop. He lived at a time when Christianity was emerging as an important spiritual force in the Roman Empire, and many Christian intellectuals and leaders had to argue against various 'heretical' groups that claimed to be Christian but did not accept some central Christian doctrines. Irenaeus's best-known work is *Against Heresies*, which argues vigorously against a powerful ideology called Gnosticism, which claimed to have secret knowledge of God. As one of the greatest of the early Christian theologians, Irenaeus upheld traditional Christian beliefs. A number of Irenaeus's works have been lost and are known only through fragments. He is largely known now for his theodicy, the attempt to justify the goodness of God in the face of evil in the world.

The Irenaean theodicy

Although it is not strictly on the specification, it is quite important to know what Irenaeus said in his theodicy, as it is the basis for John Hick's re-working of it in his own theodicy.

Irenaeus was the second Bishop of Lyons in France during the second half of the second century. He was one of the first Christian theologians and attempted to defend Christian ideas against a number of groups who claimed to be Christian but who did not believe the most important doctrines. Irenaeus begins his theodicy by going back to the book of Genesis, especially the section where the creation of humans is discussed (1:26). He wondered why the author wrote that, when God created humans, he said: 'Let us make humankind in our image, in our likeness.' Because Irenaeus considered the Bible to be the word of God, he thought that there was an important point being made here. He concluded that all humans were made in the 'image' of God but are not yet in God's 'likeness'. All humans are made in God's image, both holy and morally good people and unholy and morally bad people, such as Pontius Pilate (who sentenced Jesus to death) and Judas Iscariot (who betrayed Jesus to the authorities). For Irenaeus, being made in God's image has to do with being a rational creature, having the ability to make choices, and showing compassion and love towards others. But, sometimes, people fail to do good things and do very bad things instead. Being made in the 'image' of God does not guarantee moral perfection. To become in God's 'likeness' is a much longer journey for humans; it is a privilege and not an automatic right. If a positive free choice for God is made, then Christians, by doing good actions such as showing love and compassion for others, may eventually become in God's 'likeness' and achieve moral perfection. They will then become spiritual beings with God in heaven. As we will see shortly, Irenaeus's view concentrates on the creation of humans by God, not on their fall from grace, which is the focus of Augustine's theodicy.

Irenaeus goes on to show that evil is the result of free will. This means that, for him, God is partly responsible for the existence of evil. God created humans imperfect – in his own 'image', but not in his 'likeness'. God did this deliberately because he wanted humans to grow and develop in order to reach moral and spiritual perfection. God had to make humans with free will so that they could freely decide to do this. Giving humans freedom of choice, however, meant that God had to accept that they would sometimes make wrong choices and go against his intentions and will. God had to permit evil and suffering to take place. As Irenaeus said: 'How, if we had no knowledge of the contrary, could we have instruction in that which is good?' (*Against Heresies*, 4, xxxix, 1). In other words, God had to allow the existence of evil so that humans would understand what good was. If God had intervened, humans would have lost their freedom and therefore their distinguishing characteristic.

In Irenaeus's view, God created the world with the possibility of good as well as suffering and evil. Evil is necessary so that humans can exercise their free will and, in doing so, show their capacity for care, compassion and love for their fellow human beings and for the rest of the created world. For Irenaeus, suffering is cathartic – that is, it enables good to come into the world, as people who see suffering try to help by giving their time and using their skills to turn suffering into a positive and good outcome.

Irenaeus may have got this idea from some passages in the Bible. St Paul said: 'Not only so, but we also glory in our sufferings, because we know that suffering produces perseverance, character; and character, hope' (Romans 5:3). Irenaeus would also have known the book of Revelation (21:4): 'God will wipe every tear from their eyes. Death will be no more; mourning and crying and pain will be no more, for the first things have passed away.' This seems to suggest that, until God comes at the end of time to bring in his Kingdom, suffering is a normal and expected part of life on earth.

English philosopher Richard Swinburne follows up on this idea of the positive value of suffering:

> My suffering provides me with the opportunity to show courage and patience. It provides you with the opportunity to show sympathy and to help alleviate my suffering. And it provides society with the opportunity to choose whether or not to invest a lot of money in trying to find a cure for this or that particular kind of suffering. . . . Although a good God regrets our suffering, his greatest concern is surely that each of us shall show patience, sympathy and generosity and, thereby, form a holy character.
>
> (Quoted in Dawkins, *The God Delusion*, p. 64)

Could a perfect God not have prevented this natural disaster from killing people?

Many philosophers and religious believers have decided that God would have to allow such horrific suffering for so many people in order for them to find a 'holy character'. Supporters of Swinburne might reply that there have been some significant outcomes from the Holocaust, such as Holocaust Memorial Day, the Yad Vashem Holocaust History Museum in Jerusalem, many books on the subject, inclusion in many History specifications in schools, and a much greater recognition throughout the world of the evils and dangers of anti-Semitism.

John Hick's Vale of Soul Making theodicy

> **Vale of Soul Making:** Hick's attempt to justify both moral and natural evil, saying that evil will disappear at the end of the world.

A modern presentation of the Irenaean theodicy is Hick's **Vale of Soul Making** theodicy. Hick follows along the same lines as Irenaeus but makes an attempt to strengthen his argument. He argues that both moral and natural evil are essential to 'soul making' – therefore, they have a good purpose, and an omnibenevolent and omnipotent God is justified in creating a world that allows both nature and humankind to perform evil acts. Hick's theodicy is decidedly eschatological – it focuses on humanity's future perfection in God's Kingdom.

Although Augustine, Irenaeus and Hick all trace the root of evil back to the existence of human free will (but with Augustine believing this is totally at odds with God's original plan for mankind), Hick develops this theme and provides a discussion of the implications of the Problem of Evil for both God and humanity.

Key ideas in the theodicy

Firstly, Hick states that, instead of being created morally perfect, humans must be created in *moral imperfection* in order for them to continue the process of creation for themselves. Hick follows Irenaeus and argues that humans are created in the *image* of God, with the potential to move towards his moral *likeness*. Humankind exists already as personal, moral beings; however, it has not fulfilled the potential for the finite 'likeness' of God, morally reflecting the divine in a more accurate manner. This transition represents the perfecting of man: 'In bringing many sons and daughters to glory, it was fitting that God, for whom and through whom everything exists, should make the pioneer of their salvation perfect through what he suffered' (Hebrews 2:10).

The key question is whether God is responsible for evil in the world if he is, indeed, the one who has allowed it to occur. One may argue that this does make God partly responsible, as it is through these means that humans will become 'children of God'. However, if there is sufficient reason for God to allow the extent of suffering, then it may not question the loving nature of God. As Stephen T. Davis says:

> But if God could, without logical contradiction, have created humans as wholly good, free beings, why did God not do so? Why was humanity not initially created in possession of all the virtues, instead of having to acquire them through the long, hard struggle of life as we know it? The answer, I suggest, appeals to the principles that virtues that have been formed within the agent as a hard won deposit of right decisions in situations of challenge and temptation, are intrinsically more valuable than ready made virtues created within her without any effort on her own part.
>
> (Davis, ed., *Encountering Evil*, p. 43)

> **Epistemic distance:** Epistemic distance is the idea that there is a gap between God's knowledge and human knowledge. Because they do not have innate knowledge of God, humans must seek God through faith.

Humanity must be distanced from God in order that they may have human autonomy over the Creator (i.e. it is possible for humanity to know God, but only through the exercise of free choice and faith). The natural world must contain the capacity to cause suffering in order to preserve this **epistemic distance** and so as not to frustrate man's desire to do evil as this would limit his freedom. Humans must encounter some suffering in life as without suffering and evil there would be no difficulty in following God's laws. Also, certain virtues, or moral perfections, can only be acquired through successfully encountering evil (i.e. without need, there would be no generosity – as seen, for example, in a rape victim becoming a counsellor and helping other victims, etc.).

Hick argues that God's purposes would not be fulfilled in a world without pain or suffering. He concludes that while our world is not 'designed for the maximisation of human pleasure and the minimisation of human pain, it may nevertheless be rather well adapted to the quite different purpose of "soul making"' (Hick, *Philosophy of Religion*).

Why must there be universal salvation?

Often, evil and suffering in the world do not lead to genuine human development, so if life were to end at death then God's purpose for man to grow into his likeness would have been frustrated (which would in turn raise questions about God's omnipotence). When one considers the magnitude of suffering in the world (such as the Holocaust), then only a supreme future in heaven can justify this.

Hick accepts that there are 'victims of the system' ('evil' people who perhaps have not been brought up properly, so therefore cannot be held fully accountable for their actions). In order for there to be justice for these people, Hick argues that nobody should be overlooked when heaven's doors are opened, so an essential aspect of Hick's theodicy is that all people will become 'children of God' and will inherit eternal life.

Strengths of the Irenaean/Hick theodicy

Both Irenaeus and Hick provide important insights into human personality and moral development.

Irenaeus acknowledged that evil really existed in the world and he admitted that God seemed to allow evil to continue to exist. His argument centres round the idea that God allows evil to exist and he has a positive reason for doing so. He says that God deliberately created the world with a mixture of good and evil so that humans can grow in maturity and knowledge of God so that they can be in a relationship with him. Irenaeus has a positive view of human beings, because they have the capacity to do good deeds and improve themselves morally and spiritually.

Irenaeus believes that things are worth more if one has to work hard and struggle for them than if they come naturally. For example, if you are a single mother with a pre-school child and your family does not support you in your desire to go to university, you will appreciate the opportunity to study much more when you actually acquire your university place and gain your degree.

When Irenaeus discusses the phrase in Genesis 1:26 about how humans are made 'in the image and likeness of God', he uses the two-stage process of moral development to show that humans must make an effort to become like God. This is the main purpose of evil in the world. Irenaeus made a distinction between God's image and God's likeness. He argued that God made us in his own image, but that humans must grow morally and spiritually into God's likeness. As humans are in God's image, they are able to choose freely, and this means that they are authentic moral agents, capable of making real choices. Freedom of choice is essential to acting morally, as Kant was to confirm in the eighteenth century. In order to become in the likeness of God, humans have to mature and develop morally so that they can reach their potential. Irenaeus taught that if humans can overcome difficulties to realize their potential, then they can resist the temptation to do wrong. As Irenaeus says: 'It was possible for God himself to have made man perfect from the first, but man could not receive this perfection, being as yet an infant' (*Against Heresies*, 4, xxxix, 1).

Being created in God's image, humans can make real moral decisions for themselves, but they are not yet like God – that is, they do not have his moral perfection. As they are made in God's image, however, they have the potential to attain it. In order to do this, they must endure evil and suffering.

Irenaeus's theodicy can be understood in the light of modern evolutionary theory, which supports the idea of humans being made for growth and development towards morality and spiritual awareness, therefore being compatible with modern scientific theory.

Irenaeus and Hick make no attempt to deny either the real existence of evil in the world or that God can use evil as a tool to help humans to develop towards godliness. Irenaeus's argument takes a positive approach to evil. It looks to the future for the purpose that evil serves and the good that can come from it. Evil is the means to a greater end. Irenaeus has a forward-looking solution to the problem, in which humans can rise towards God. This may help people who are enduring suffering by giving them reason for their suffering and hope that it will be beneficial in the end.

Weaknesses of the Irenaean/Hick theodicy

Irenaeus's arguments have not been very well received by many Christians because his 'positive' view of evil downplays the importance of the Fall as the point at which evil and suffering entered the world.

He seems to ignore the idea expressed in Genesis 3 that sin (and therefore suffering and evil) came about as a result of Adam and Eve's choice to disobey God's command, which goes against the literal interpretation of Genesis.

As a result, he makes Jesus into little more than a great moral role model. This seems to go against mainstream Christian teaching that Jesus was the saviour of the world who brought forgiveness and reconciliation with God through his crucifixion and resurrection.

Irenaeus did not believe in universal salvation, but Hick did. Hick's belief in universal salvation seems to contradict Bible teaching – making Christ's atoning for the sins of mankind an irrelevance. This appears unjust and may arguably be a disincentive for free moral agents to choose good over evil. It undermines the suggestion that we can only progress towards God's moral likeness by an engagement with suffering within the world, given that that job is completed in heaven regardless.

Is the theodicy even morally acceptable? The idea of universal salvation would mean that a mass murderer who converts on his death bed would achieve moral perfection as much as a person who had tried to live a genuine morally good life.

The theodicies of Hick and Irenaeus do not really solve the problem of why many 'innocent' individuals suffer terribly through their lives. They treat people as a 'means to an end' and do not account for the unfair distribution of suffering. If the tragic death of a child facilitates moral and spiritual growth for the family of the child, it is little consolation for the suffering of the innocent child. This point is well stated in Dostoyevsky's great novel *The Brothers Karamazov*:

> Is there in the whole world a being who would have the right to forgive and could forgive? I don't want harmony. From love for humanity, I don't want it. I would rather be left with the unavenged suffering. I would rather remain with my unavenged suffering and unsatisfied indignation, even if I were wrong. Besides, too high a price is asked for harmony; it's beyond our means to pay so much to enter on it. And so, I hasten to give back my entrance ticket, and if I am an honest man I am bound to give it back as soon as possible. And that I am doing. It's not God I don't accept, Alyosha, only I most respectfully return him the ticket.

For these theodicies to be successful, one has to have a theoretical idea that a state of moral perfection actually exists. Irenaeus says that it is possible for all humans to reach the 'likeness' of God, but not all will achieve this state during their physical life. There must, therefore, be some form of life after bodily death so that all humans can reach moral perfection. Irenaeus does not give any evidence for this idea, so this is a serious weakness.

The theodicy fails to explain the sheer extent of suffering which is required for God to achieve his will for mankind. Could an omnipotent God have found a way in which the spiritual and moral growth of mankind could be encouraged without the need for such widespread, devastating moral and natural evil? Surely an omnibenevolent God would want this also? Therefore, does one have to question the attributes of God if this theodicy is to be accepted?

The Free Will Defence

The notion of free will plays a central role in the theodicies covered so far; however, it can also be considered as a stand-alone defence (though it fails to meet the challenge of natural evil if understood in this manner).

The free will of humanity is a fundamental, essential good. Faith in God and genuine worship of God depend upon free will, especially given the epistemic distance between humans and God – mankind have to choose freely to worship God, should they so wish. Free will necessarily involves the capacity to choose evil – hence evil and suffering exist as a product of human choice. However, it can be argued that suffering is a small price to pay for this human freedom.

For the Free Will Defence to be successful, two conditions have to be in place:

1. Free will must be understood in a non-compatibilist sense
2. Omnipotence must be understood as the ability to do anything *logically possible.*

To maintain the Free Will Defence, we must understand freedom in a non-compatibilist sense. According to the Free Will Defence, human actions are determined by God. Humans can, however, retain the capacity to make free decisions without limiting our freedom, because if we can still have free will, despite our actions being determined, then God could have created us always to do good and never evil, without limiting our freedom.

Also, omnipotence must be understood to be the ability to do anything logically possible as opposed to 'anything at all' because if God's omnipotence meant he had the ability to do anything 'at all', then he should have the power to achieve the logically impossible task of giving us genuine free will whilst predetermining that our actions are always good. Only if God's omnipotence is understood to extend to the 'logically possible' can we show that he could not have preserved free will whilst at the same time determining our actions as being wholly 'good'.

FURTHER READING

Brian Davies, *The Reality of God and the Problem of Evil*. Continuum International Publishing, 2006

Stephen T. Davis, ed., *Encountering Evil: Live Options in Theodicy*. John Knox Press, 1981

Gillian R. Evans, *Augustine on Evil*. Cambridge University Press, 1990

John Hick, *Evil and the God of Love*. Macmillan, 1966

Philosophy of Religion, 4th edn. Prentice Hall, 1990

Peter van Inwagen, *The Problem of Evil*. Oxford University Press, 2008

Charles T. Mathewes, *Evil and the Augustinian Tradition*. Cambridge University Press, 2008

William L. Rowe, *God and the Problem of Evil*. John Wiley & Sons, 2001

Thought Points

1. Make a summary of what the 'problem' of evil is.

2. Make a grid of similarities and differences between Augustine, Irenaeus and the Free Will Defence.

3. How convincing do you find the Free Will Defence?

4. Do you think that, if the Augustinian and Irenaean theodicies and the Free Will Defence are taken together, they 'solve' the Problem of Evil?

5. 'God is responsible for evil and suffering in the world.' How far do you agree with this statement?

6. Plan a class debate on the motion 'This house believes that God is the only cause of evil and suffering in the world.'

7. Explain the idea of a 'vale of soul making' and decide whether you think it solves the 'problem' of evil.

8. 'The existence of evil in the world proves that God does not exist.' Discuss.

CHAPTER 8

God's Attributes

LEARNING OUTCOMES

In this chapter, you will be learning about some of the central theological and philosophical terms used in Philosophy of Religion:

- omnipotence
- omniscience
- omnibenevolence
- eternity
- free will

You will also be discussing issues such as:

- whether or not it is possible, or necessary, to resolve the apparent conflicts between divine attributes
- whether Boethius, Anselm or Swinburne provides the most useful understanding of the relationship between divinity and time
- whether or not any of these thinkers are successful in resolving the problems of divine knowledge, benevolence, justice, eternity and human free will
- whether the attributes should be understood as subject to the limits of logical possibility or of divine self-limitation

Introduction

The New Testament, having emerged from a Roman Empire which had adopted much of the ancient Greek philosophical tradition, is written in a Hellenistic context, but is also heavily influenced by Jewish concepts and understandings of the world. It brings Greek philosophy and the Judaeo-Christian understanding together to form a broader context of the nature and meaning of God.

134 | GOD AND THE WORLD

```
        Omnipotence
    ↗              ↘
Eternity          Omniscience

Free Will      Omnibenevolence
```

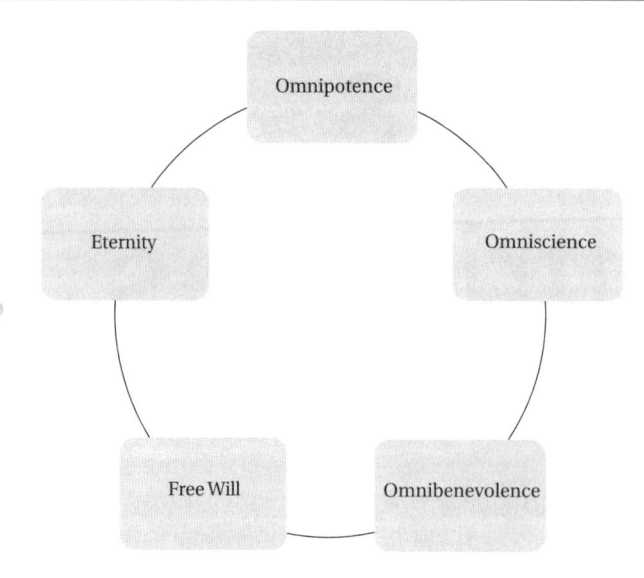

Whilst parallels may be drawn between the Judaeo-Christian God, Plato's Form of the Good and Aristotle's Prime Mover, the Ancient Greeks have a markedly different approach from that of Judaeo-Christianity.

The key difference here is that of Faith and Reason. Whilst both Plato and Aristotle adopted a very philosophical approach to explaining the existence of humans and providing a purpose for life, the Judaeo-Christian tradition is based on a premise of faith. Where Plato and Aristotle have the starting point of forming a rational, coherent argument as to why God may exist, the Judaeo-Christian approach is to have an abiding belief and trust in the writings of the Bible. The Bible does not adopt a philosophical approach. It is quite simply a collection of written work in different styles by people who all share the same faith. Furthermore, it adopts a non-cognitive approach, using metaphors, analogies and symbolism to explain its concepts. This is a marked difference from the well-reasoned lines of argument of Ancient Greek philosophy.

This difference in approach has led to a conflicting understanding of God and the divine compared to that of Plato and Aristotle. For Plato, the Form of the Good was an impersonal and remote entity that does not interact with his creation or have the capacity for love. Aristotle's understanding of the Prime or Unmoved Mover is that he is unaware of his creation and only has the capacity to think about himself. This is as far removed from the personal and interactive God of classical theism as one could get. The Judaeo-Christian God is concerned with the actions of humans and he makes demands; he intervenes in the world and responds to human behaviour, making actions such as prayer more prevalent than with the Ancient Greek idea of God.

The Greek influence on the Judaeo-Christian concept of God is evident throughout the Bible and early Christian writings. For example, we see the following influences.

Influence of Plato

- Sense pleasures should not be the sole purpose of one's existence
- The soul will be released from the body upon death (concept of Dualism)

- There is an eternal realm where we shall live after death (Realm of the Forms)
- The Form of the Good has led Christians to perceive God as perfect and the source of all goodness

Influence of Aristotle

- God is unchanging, eternal and beyond time and space (transcendent)
- The universe (and everything in it) exists for a purpose (*telos*)
- God is the cause of the creation of the universe (Prime Mover)
- A pattern of design and purpose in the universe only capable of coming from God is evident in the universe

The concept of God as creator

> **Exercise**
> How would you define 'Creator'?

In his book *The Coherence of Theism*, Richard Swinburne describes God as: 'A person without a body (i.e. a spirit), present everywhere, the creator and sustainer of the universe, a free agent, able to do everything (omnipotent), knowing all things, perfectly good, a source of moral obligation, immutable, eternal, a necessary being, holy and worthy of worship' (2nd edition, Oxford University Press, 2016, p. 2).

The Judaeo-Christian belief that God is the creator of the universe is derived from the Bible and is a central and necessary doctrine. For example, an early summary of Christian belief called the Apostles' Creed opens with the statement 'I believe in God, the Father Almighty, Creator of Heaven and Earth.' This creed is still recited in many Christian denominations during the Eucharist service.

As may be seen in the diagram, God is the creator of everything that exists in the universe, and is necessary for the continuation of everything in the universe from moment to moment, so that, if God were ever to cease to exist or were to be diverted from his loving care for the universe, the universe would cease to exist. Christians also believe that God is responsible not only for existence of the physical universe as a whole, but for every single element within it. Without God, there could not ever have been a universe and would not continue to be one. God is absolutely necessary for every aspect of the existence of the universe.

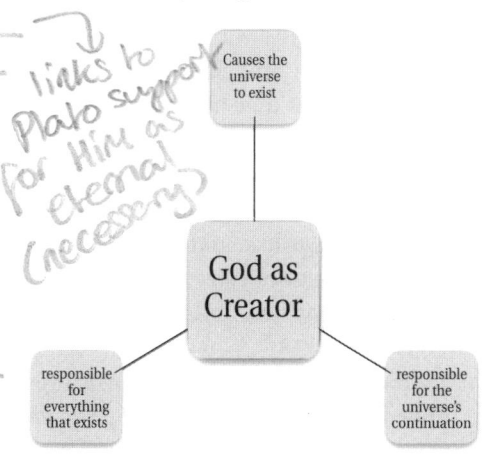

Genesis

All of these beliefs stem from the Bible, focusing mainly on the book of Genesis. Genesis is the first book of the Pentateuch (the five books of Moses). It is split into two sections:

- Section one (chapters 1–11) – this deals with the beginnings of human history
- Section two (chapters 12–50) – this deals with the beginnings of Israel's history

Although parts of the book were traditionally attributed to Moses, most of it has been written by a number of sources, now known as 'J', 'E', 'D' and 'P'. (For more details on this, see chapter 9, p. 181). These sources (and, as a result, the book) are believed by many Jews and Christians to be divinely inspired.

Genesis begins with the confident statement: 'In the beginning God created the heavens and the earth' (Genesis 1:1).

Genesis 1 offers the first account of creation. The narrative is an expression of the supreme Judaeo-Christian belief that God is the divine author of the universe. Genesis describes God as a deliberate organizer of the earth, and he issues commands for each day of creation. God is seen to be responsible for each new thing and hovers above His creation, breathing new life into the world. God creates the idea of time through the sun and moon marking each new day, and it is through time that humanity can know when to observe festivals and the Sabbath. God also pronounces his creation of animals to be 'good', and through his creative power he divinely commands them to multiply.

The creation of humans is God's crown and glory of the universe, as they were brought into being on the final day of God's creative activity. Humans alone resemble God and they are placed on the earth and given 'dominion' to rule over the fish in the sea and the animals on the land.

This process occurs over six (non-literal?) days and on the seventh day God rests. This seventh day is to be holy and separate, set apart from the rest. Humans must set apart the tasks of their ordinary life on this day and offer thanks and praise to God instead. This day is known as the Sabbath.

Genesis 2 is not really a 'creation' account, as it has traditionally been understood. The account begins with the earth already in existence – it is a paradise garden (Garden of Eden) and God then creates a man, Adam (this just means 'a man' in Hebrew), from the dust of the earth. Adam is given control of everything on the earth and God then creates woman, to be Adam's helper and partner. The story is actually about the relationship between God and humans, between humans and other humans, about temptation and the resultant punishments for disobeying God's command. It is written in the form of an aetiological myth that gives answers to why, for example, humans have to work for a living, why women have pain in childbirth, and why humans are mortal (and why snakes do not have legs!). (For more on this, see chapter 9, p. 181).

The creation narratives of Genesis are only the tip of the iceberg when it comes to biblical expression of God being the creator. The theme runs throughout the Old

God's Attributes 137

Testament and is expressed clearly throughout the Psalms and Wisdom Literature. For example, when Job questions God's plans and purposes as a result of the horrendous suffering he has experienced, God responds 'Where were you when I laid the foundations of the earth?' (Job 38:4).

> **Exercise**
>
> Compare Genesis 1 with Genesis 2. How many similarities can you find? How might you explain the differences?

Genesis is not the only biblical description of God as a creator. He is also described as intervening with the world on a regular basis throughout the Bible, as seen by passages such as:

- **John 1:3** – 'All things were made through him'
- **Genesis 3:8** – 'Then the man and his wife heard the sound of the Lord God as he was walking in the garden in the cool of the day, and they hid from the Lord'
- **Genesis 19:24** – 'The Lord rained down burning sulphur on Sodom and Gomorrah – from the Lord out of the Heavens'
- **Joshua 10:14** – 'There has never been a day like it before or since, a day when the Lord listened to a human being. Surely the Lord was fighting for Israel!'
- **Genesis 6:13** – 'So God said to Noah, "I am going to put an end to all people, for the earth is filled with violence because of them. I am surely going to destroy both them and the earth"'
- **Psalm 139:13** 'For you knew me in my mother's womb'

> **Exercise**
>
> Look up Psalm 104 in the Old Testament. Count the number of references to God as creator and list the five most important ones (in your opinion).

Isaiah 40 describes God as tending to his flock (his creation) 'Like a shepherd. He gathers the lambs in his arms and carries them close to his heart; he gently leads those that have young' (Isaiah 40:11). Here we see that God is in control of his creation and he watches over and is responsible for it each and every day. This is vastly different from the impersonal and absent 'Gods' of Plato and Aristotle.

This involvement in creation may raise questions over the free will of humanity. How can God (omnipotent and omnibenevolent) be *involved* in creation at an intimate level, yet stand back and allow humankind free will which then causes such mass suffering and devastation? Rudolph Brun addresses this issue:

> We face the Christian paradox that God is involved in all cosmic and human history but in ways that do not prevent creation from becoming itself. On the one hand, God is intimately

involved in His creation, is at the centre of its becoming, yet lets creation, and with it human beings, become themselves in freedom. A shadow of God's nature falls on those who raise children: what a constant involvement in letting go!
(Brun, *Creation and Cosmology: Attempt at Sketching a Modern Theology of Nature*, Xlibris Corp., 2009, pp. 29–30)

Here, Brun compares God's involvement with creation to that of parental involvement in the lives of their children. As much as a loving parent may want to control each and every aspect of their child's life, at some point the most loving thing to do is to let go and let their children make mistakes, whilst still being there and ready to help out if needed. This process is a huge learning curve for the child, but helps him/her to grow into a strong and independent adult. Therefore, God can be actively involved within his creation without the need to control each and every aspect. Hence, God can be involved with his creation whilst still allowing total freedom for humans.

The place of human beings in God's creation

You have made them [humanity] a little lower than the angels and crowned them with glory and honour.
You made them rulers over the works of your hands;
you put everything under their feet.

(Psalm 8:5-6)

One important belief throughout the Old Testament is that humanity is at the very top of the hierarchy of all life (as stated in the Psalm above). Humankind is the only animal 'made in the image of God' (Genesis 1:26), but there is no further explanation as to what this may mean in reality, other than humanity taking charge of the earth God created for them.

In Genesis 2, no cosmology of creation is offered as it is primarily concerned with the place of human beings in God's creation. Humans are given a set purpose and duty given by God – working on the land, growing fruit and crops, etc. Man is also commanded not to eat from the tree of the knowledge of good and evil. However, in Genesis 3, Adam and Eve are tempted by the serpent's misrepresentation of God denying them some of the advantages of the garden and they give in to this temptation. As a result, they do gain knowledge, but not knowledge of God – merely knowledge of their own sexuality. They suddenly feel shame in their nakedness which represents a form of fall from innocence.

As a result of their disobedience, God punishes them in the following ways:

- The serpent will now crawl on the ground and eat the dust
- The woman will now experience severe pains during childbirth
- The man's work will be exhausting and futile, experiencing a life of struggle followed only by death

The interpretation of humankind's disobedience has been discussed in chapter 7, but it is obvious that the place of humankind in the Garden of Eden is very clear – God is in charge. God provides a paradise for humanity as long as they obey the commands he lays down. God provides for humans and puts them in charge of creation – it is then up to them. Humans are to be responsible tenants of the earth God provides, but, as seen in Genesis 2–3, it is ultimately God who is in control.

Aspects of God's character as shown through Genesis

Much knowledge of God's attributes can be found through the account of creation in Genesis. Below is a summary of the key points raised:

- Humans are inferior to God and do not have the same power and status
- God is the supreme creator, leader, and is in control of the destiny, of humans
- Humans must submit to God's laws and acknowledge God's authority, law and divinity, maintaining God's superiority over humans
- God is omnipotent – he gives life through his spirit and maintains his creation
- God is infinite – he has no beginning or end and is the only eternal being
- There is one creator and one creation
- God creates immortal forms of beauty and goodness and creates a world that has no pain or suffering
- Genesis could be viewed as being an indication of God's divine intentions. There is no sin, death or disease recorded in Genesis 1.

Imagery of God as a craftsman

> **Exercise**
> What do you understand by the word 'craftsman'? What qualities does a craftsman have? List at least five examples of craftsmen. Discuss your views with your classmates.

In his book *The Power of God*, Aquinas states: 'Natural things are in the first cause of motion, that is, God, as craft products are in a craftsman, and so God acts as a craftsman' (p. 17).

Throughout the Old Testament, there are a number of occasions where God is compared to a craftsman. When we consider the term 'craftsman', we think about a person who creates or performs a particular skill with dexterity – a person skilled in a particular craft. Through our examination of God as a creator, so far, we have seen biblical evidence of a God who has an intimate and loving concern for his creation. However, the concept of God as a craftsman permeates the whole Old Testament. Jeremiah compares the concept of God as a craftsman with that of a potter. Jeremiah says, in the House of the Potter: 'the word of God came to me as follows, "House of Israel, can I not do to you what this potter does? Yes, like clay in a potter's hands, so you are in mine"' (Jeremiah 18:6).

God is also compared to a potter in Isaiah, where the prophet says: 'And yet, Yahweh, you are our father; we the clay and you the potter, all of us the work of your hands' (Isaiah 64:8).

Both of these quotes show that, from the beginning of the process of creation, there has been an intimate connection between God and his creation, and each being is crafted as an individual work of art, as with a potter and his creations.

This comparison of God being a 'potter' presents an anthropomorphic image of God – an image of God which likens some aspect of God's nature to that of a human being. Although there are many philosophical problems with anthropomorphism, likening God to a potter is an effective way to understand his nature as a creator.

God as omnipotent

Omnipotence is regarded as one of the most crucially important aspects of faith, because it is through God's power that the existence of the universe came into being, as a result of God's will. It may be said, therefore, that God is worthy of worship, as people have faith that God has the power to bring about his will, and in doing so he can secure a just world for all.

In order to contemplate the omnipotence of God, we firstly need to consider exactly what omnipotence means. According to the *Oxford English Dictionary*, omnipotence is 'the quality of having unlimited power'. The concept of the God of classical theism is viewed to be an omnipotent (or 'all-powerful') being, although the understanding of this omnipotence is widely debated. The difficulty is presented by the following three questions:

1. Does God's omnipotence entail that God has the power to do literally anything?
2. Is God's power limited by logic and God's nature?
3. Is omnipotence even a coherent concept?

There are many biblical references to God's omnipotence. As discussed above, the creation story is arguably the most telling example of God's omnipotence, as he had the power to create the universe *ex nihilo* (from nothing). Following from this, we can consider the miracles of the Old Testament (for example, the parting of the Red Sea in Exodus 14 and making the sun stand still in Joshua 10).

There are many more examples of miracles in the New Testament. One example is the virgin birth as detailed in Luke 1:34-7, where it states:

> Mary said to the angel 'How can this be, since I am a virgin?' The angel said to her, 'The Holy Spirit will come upon you and the power of the most high will overshadow you; therefore the child to be born will be holy; he will be called the Son of God. And now, your relative, Elizabeth in her old age has also conceived a son; and this is the sixth month for her who was said to be barren. For nothing will be impossible with God.'

Also, Matthew 19:23-2 states:

> Then Jesus said to his disciples, 'Truly I tell you, it will be hard for a rich person to enter the kingdom of heaven. Again, I tell you, it is easier for a camel to go through the

God's Attributes

eye of a needle than for someone who is rich to enter the kingdom of God.' When the disciples heard this, they were greatly astounded and said, 'Then who can be saved?' But Jesus looked at them and said, 'For mortals it is impossible, but for God all things are possible.'

> **Exercise**
>
> What can God do? Are there any limits to what God can do? Consider the following examples and discuss them with your classmates: can God –
> - Change his mind?
> - Turn water into wine?
> - Eat an ice cream?
> - Commit suicide?
> - Make a rock too heavy for him to lift?
> - Change the past?
> - Create a square circle?
> - Go swimming?
> - Tell jokes?
> - Get rid of terrorism?
> - Cook dinner for everyone in the world at the same time?

There are many questions raised by the concept of God's omnipotence. For example:

- Is omnipotence compatible with omnibenevolence?
  - Surely if God is all powerful then he would have the power to do evil?
- Is omnipotence compatible with immutability?
  - An all-powerful God would surely have the power to change?
- Is omnipotence compatible with omnipresence?
  - Could an all-powerful God choose where to be?
- Is omnipotence compatible with being eternal?
  - Could an all-powerful God not have the power to kill himself?

These questions may appear glib, but, if God cannot do these things, surely his power is limited? Indeed, if God can do these things, then it would appear that God's nature is not fixed.

This poses the question: is omnipotence limited by God's character? One possible response is that God could do all of the above things – however, he would choose not to, as that is not part of his nature. This suggests that God's omnipotence means that God has the power to do anything that he *wills*. Another response might be to suggest that God does not have the power to contravene his nature because it would be a logical contradiction. God's power means that God has the power to do anything that does not contravene logic, and going against his fixed nature would contradict logic.

GOD AND THE WORLD

This view then raises another question: is God's omnipotence limited by logic?

- Can God create a square circle?
- Can God be wholly good, yet commit sin?
- Can God create a stone too heavy for him to lift?
- Can God make 2 + 2 = 5?
- Can God make the sun shine in Manchester?

René Descartes states: 'There are many such things that, although we recognise some perfection in them, we also find in them some imperfection or limitation, and these therefore cannot belong to God' (Descartes, *Meditations* 5, 67, in Descartes, *Key Philosophical Writings*, Wordsworth Editions, 1997, p. 173).

Descartes would argue that God is perfect in every way and therefore unlimited – meaning he is not bound by the laws of logic and, as he is the source of logic, he can suspend it or replace it at his will. Therefore, for Descartes, if God wills it, God can make 2 + 2 = 5.

Biblical support for God's power defying logic

Creation *ex nihilo*

'Ex nihilo nihil fit' – 'Nothing comes from nothing'. In Genesis 1, we see an argument for God creating the universe 'from nothing'. If God is the exception to this logic and is a being who can create something from nothing, then is it possible that God has the power to defy reason and commit the logically impossible.

The Incarnation

Christians view Jesus as 'wholly human' and also 'wholly God'. Logic would dictate that one single being cannot be in two contradictory states at once. Again, this would appear to provide support that God has the power to defy logic, as in Christian belief Jesus was both human and divine at the same time.

There is an argument to suggest that, as mortal humans, we do not have the power to understand how God can defy logic – rather, we should have faith and accept that God's omnipotence is ultimately beyond our limited human comprehension.

Many theologians have argued that God's omnipotence should be accepted as operating within the realms of logical possibility. Aquinas is one philosopher who holds this belief. As Richard Muller states: 'Aquinas refuses to allow the powers of God to be restricted in its creation to the actually existing order of things. Divine liberty, freedom and power are released from the restrictions of the actual and allowed scope in the realm of the possible' (Muller, *Divine Will and Human Choice*, p. 167).

Theologians who support this view argue that to say that God cannot do nonsensical things such as creating a square circle in no way limits God, as these are not viable options. Therefore, there is no way even an ultimately powerful being could carry

> **Incarnation:** The Christian view of Jesus as 'wholly human' and yet 'wholly God'.

links to Swinburne's view

God's Attributes

them out. Also, doing something that is logically impossible is literally inconceivable because God's omnipotence is viewed as meaning that God has the power to do *anything that can be conceived to be done*.

Once again, this links back to God's nature. The reason that God cannot change or be sinful is not that God lacks power, but rather that it would go against logic for God to do so. By definition, God has certain qualities that cannot be contradicted. As William L. Rowe states in his book *Philosophy of Religion: An Introduction*, 'God could no more cease to be perfectly Good than a triangle could cease to have three angles' (p. 7).

[handwritten note: links to Mavrodes' criticism of the paradox of the stone]

> **Exercise**
> If it is true that God is omnipotent, why does God not put a stop to all the evil and suffering in the world? Discuss.

God as omniscient

There are many accounts in the Bible which describe God as omniscient, as we see below: 'Before a word is on my tongue, you know it completely, O Lord. . . . . .Such knowledge is too wonderful for me, too lofty for me to attain. . . . . .All the days ordained for me were written in your book before one of them came to be' (Psalm 139).

This shows the Christian belief that, even before events happen, God knows about them, and before we were even born God had already written the plan for our lives. This omniscience poses a number of philosophical questions which are examined below:

- *Is it right to apply the word 'knowledge' to God?*

  - For humans, knowledge can be said to be 'justified true belief'
  - At times, however, this belief – no matter how justified – may be wrong. (For example, the ancient theory of the earth being flat – this knowledge was justified and supposedly 'accurate' until modern science – and indeed philosophy – proved the theory wrong.)
  - If God's knowledge is unlimited and beyond human comprehension, is it right to apply the word 'knowledge' to God, whose knowledge and wisdom seem incomparable to our own?
  - Aquinas argues that, as God is so far beyond our limited human comprehension, when we speak of God we must do so using analogies, as using these is the only way we can truly begin to understand the qualities of God. Mortal beings only understand human wisdom, and our understanding is like the imperfect shadow of God's ultimate knowledge and wisdom.
  - As Aquinas states: *[handwritten note: so we should not apply our limited language & knowledge to Him]*
    - 'Nothing can be found that is common to these kinds which would be their genus and univocal; that which is common to them is not contained

under a certain category: but being common to them according to analogy, as shown in *Metaphysics IV*' (McInerny, *Aquinas and Analogy*, Catholic University of America Press, 1999, p. 32).

- *Is it 'right' for God to know details of our lives without permission?*

  - In Nietzsche's preface to *The Gay Science* (Cambridge University Press, 2001), a little girl asks her mother if God is everywhere. The mother answers 'yes', to which the little girl replies 'I think that's indecent!'
  - For Nietzsche, this omniscience is indecency on God's part.
  - However, one may respond that God is the creator (as discussed earlier in the chapter) and not only is God's knowledge for our benefit, but, as God crafted us, he can no more be separated from knowledge about us than a painter can be separated from knowledge of his painting.

- *What types of knowledge can God have?*

  - Can God have practical knowledge gained through experience – e.g. could God learn how to ride a scooter? To tie shoelaces? To know what ice cream tastes like?
  - These questions link to the debate on omnipotence as discussed earlier in the chapter – if God is all-powerful, why can he not perform these actions? However, if he can be subject to change through experience, can he be immutable?

The problem of omniscience and free will

Brian Davies sets out this problem in the following way:

> The first [problem] is the view that if God is omniscient he cannot know only what has happened, is happening or will happen. For there is more to be known than that. What about what could have happened, what could be happening and what could happen in the future? These, so the argument runs, are things that can be known, and if God is omniscient then he must know them.
>
> The second is the view that God must know what will happen, but his knowledge of this must not interfere with human freedom. The argument then states:
>
> 1. God must know future free actions
> 2. He can only know these if he first has knowledge of them as 'uncreated possibilities'
>
> (Brian Davies, *Thinking About God*, Geoffrey Chapman, 1985, p. 183)

Here, Davies argues that, if God is truly omniscient, then he knows all that will be true in the future (categorically true, as God cannot be wrong). It follows that, if a person *knows* 'x' will happen, then 'x' *has to happen*. So, if God knows that a future event is going to happen, then that future event has to happen otherwise God would be wrong (which is a contradiction in terms – an *omniscient* God cannot be wrong). So, if God is aware that a future event is going to happen, then as a result of his omniscience that event *has* to happen, otherwise God would not be omniscient – therefore the event is *necessary* (cannot be thought not to happen). If human action is truly free, then it can never be seen to be necessary. Therefore, for Davies, if God is omniscient, then there can be no free human actions. Davies concludes this theory by stating: 'If God knows that someone would have done such and such if created, and if he knows that the person will be created, will he still not show in advance what the person will do as created? And will that not mean that the person's action will not, then, be free after all?' (Davies, *Thinking about God*, p. 183).

> **Exercise**
> Write a summary of, and a response to, the above argument.

The importance of free will

The argument above, as presented by Davies, may prompt the question: 'Why is free will so important?' For most theists, the belief that God gave us free will is of great importance because most theodicies rely on the fact that God gave humans free will – this free will is then used to justify the existence of evil and suffering in the world, allowing for God to remain omnipotent and omnibenevolent (but may therefore question his omnipotence?). Also, if we are simply playing out what has already been decided for us, are we no more than puppets in a theatre being controlled by a puppet-master? Would that then make our lives devoid of any true meaning? Further, if God works on commandments, rewards and punishments, it would appear decidedly immoral that God should punish a person for behaving in a way he predetermined them to behave. Does that then make God's commandments redundant? Finally, if humans are not truly free, then they can take no blame for (and indeed accept no consequences for) their actions.

Why is predestination a problem?

Most theists think that, because we believe that a person acts freely, we may attach praise, blame, reward and punishment to their actions. If all of our actions were predetermined, however, there would be no point in being thankful to a person for doing a kind deed, as they were always going to do that deed. Equally, it is pointless being angry or upset if somebody hurts us – their actions were predetermined, so they had no choice in the matter.

Also, most monotheistic religions work on the basis of moral responsibility, reward and judgement. How can God possibly judge the moral actions of a person if it were he who determined the way in which a person would behave? Surely, therefore, all people should be allowed to enter the kingdom of heaven if they are not responsible for their actions?

Responses to the problem of omniscience and free will

1. Doctrine of Double Predestination

John Calvin (1509–64), a Protestant reformer, wrote: '(God) in accordance with his wisdom has from the farthest limit of eternity decreed what he is going to do, and now by his might carries out what he has decreed' (John McNeill, *Calvin – Institutes of the Christian Religion*, Westminster / John Knox Press, 1960, p. 207).

Here, Calvin argues that our decisions and each choice we make are intermediate causes which fulfil God's primary cause and plan. Calvin also goes on to state: 'He (God) predestined what he wished to make of every man. For he does not create everyone in the same condition, but ordains eternal life for some and eternal damnation for others' (McNeill, *Institutes*, p. 109).

This is known as the *Doctrine of Double Predestination*. God knows, so therefore determines, who will receive his grace and be saved and who will be damned to hell. Romans 8:28-30 states:

> We know that all things work together for those who love God, who are called according to his purpose. For those whom he foreknew he also predestined to be conformed to the image of his son, in order that he might be the firstborn within a large family. And those whom he predestined he also called; and those whom he called he also justified; and those whom he justified he also glorified.

For Calvin, God knows his plan for each person. Before a person is born, he knows whether or not that person will be saved. God does not get involved with some sinners and leaves them in their sins awaiting eternal damnation – a philosophy known as *The Doctrine of Retribution*. Although this may seem unfair for some, Calvin argues that the nature of God is just, and that even though humans may not understand the works of God, they should not question his infinite wisdom.

John Calvin (1509–64)

God's Attributes

Defence of Calvin

One may argue that human free will is often misunderstood and that humans can have free will even if they are predetermined. Freedom does not necessarily need to be understood as having absolute open choices ahead – freedom could be seen to be acting upon one's choices and desires. It may be argued that, as God created us and knows us inside out, he knows the choices we will make before we even make them. To illustrate this example, when I take my son out for dinner, even though he has absolute free choice of anything he wants from the menu, I can guarantee that, given a choice, he will choose to eat margherita pizza for main and strawberry and chocolate ice cream for dessert. This is not because I have determined him to choose this – I have not shaped or influenced his decision on the way to the restaurant. I simply know him well and know what he likes. The same can be said (on a *much* greater scale) for God. He knows his creation and is involved with his creation. Although our actions are free, God knows us so well he knows which free choice we will make before we even know ourselves.

God as omnipresent

The attributes of God, taken together with what is written in the Bible, seem to suggest that God is *omnipresent* (present everywhere at the same time). From our examination of the creation story in Genesis, we can reach the conclusion that God must be outside both the universe and time in order to create them.

Aquinas states:

> But God, as has been proved, is absolutely without motion, and is consequently not measured by time. There is, therefore no before and after in Him: He does not have being after non-being, or non-being after being, nor can any succession be found in His being. For none of these characteristics can be understood without time. God, therefore, is without beginning and end, having His whole being at once. In this, consists the nature of eternity.
>
> (Aquinas, *Summa Contra Gentiles: Book One: God*, I, 20)

In his *Summa Theologica*, Aquinas refers to Isaiah 57:15, which argues for God's omnipresence by stating (God is) 'The one who is high and lifted up, who inhabits eternity, whose name is holy.' Aquinas illustrates this by considering a person sitting at the top of a hill. From this high vantage point, they are able to see a vast section of the road ahead of them, whereas for a person on the road below, they can only see what is directly in front of them or directly behind. Relating this concept to God, he is so far removed from time and space that he has the ability to view the whole of time simultaneously.

Omnipresence and immanence

If God is timeless and transcendent, how does this fit in with the Judaeo-Christian belief that God is immanent and active within the world? How do such events as miracles happen if God is transcendent? Also, does prayer become invalid? If God is outside and unconcerned with time, then surely prayer is redundant as God is too far removed from the constraints of this world to be affected by human prayer?

Throughout the Old Testament, God is described as having no beginning and no end, as seen from the passages below:

- Isaiah 57:15: 'For this is what the high and exalted one says – he who lives forever, whose name is holy.'
- Deuteronomy 33:27: 'The eternal God is your refuge, and underneath are the everlasting arms. He will drive out your enemies before you, saying "Destroy them!"'
- Genesis 21:33: 'Abraham planted a tamarisk tree in Beersheba, and there he called on the name of the Lord, the eternal God.'

The above passages are consistent with the idea that God is omnipresent and eternal; however, there may be another way of interpreting the passages – that God is everlasting. With this view, one could suggest that although God is eternal – he *has* always existed and *will* always exist – he can live alongside and within his creation. The only reason God works outside of time is because if he existed within time, then he could have not created it (which would then have implications for his omnipotence). If God were to work within time, then it may be argued that he would be unaware of the future as it has not happened yet, which would then raise questions for God's omniscience.

The goodness of God

Introduction

> **Exercise**
> How would you define 'goodness'? What would you understand as a 'good' act?

God saw everything that He had made, and indeed, it was very good

(Genesis 1:31)

Throughout the Bible, there are two key ideas:

1. God is good
2. God's actions are good

The story of creation in Genesis 1 repeatedly states 'and God saw that it was good', so Christians may see something of the nature of the 'goodness' of God in nature (Natural Theology). God is clearly good throughout the creation story, and many

God's Attributes

Psalms state the nature of God's goodness. God creates and sustains the world, and throughout the Bible there are many occasions where God performs healing miracles or supports his followers in battle. This paints a picture of a 'good' God who is both present and active within his creation.

However, the question can be posed as to what makes an action 'good'? Is an action 'good' because (a) God commands it, or (b) God commands what is good? This is known as the classical problem of the **Euthyphro Dilemma**.

What is the Euthyphro Dilemma?

> **Euthyphro Dilemma:** The question of whether certain acts are classed as good/bad because God has chosen them to be so, or because they are intrinsically good or bad.

In Plato's *Euthyphro* dialogue, Socrates asks Euthyphro: 'Is piety loved by the Gods because it is pious, or is it piety because it is loved by the Gods?' That is, are certain acts classed good/bad because God has chosen them to be so, or because they are intrinsically good or bad?

If we acknowledge that the former is correct (good or bad because God has chosen them to be so), then it can be said God's goodness is not significant. It is entirely arbitrary and, if God had chosen differently, then torture could be good and kindness could be bad. This then raises questions over why God's goodness should be revered and worshipped.

If the latter is correct (acts are good because they are intrinsically right or wrong), then it could be suggested that there is a standard of goodness in the world which is independent of God, therefore undermining God as the ultimate source of goodness and making his goodness redundant. God could be said to be subject to a greater standard of morality which transcends him, which would then raise questions over his omnipotence and arguably his omnibenevolence.

In this dialogue, Plato seems to suggest that Socrates demonstrated that there is no meaningful sense in which God can be considered to be the perfect source of all goodness.

Response to the Euthyphro Dilemma

Aquinas states that this is not a dilemma at all as both sides can be accepted. As Anders Kraal explains:

> The doctrine of divine simplicity says, in its classical Augustinian explication found in The City of God, that God's simplicity means that the being or substance of God and the attributes or intrinsic properties of God are identical. In the classic Augustinian phrase: God is what he has (quod habet, hoc est). God is his goodness, his love, his power and so on.
>
> If this doctrine is accepted, then the Euthyphro dilemma can be diagnosed as *a false dilemma*. This is because there is a further alternative: that the good is neither the good independently of God's will, nor because God wills it, for God and goodness are identical.
>
> (Harris, *God, Goodness and Philosophy*, p. 101)

In other words, God commands things because they are good, and he knows what to command due to his perfect knowledge of goodness because his nature is entirely good. God *is* goodness, so God's commands will always reflect goodness – they are not arbitrary.

Does supreme goodness make sense?

Theists generally accept that God embodies absolute moral perfection; however, the meta-ethical relativist position would question whether such absolute moral standards are possible. Throughout different cultures and religious practices, there are different moral standards, which demonstrate that there can be no objective right or wrong. Even if you take the example of your next-door neighbour – what is deemed acceptable behaviour in your house may be deemed unacceptable in theirs. Does it make sense, therefore, to view God as the source of *all* goodness, if goodness is not an objective concept that is shared by all of humanity?

Dawkins on God's goodness

In his work *The God Delusion*, Richard Dawkins argues that the God presented in the Bible does not set an example of moral goodness that people can look up to (for example, when God tests Abraham's faith by commanding him to kill his son Isaac – God only intervenes to stop this when Abraham is about to carry out the command).

For Dawkins, this is an example of God's immorality – a clear distance from God being the ultimate source of Good. God puts man and son through an awful ordeal to satisfy his own curiosity – certainly not demonstrating love or goodness. Dawkins describes God as 'obnoxious'.

> **Exercise**
> Do you agree with Dawkins's conclusion that God must be 'obnoxious'? Give reasons for your answer.

Boethius, Anselm and Swinburne on God's attributes

> **Boethius** (full name Anicius Manlius Severinus Boethius) lived from c.480 to c.524. He was a Christian philosopher and statesman from a noble family, who befriended the Gothic emperor, Theoderic. As part of his upbringing, Boethius learned Greek and read much Platonic philosophy, and he translated many Greek philosophical works into Latin and composed commentaries on them. Also as part of his aristocratic upbringing, Boethius was brought up as a Christian and he became involved in many debates and disputes about doctrine. He was appointed by Theoderic to the post of 'Master of Offices', roughly equivalent to Prime Minister. He did not hold this post for long, however, because he angered other senior officials at court by attacking their corrupt practices. They conspired to have him imprisoned and he was executed, probably by strangulation or crushing of the head followed by clubbing. Before this, however, Boethius was able to write his most famous book, *The Consolation of Philosophy*. This literary masterpiece is a dialogue between Boethius and 'Lady Philosophy', which tries to explain why he had apparently been abandoned by God to his fate. This book became very influential during the Middle Ages, being referenced by many scholars, including St Thomas Aquinas.

God's Attributes | 151

Boethius's *Consolation of Philosophy*

Boethius was one of the first Christian philosophers to tackle the question of the relationship between God's eternity, omniscience, human freedom and evil. He wrote the book as a dialogue between himself and 'Lady Philosophy'. He regales her with his tales of unjust arrest and punishment by imprisonment, and impending death on fabricated charges. In reply, the lady provides reasons why his experiences reflect the existence of a loving and benevolent God. She tells him that the world is not a random, chaotic place where rewards and punishments are given out on a whim. He only thinks this is the case because of his limited perception of the world – it is not reality.

Lady Philosophy proves that not only is God good but he is the source of goodness. Humans are good because they share in God's goodness; conversely, they are evil because they reject it. To be fully human is to accept the good; to reject it makes one sub-human. Boethius's perception that evil people are ruling the world is a false one. In fact, God is in perfect control of the world.

In book 5 of the *Consolation*, Boethius puts forward a strong and important discussion concerning the philosophical problems that arise from the belief that God is omnipotent, omniscient, eternal and omnibenevolent, and how these divine attributes relate to human free will.

Boethius on God's eternity

Almost all theists and philosophers of religion believe that, if God exists, he must exist eternally – that is, that God has neither a beginning nor an end. The difficulties start, though, when it turns to attempting to define what is meant by 'eternity'. What does it mean to be 'eternal'? Following from this is the vexed question of what God's relation to time is and to the universe that exists in time and space. There are three main positions on this issue – God is timeless, God is everlasting or eternal, and God is temporal.

1. God as timeless

In this view, God exists outside time and space. God has no temporal body or temporal location. For God, there is no 'before', 'during' or 'after'. Most of the early Christian thinkers, such as Augustine, Anselm and Aquinas, took this view. They decided on this as the most appropriate view to take because it seemed to solve the problem of God's omniscience and human free will. If God is outside time, he cannot know any facts about the temporal world or the actions of human beings. God is therefore alive in his own eternity and simply knows all events timelessly – past, present and future all together – including all the actions of humans.

Boethius took this view. He says: 'That God is eternal . . . is the common judgement of everyone who lives according to reason. Let us consider what eternity is, because this will make it clear to us both God's nature and his knowledge. Eternity is the complete possession all at once of life without limit' (*Consolation*, book 5, section 6).

Another reason for viewing God as timeless is that, if God is a perfect being, it must follow that God must have the perfect form of existence. The perfect form of existence would be timeless rather than in time, because a temporal being would not be able to experience all of life at once in the way a non-temporal being would. If God were temporal, there are many things in God's life that have passed and cannot occur again, such as creating the universe. These events would only be in God's memory. Such a transitory life is not compatible with the being of God, because even a perfect memory of events is not as perfect as a present reality.

American philosopher Chad Meister adds a further argument in favour of God as timeless:

> Another argument in support of timelessness is based on relativity theory. According to the theory, time and space are conjoined; one does not exist without the other. Now most theists believe that God is non-spatial. If this is the case, then to be consistent with relativity theory one would need to believe that God is non-temporal (or atemporal) as well.
>
> (Meister, *Introducing Philosophy of Religion*, p. 57)

Criticisms of God as timeless

A number of criticisms have been made about Boethius's theory of God as timeless. One is that God's timelessness would mean that God could only have knowledge of timeless truths such as mathematical truths – 'a triangle is a three-sided figure with internal angles adding up to 180 degrees' – or tautologies like 'a bachelor is an unmarried man'. God would not – and could not – have any knowledge of any human activities. If I were to say that I am going to the gym for an hour tonight after work and will be going again on Saturday, God could have no idea about the temporal references – an hour, tonight, Saturday – because all of these are in God's eternal present.

A second criticism is that it appears to contradict the teaching of Christianity. Nearly all the narratives in the Old Testament and New Testament describe God as acting in specific times and places. For example:

- God *did* create the world in six days (Genesis 1:19)
- God *is* sustaining the world (Psalm 65:9-13)
- God *will* judge the world (2 Corinthians 5:10)

If God acts in time as the Bible teaches, then God must be in time, and therefore not eternal.

2. God is everlasting

This is really a response to the previous idea that developed in order to avoid the criticisms we have looked at above on God as timeless. In this view, God exists without beginning or end, but is in existence in time – forever. It may be observed that, in the Bible, God is directly involved in the world. This means that God has had relationships with the world and the people in it, where God performed various actions – creating the world, talking to people, going to war, punishing wrong-doing, and so on. These examples show that God interacts with creatures in the temporal world, so God must, in some sense, be temporal. The benefit of this view is, of course, that God may be seen to interact meaningfully with his creation and understand actions and temporal ideas as individual items.

3. God is eternal and temporal

This view explains that God was originally eternal up to the point of the creation of the universe, and was therefore outside time. After he created the universe, however, God was drawn into temporality. The Christian philosopher William Lane Craig holds this view. He maintains that there are good theological and philosophical reasons for affirming both views. Rather than choosing one of the positions, Craig presents a third point of view – a position in which God is timeless before the creation but becomes temporal at the creation.

Clearly, Craig's view is open to criticism. One is that it is incoherent, because it is not possible for God to be *fully* timeless because, as Craig claims, God was capable of changing to be temporal even while in the timeless state. God did change at the moment of creation, at least in terms of his relationship with the world and humans, and, since time and change are two sides of the same coin, God can only be partially timeless, not fully so.

Boethius on God's foreknowledge

Traditionally in Christian theology, God is believed to be omniscient (all-knowing). There are several ways in which this term may be taken – God knows everything that there is to know; God knows everything there is to know within the laws of nature; or God may know every event that occurs, has occurred or will occur in the future at the same time.

There is a problem with God's foreknowledge, however. Specifically, the problem concerns human free will. We generally believe that we have free will to say and do what we want to. For example, I might say that Manchester City is the best soccer team in the English Premier League. I am free to say this although many soccer supporters in Manchester will disagree with me, and they, of course, are free to do that too!

For Boethius, the problem with God's foreknowledge and free will was that, if God knows what human individuals are going to do before they freely choose to do an evil action, should not God be held at least partly culpable for letting it happen, and responsible for the results of the evil?

Boethius's answer to this problem is to say: 'when God knows that something is going to happen in the future, he may know a thing which will not happen out of necessity, but voluntarily; God's foreknowledge does not impose necessity on things' (*Consolation*, book 5, section 6).

Boethius makes a distinction here between knowing what someone will do and causing it to happen. For example, it is known that you will sit your A Level RS exam in the summer term of Year 13, but the grade you will achieve is not yet known. In a similar way, even if God already knows what actions I may do in the future, it does not mean that God causes them to happen.

Anselm's four-dimensionalist approach to eternity and God's actions in time

Anselm was familiar with the works of Boethius and had studied his views on God's eternity and foreknowledge. Anselm was deeply concerned about the issue of God's free will and wrote about this in several works, including the *Monologion* and his last book, *De Concordia: On the Compatibility of God's Foreknowledge, Predestination and Grace with Human Freedom*. Like Boethius, Anselm believed that God was timeless, and this was because God was omnipotent. As Anselm said in the Ontological argument, God is 'that than which nothing greater can be conceived'. Part of the meaning of this definition of God is that God is eternal. Anselm therefore has the same problem as Boethius regarding whether humans have free will or our existence in time is predetermined because God knows our future.

For Anselm, human freedom is linked to moral action. For example, I choose to do a good deed for someone in need. In this case, I show my goodness. If, on the other hand, I am told to help someone in need, then I am not showing my goodness because I have not chosen to do it. Here, the element of choice is crucial, for making a free choice is what 'good' people do. Anselm thought that making an incorrect choice is to choose nothing at all. He takes the view that God cannot choose to do evil, so must always make good choices, but God does have free will because to make a good choice is to demonstrate one's free will.

On the question of God's foreknowledge, Anselm argues that God knows what will happen beforehand because he can see all moments of time at once. Humans, on the other hand, only know what happens after it has happened, because our minds work in a linear way. We can only see what happens today, we cannot change what happened yesterday and we cannot see what will happen tomorrow. This view is now called 'presentism'. It contrasts with Anselm's understanding of how time works for God. God is timeless and spaceless, whereas humans are limited by both time and space. This is Anselm's 'four-dimensionalist' view of the timelessness of God. According to Anselm, God sees the past and the future in the same way that he sees the present. It can be difficult for people living now to understand this but it might be analogous to you watching a movie that switches time between the past, present and future – for example, the classic *Back to the Future* movies in which Doc Brown transports himself and his friend Marty McFly backwards and forwards in time in his DeLorean car to avert various disasters. Here, you know that you are living in the present, but, when you immerse yourself in the movie, you almost feel as if you are in the past/future alongside the characters. When it ends, you know that you are firmly in the present again and looking forward to whatever you are going to do next (in the future).

For Anselm, his four-dimensionalist understanding of time and eternity meant not only that God can see everything in time and space but also that all time and space is 'in' God. This is because God created everything that exists and he sustains all that exists. Anselm's view also means that humans do have real free will. God can see the choices that individuals have made in the past, make in the present and will make in the future. At this point, Anselm differs from Boethius, in that Anselm talks of God's *eternal present*. This is different from the human concept of 'the present', because we can compare 'the present' with 'the past' and 'the future', whereas God sees them all at once. For Anselm, 'eternity' is not a temporal idea like past, present and future. Eternity is Anselm's fourth dimension and this is what sets God apart from his creation and the creatures in it.

Richard Swinburne on God's timelessness and human free will

Swinburne takes a radically different approach from Boethius and Anselm to the issue of God's timelessness and human free will. He argues that the concept of timelessness as applied to God has no meaning. First of all, he looks at the Bible and declares that there is no evidence of a timeless God in it. He says: 'The Hebrew Bible shows no knowledge of the doctrine of divine timelessness . . . The same applies in general to the New Testament writers' (Swinburne, *The Coherence of Theism*, p. 230).

He comments on one statement in the book of Revelation in the New Testament that might be interpreted as relating to God's timelessness, where God says: 'I am Alpha and Omega, the first and the last, the beginning and the end' (Revelation 22:13). It is Swinburne's judgement, however, that this single statement does not provide sufficient evidence for a doctrine of divine timelessness in the Bible.

Swinburne also concludes that the very idea of God's timelessness does not make sense, because God 'would have to be aware simultaneously of all the events of human history that happen at different times as they happen' (*The Coherence of Theism*, p. 239). But Swinburne finds this a logically impossible idea. For it to be true, God would have to have simultaneous knowledge – at the same time – of two events happening at different times. This is not logically coherent. He cites the example of two different events concerning the destruction of Jerusalem: 'How could God be aware of the destruction of Jerusalem by the Babylonians in 587 BCE as it happens, and of its destruction by the Romans in 70 CE as it happens, when these two times are not simultaneous with each other?' (p. 239).

Swinburne's conclusion is that there are no convincing reasons for believing in the timelessness of God. To maintain this view is both against the evidence of the Bible and logically incoherent. For him, the idea of timelessness as a characteristic of God is not necessary.

Exercise

1. Explain Boethius's views on God and eternity.
2. Do you think the criticisms of Boethius's view of eternity are justified?
3. In your opinion, is Boethius successful in solving the problem of God's foreknowledge and human free will?
4. Construct a short dialogue between Anselm and Swinburne on the topic of God's timelessness and human free will.

FURTHER READING

Aquinas, *On the Power of God*. Wipf & Stock, 2004

Harriet A. Harris (ed.), *God, Goodness and Philosophy*. Routledge, 2011

C. Hartshorne, *Omnipotence and Other Theological Mistakes*. State University of New York Press, 1984

J. Hick (ed.), *The Myth of God Incarnate*. SCM Press, 1977

(ed.), *The Myth of Christian Uniqueness*. SCM Press, 2012

John Marenbon, *The Cambridge Companion to Boethius*. Cambridge University Press, 2009

R. Muller, *Divine Will and Human Choice*. Baker Academic, 2017

W. L. Rowe, *Philosophy of Religion: An Introduction*, 4th edition. Wadsworth/Thomson, 2006

E. Stump and N. Kretzmann, 'Eternity', in Eleanore Stump and Michael J. Murray (eds.), *Philosophy of Religion: The Big Questions*. Blackwell, 1999, pp. 42-53

M. Wiles, *The Remaking of Christian Doctrine*. SCM Press, 1974

The Making of Christian Doctrine: A Study in the Principles of Early Doctrinal Development, new edition. Cambridge University Press, 2009

Thought Points

1. Describe each of the attributes of God dealt with in the chapter: omniscience, omnipotence, omnibenevolence, eternity and free will.

2. Try to create a mind map of the relationships between the attributes of God.

3. Which of these attributes of God do you think is the most important? Give reasons for your choice.

4. Which, in your opinion, is the most significant criticism of God's attributes? Why?

5. 'It is impossible to believe that God can possess all of these attributes at the same time, because they contradict each other.' Discuss.

6. 'The problem of God's foreknowledge is the most difficult attribute of God to defend.' How far do you agree with this statement?

7. 'To believe that God knows everything and also to believe that humans have free will is logically contradictory.' Critically assess this statement.

8. 'Anselm's four-dimensionalist view is unconvincing.' Do you agree? Give reasons for your answer.

9. 'Swinburne's argument on God's attributes is more successful than either Boethius's or Anselm's.' To what extent do you agree with this statement?

SECTION IV
RELIGIOUS LANGUAGE

CHAPTER 9

God-talk: Negative, Analogical, Symbolic

LEARNING OUTCOMES

In this chapter, you will be learning about:
- religious language –
  - the apophatic or negative way
  - the cataphatic or positive way
  - the symbolic way

You will also be discussing
- the usefulness of each response to religious language
- whether or not the apophatic way brings effective understanding of religious language
- whether or not Aquinas's analogical approaches support effective expression of language about God
- whether or not discussion about religion is comprehensible if religious language is understood as symbolic

Introduction: different kinds of language

Language is about communication. It is not unique to humans. All creatures communicate with each other using their own language. Sometimes this is verbal, sometimes it is non-verbal. Without language, we would not be able to interact with others. Sometimes, language can be very straightforward, so, for instance, we might say 'I've written an essay about religious language.' This is a description of what you claim to have done and its meaning is clear to anyone listening. The person you are talking to knows what the terms you are using mean and they can check whether what you have said is correct. You might later have a discussion about whether the essay you wrote was awarded a high mark by your teacher. This statement could be easily checked by looking at the end of the essay.

> **Exercise**
>
> Look at the following statements and try to communicate them to someone else without using any words:
> 1. 'I love RS'
> 2. 'This textbook is really good'
> 3. 'I'm looking forward to the weekend'
> 4. 'It's my birthday today'
> 5. 'Philosophy of Religion is really interesting but quite hard'

Most language is what we would call 'public', which means that it is accessible to everyone. Sometimes, however, people might have their own 'private' language. So, for example, I might say: 'Spligs are just ootbveqlc, they're even woozer than Splogs. Spligs are ucorsy quxziww!' In this case, because I am using words that might mean something to me but would not be found in any dictionary, no-one else would understand my meaning. Communication could not happen.

When it comes to religious language, there are major problems concerning meaning. David Hume, in his *Enquiry Concerning Human Understanding*, wrote:

> When we run over libraries.... What havoc must we make? If we take in our hand any volume; of divinity or school metaphysics, for instance; let us ask, Does it contain any abstract reasoning concerning quantity or number? No. Does it contain any experimental reasoning concerning matter of fact and existence? No. Commit it then to the flames: for it can contain nothing but sophistry and illusion.
>
> (Hume, *An Enquiry Concerning Human Understanding*, Oxford University Press, 2008, p. 165)

Hume's point here is that, when we encounter a form of communication that appears to make statements about the way things are but that has no grounding in experience, and it cannot be checked by our experience, then it is meaningless. For Hume, the language of religion is of this sort: it is meaningless. Hume's statement here points up an important difficulty concerning religious language. How can religious believers talk about God when human language is made up of words that can only relate to *this* world, whereas religion talks about so-called 'realities' *beyond* this world? For religious believers, God is totally different from humans, so how can we say anything meaningful about God's nature? Atheists argue that the concept of God is not accessible to testing and no human vocabulary could be adequate to describe anything about God's nature. For empiricists, there is little point in discussing

God-talk: Negative, Analogical, Symbolic

anything about God because it is just like speaking nonsense. Any language about God is pointless and meaningless.

The main problem for religious language is that there is little language that is reserved exclusively for God. Religious believers use ordinary language to try to explain divine concepts. This is a very difficult task and has led to many philosophical differences and debates within the religious community. Another related problem with religious language is that some of the terms that are used to describe God, and his character and actions, are very obscure, and this raises its own problems in communicating their alleged meaning. Many religious statements sound as if they are literal statements – so, for instance, 'Jesus came to redeem the sins of the world' or 'God gave the 10 Commandments to Moses' might appear to be factual statements but, for many people, they are clearly not intended as such. Thinking rationally about these or similar statements, how could Jesus, a human, save all the sins of everyone in the world? What is meant by 'sins'? God presumably did not have a physical body with vocal chords that could be heard by Moses. Philosophers of religion have attempted to solve these problems and we will be looking at some of their ideas in this chapter.

Religious language as negative

At first sight, it may seem very odd that religious language should be described as 'negative', but the term is used in a very specific way. It comes from early medieval philosophy and is particularly associated with **Pseudo-Dionysius the Areopagite** in the sixth century CE, though its roots may be traced back to the mystical theology of Origen in the third century CE and, more generally, to neo-Platonic philosophy. It has had an enormous influence on the development of Christian theology, particularly in the Eastern Orthodox tradition, though it has also been important in the thought of St Thomas Aquinas, in *The Cloud of Unknowing*, and in the twentieth century with Orthodox theologians such as **Vladimir N. Lossky (1903–58)**.

Development of Apophatic theology

Apophatic theology: (*Via negativa* in Latin) Also known as 'Negative theology', attempts to come to a knowledge of God indirectly, by removing those things that God is not.

Negative theology has its roots in the philosophy of Plato. Plato's insights are found mainly in the *Republic* (VII, 509 b), the *Seventh Letter* (ep.7, 341 c–e) and the *Parmenides* (137d–146a). Middle Platonist and neo-Platonist philosophers developed these ideas into a systematic form. When Christianity began to develop, neo-Platonic philosophical concepts were used to describe emerging Christian ideas and doctrines. Among the burgeoning Christian community, a number of the early theologians, such as Tertullian in the third century, and Cyril of Jerusalem and the Cappadocian Fathers in the fourth century, developed **Apophatic theology**. Gregory of Nyssa, one of the Cappadocians, said: 'The true knowledge and vision of God consists in this – in seeing that He is invisible, because what we seek lies beyond all knowledge, being wholly separated by the darkness of incomprehensibility' (*The Life of Moses*, II,163).

> **Exercise**
> Explain how the Cappadocian Fathers could say that they believed in God, but that they did not believe that God exists, at least in the same sense that humans exist (despite believing in the Incarnation).

Beginnings of Apophatic theology

The beginnings of Apophatic theology in Christianity go back to the Bible. There are a number of passages in both Old and New Testaments that recount incidents where significant figures experience God in a direct way that appeals to their emotional or spiritual side rather than through the use of rational arguments. For instance:

- No-one has seen or can see God (John 1:18)
- He [God] lives in unapproachable light (1 Tim. 6:16)
- His ways are unsearchable and unfathomable (Job 11:7-8; Romans 11:3-36)
- Abraham is told in a vision to sacrifice his son Isaac (Gen. 18)
- God appears to Moses at the Burning Bush (Ex. 3), in a non-physical form, yet speaking in a voice he could hear and understand
- Moses is also given the sacred, ineffable, name of God (YHWH) (Ex. 3:14)
- The prophet Elijah 'hears' the 'still, small voice' of God (1 Kings 19:11-13)
- St Paul refers to the 'Unknown God' in his debate with Athenian philosophers (Acts 17:23)

The life of Jesus shows several examples of apophatic speech. The Synoptic Gospels often describe Jesus as being in the constant presence of God. So, for example, his public ministry begins with a prayer and a vision: 'While Jesus after his baptism was at prayer, heaven opened and the Holy Spirit descended on him in bodily shape like a dove' (Lk. 3:21-2). Jesus spent forty days in the wilderness being tempted by the Devil (Mk 1:12f.).

At the end of Jesus' life, he prays: 'Father, into your hands I commend my spirit' (Lk. 23:46). Jesus begins all the important public acts of his ministry with a prayer. He often withdraws from the crowd for periods of solitary prayer. He interprets his entire existence by reference to God, whom he calls 'father'.

These instances all show that Jesus and other biblical characters felt that God communicated with them directly using non-physical, non-verbal means. They did not need empirical evidence of God's existence, but accepted that God could speak directly to them. These examples emphasize God's **ineffability**, showing that God is unknowable by humans except by a spiritual readiness by those involved to listen for the voice of God.

The other side of the idea of ineffability is that, when theologians begin to explain God's essential nature, they want to make a distinction between God's transcendence and his immanence. All Christians accept the truth that God is immanent and that the supreme example of this is shown by the Incarnation, whereby God voluntarily sends his only Son to earth as a human being in the form of Jesus. The difficulty

> **Ineffability:**
> The idea that God cannot be spoken of truly or described accurately.

with attempting to describe God's transcendence is that, by definition, anything that is transcendent cannot be described adequately in human language without diminution of its meaning. So, as we will see with Pseudo-Dionysius, God cannot be described meaningfully as 'good', because we would compare this with human goodness and this would be inadequate to describe God's goodness. To get round this difficulty, Apophatic theologians had to describe God's characteristics 'negatively', so, to describe God's goodness, they could say only that 'There is no evil in God.'

Pseudo-Dionysius

Apophatic theology derives its meaning from the Greek word 'apophatikos', meaning 'negative' or 'to deny'. It stresses the idea that it is not possible to use human language to describe or refer to God, because God is completely different from humans and human language is inadequate for the purpose. In fact, human language about God is harmful because it could lead to the conclusion that God is less powerful, loving, creative and so on than God actually is. Ultimately, God's reality is beyond human language or understanding and can only be adequately described by saying what God is not.

In his most famous and important book, *The Divine Names*, Pseudo-Dionysius attempts to describe God positively. He shows how words such as goodness, wisdom and power are applicable to God, and how these words relate to humans only because they are derived from God. For example, he begins with the idea of goodness, which expresses the nature of God. Humans share in this idea only inasmuch as it is a reflection of God's goodness. As he says, 'None is good save one, that is, God.' Ultimately, however, he believes that the positive way of attempting to describe God's qualities fails. It fails because God's qualities and characteristics are of a much superior level to those of humans and this can only lead to misunderstanding of the nature of God. So he turns to the negative way in his *Mystical Theology*, looking for greater clarification of how God may be described and understood.

Pseudo-Dionysius begins by denying those characteristics that are furthest removed from God, such as hatred and drunkenness. Neither of these can be attributes of God. He proceeds to discuss other attributes and qualities of the divine. Some of these were 'goodness', 'truth', 'creator' and other traditionally central properties of God, but Pseudo-Dionysius rejects these because they can all be compared to human goodness, truth and creating, which are necessarily much less 'intense' or 'real' than the way God experiences them.

He reaches what he calls 'the super-essential darkness'. He writes that, because God is utterly transcendent, humans can understand God best, by denying or removing all things that are – just as men who, carving a statue out of marble, remove all the impediments that hinder the clear perception of the latent image and by this mere removal display the hidden statue itself in its hidden beauty' (quoted in F. C. Copleston, *A History of Philosophy*, vol. II, Doubleday, 1948, p. 198).

Pseudo-Dionysius believed that humans could only speak meaningfully about God apophatically (negatively) because to attempt to speak of God in any other way would lead to misconceptions and inadequate understanding of God's nature. Human beings, he says, are prone to form **anthropocentric** ideas of what God is like, but this would not mean that humans would have a clear view of what God is in reality. Religious believers must strip away any human ways of thinking and inadequate conceptions of God. When this happens, they will enter what Pseudo-Dionysius calls the 'Darkness of Unknowing', when the human mind 'renounces all the apprehension of the understanding and is wrapped in that which is wholly intangible and invisible . . . united . . . to Him that is wholly unknowable' (Copleston, ibid., p. 199).

At this point, Pseudo-Dionysius demonstrates his neo-Platonic background. Plato and his neo-Platonic interpreters believed in Dualism, in which there was a division between the physical realm of the body and the spiritual realm of the soul. The physical body was, in many ways, an obstruction to the soul's wish for real understanding of God, who was beyond 'mere' human knowledge and rational thought. Only the soul could have any real understanding of God. For Pseudo-Dionysius, humans had to move beyond rational arguments and logic to seek for God through achieving the mystical union of the human soul with God that can only occur by using Apophatic theology.

> **Anthropocentric:** Human-centred. The view that words and ideas are focused on human thoughts and characteristics.

Exercise

The ninth-century philosopher and theologian **John Scotus Erigena (815-77)** said: 'We do not know what God is. God Himself does not know what He is because He is not anything [i.e. 'not any created thing']. Literally God is not, because He transcends being.'

What do you think this means? Try to explain it in terms of Apophatic theology.

Thomas Aquinas

Although St Thomas Aquinas is better known for his views on religious language as analogy (see below), he also writes about the *via negativa*. We will discuss the relationship between his use of apophatic and cataphatic language later in this chapter.

In several of his writings, Aquinas uses negative terms to describe God. For example:

> The most we can know of God during our present life is that He transcends everything that we can conceive of Him.
>
> (Aquinas, *De Veritate* 2, 1–9)

> For, by its immensity, the divine substance surpasses every form that our intellect reaches. Thus we are unable to apprehend it by knowing what it is. Yet we are able to have some kind of knowledge of it by knowing what it is not.
>
> (Aquinas, *Summa Contra Gentiles*, I, 14, 2)

> We cannot grasp what God is, but only what He is not and how other things are related to Him.
>
> (Ibid., I, 30, 4)

> This is the ultimate in human knowledge of God: to know that we do not know Him.
>
> (Aquinas, *Quaestiones Disputatiae de Potentia Dei*, 7, 5–14)

Aquinas, then, denies that God has being or existence like a creature. He prefers to talk of God as 'Being Itself' – he uses the phrase *Ipsum Esse Subsistens* ('Being in and of Itself'). In the view of philosopher Brian Davies, 'We cannot, he (Aquinas) argues, know what God is. We must content ourselves with considering the ways in which God does not exist, rather than the ways in which he does' (Brian Davies, ed., *Thomas Aquinas: Contemporary Philosophical Perspectives*, Oxford University Press, 2002, p. 87). In this sense, Aquinas's Five Ways can be understood less as arguments *for* God's existence and more as arguments *against* God's existence. In the Five Ways, Aquinas's purpose is to demonstrate that God is not a creature and is therefore wholly different from every other created thing. He does this by using the *via negativa*.

> **Exercise**
> 1. What does Aquinas mean by the phrase *Ipsum Esse Subsistens*?
> 2. Explain briefly why, according to Davies, Aquinas argues that 'we cannot know what God is'.
> 3. Do you agree with Davies's argument here?

The Cloud of Unknowing

Another example of anaphatic theology comes from an anonymous Christian work dating from the second half of the fourteenth century in England. *The Cloud of Unknowing* is a spiritual guidebook on prayer, drawing on the tradition of Pseudo-Dionysius, and it uses the *via negativa* method of discovering truths about God through spirituality. All knowledge and rational thought are put to one side so that contemplation may lead to spiritual union with God:

> For He (God) can well be loved, but he cannot be thought. By love he can be grasped and held, but by thought, neither grasped nor held. And therefore, though it may be good at times to think specifically of the kindness and excellence of God, and though this may be a light and a part of contemplation, all the same, in the work of contemplation itself, it must be cast down and covered with a cloud of forgetting. And you must step above it stoutly but deftly, with a devout and delightful stirring of love, and struggle to pierce that darkness above you; and beat on that thick cloud of unknowing with a sharp dart of longing love, and do not give up, whatever happens.
>
> (*The Cloud of Unknowing*, ch. 6)

The 'cloud of unknowing' is an apophatic expression declaring that God is hidden from human reason and intellect by an impenetrable cloud that is accessible to believers, but only by a spiritual and mystical love. The cloud exists between God and humans and can only be pierced by a 'sharp dart' of love. Prayer, which is in the emotional or affective part of the human psyche rather than in the intellectual part of the soul, is in some ways negative. Mystics pray, but, despite their efforts, can never fully know God without God's loving kindness.

> **Exercise**
> 1. Summarize how the author of *The Cloud of Unknowing* understands God's nature.
> 2. Research *The Cloud of Unknowing* and produce a short report on it, including its origins and importance.

Twentieth-century apophaticism

The major modern adherents of apophatic language and theology are seen in the Eastern Orthodox Church, and their views on religious language have been articulated by theologians such as John Meyendorff, Georges Florovsky, Andrew Louth and Vladimir Lossky.

Vladimir Lossky summarizes the nature and importance of Apophatic theology as follows:

> The apophatic way of Eastern theology is the repentance of the human person before the face of the living God. It is the constant transformation of the creature tending towards its completeness: towards that union with God which is brought about through divine grace and human freedom. But the fullness of Godhead, the ultimate fulfilment toward which all created persons tend is revealed in the Holy Spirit. It is He, the Mystagogue of the apophatic way, whose negations attest the presence of the Unnameable, the Uncircumscribed, the absolute Plenitude... The apophatic attitude in which one can see the fundamental character of all theological thought within the Eastern tradition, is an unceasing witness rendered to the Holy Spirit who makes up all deficiencies, causes all limitations to be overcome, confers upon the knowledge of the Unknowable the fullness of experience, and transforms the divine darkness into light wherein we have communion with God.
>
> (Lossky, *Mystical Theology of the Eastern Church*, pp. 238–9)

Vladimir Lossky

Lossky, like many other Eastern Orthodox Christians, believed that the use of apophatic language was superior to that of western churches because it reveals a more authentic expression of the nature of God as totally different from human conceptions of the divine. He defined the apophatic way as the understanding that God is radically unknowable in human and philosophical terms. The only way that humans can have any understanding of God is because of the special revelation of the Trinity and especially through the Incarnation of the Son (Jesus).

> **Exercise**
> 1. How does Lossky define the apophatic way?
> 2. What is the link between Apophatic theology and revelation?

Criticisms of Apophatic theology

Apart from its use in certain quarters of Christianity, particularly the Orthodox Church, the practice of Apophatic theology and language has all but disappeared and been replaced by other theories about religious language. There have been a number of serious criticisms of apophatic language.

God-talk: Negative, Analogical, Symbolic

First is the point that, if we speak of God only negatively, then it is very difficult even for religious believers to know what God is like. It is even more difficult for non-believers. To say that God is not-love, not-holy or not-existing is not helpful at all. The normal way that people explain things in everyday life is positive rather than negative. It would therefore make much more sense if people would talk about God in a positive way. To attempt to describe God's characteristics negatively is felt by many to be more confusing than helpful. This may go some way to explaining why most Christians have dismissed apophatic language.

A second point was made by **Anthony Flew (1923–2010)** when he argued that using negative terms for God such as 'invisible', 'non-bodily', 'unknowable' and 'formless' actually gives the impression that there is little difference between a theist's definition of God and the definition of nothingness. To explain this, he uses John Wisdom's 'Parable of the Gardener', in which two explorers come to a clearing in the jungle. They see many flowers growing there, but many weeds too. One man says that there must be a gardener who looks after the clearing; the other says that there is no gardener. They set up a fence, electrify it and have a bloodhound patrol the area and wait to see whether a gardener turns up. No-one appears and no evidence of a gardener emerges. The believer says the gardener must be invisible, intangible and insensible to electric shocks, makes no sound and has no scent. The point is clear to the sceptical companion: how would someone with all these characteristics differ from an imaginary gardener or even from no gardener at all? Using this parable with reference to apophatic language shows that this kind of negative language does not aid a person's understanding of God. It leads to more problems than it solves.

N.B. We will be discussing Flew's parable again in chapter 10, pp. 193

A third criticism of apophatic language is that many religious believers assert that the Bible is the 'Word of God'. They imply from this statement that God wrote the Bible (perhaps with the aid of various humans, such as Moses or St Paul and the evangelists). Almost all statements concerning God and God's actions are positive – God is loving, creative, just, forgiving, wise, redeeming, saving, to name just a few. How can all these positive characteristics be inappropriate for religious believers to use? To insist on using negative terms to describe God, or to claim that God cannot be described in any meaningful way, seems nonsensical and unhelpful.

> **Exercise**
> 1. Which of these criticisms do you think is the strongest?
> 2. Is it possible to argue against these criticisms? Give reasons for your answer.

Cataphatic theology: (Greek) / *via positiva* (Latin). Comes from the Greek word *kataphasis*, meaning 'affirmation'. It attempts to come to knowledge of God by using positive and direct language.

Religious language as positive

As we have seen, the 'negative' use of language to understand the nature of God did not persuade most Christians to follow it. The main alternative is known as the *via positiva* or **cataphatic theology**. The way this has manifested itself in subsequent practice and discussion of religious language is through the idea that religious language may best be understood by thinking of it as analogy. The most important proponent of this view is St Thomas Aquinas.

Introduction to analogy

An analogy is a comparison between two objects or systems that highlights ways in which they are thought to be similar or different. An analogical argument is one where accepted analogies are used to argue towards a further similarity. The use of analogies is very common throughout the world and analogical reasoning has been very important in a wide range of contexts. It has been used in scientific, philosophical and legal reasoning. Below are two examples, adapted slightly from the *Stanford Encyclopedia of Philosophy* article 'Analogy and analogical reasoning' (accessed 15 April 2017):

(a) Charles Darwin makes an analogy between artificial and natural selection to argue towards the probability of the latter:

> Why may I not invent the hypothesis of Natural Selection (which from the analogy of domestic productions, and from what we know of the struggle of existence and of the variability of organic beings, is, in some very slight degree, in itself probable) and try whether this hypothesis of Natural Selection does not explain (as I think it does) a large number of facts.
> (Darwin, Letter to Henslow, May 1860, in F. Burchardt, *Evolution: Selected Letters of Charles Darwin 1860–1870*, Cambridge University Press, 2008)

(b) In an interesting and important British legal case in 1932, the House of Lords found a manufacturer of bottled ginger beer liable for damages to a consumer who became ill as a result of a dead snail in the bottle. The court argued that the manufacturer had a duty to take 'reasonable care' in creating a product that could foreseeably result in harm to the consumer in the absence of such care, and where the consumer had no possibility of intermediate examination. The principle articulated in this famous case was extended, by analogy, to allow recovery for harm against an engineering firm whose negligent repair work caused the collapse of a lift (*Haseldine* v. *CA Daw & Son Ltd.* 1941).

> **Exercise**
> Explain the following to someone who has never experienced them before, using only analogies:
> 1. visiting Paris
> 2. eating coconut ice cream
> 3. flying in an aeroplane
> 4. not eating for 24 hours (voluntarily)
> 5. running in a 10-kilometre race
> 6. winning first prize
> 7. learning to play a musical instrument
>
> Is there anything that can be explained without using analogies? If so, what makes these things different?

Aquinas and analogy

We have already seen that Aquinas believed that God could not be described literally in human language. This was because of its limitations, so that, if a religious believer were to say 'God is good', the word 'good' cannot be understood to mean literally the same as when a parent might call her child 'good'. There is some similarity between the two uses, in the sense that there is a moral connotation in both, but there is a huge difference in the extent to which God is 'good' by comparison with human 'good'. This is why Aquinas advocated the *via negativa* or apophatic language.

Aquinas goes further than this, however, in his understanding of the nature of religious language. Influenced by Aristotle, he recognized that it was not satisfactory to talk about God solely in negative terms. He advocated the *via eminentiae* ('way of eminence'), by which he means that, while it is possible to know something of God's nature, our knowledge is only partial. It is not possible for humans to know God completely. Karen Armstrong explains this idea as follows:

> Thomas made it clear that all our language about God can only be approximate, because our words refer to limited, finite categories. We can speak of a good dog, a good book or a good person and have some idea of what we mean; but when we say that God is not only good but Goodness itself, we lose any purchase on the meaning of what we are saying.
>
> (Armstrong, *The Case for God*, p. 143)

> **Via eminentiae:** ('Way of eminence') This is Aquinas's way of arguing that humans can talk positively about God, but acknowledging that our knowledge is only partial.

For Aquinas, all human talk about God is analogical, because when we talk about God we attribute characteristics to God in a similar way to how we attribute characteristics to other humans. There are two ways of talking about things: we can use **univocal language** or **equivocal language**. When we talk univocally, we mean the word has only one definition and will therefore mean the same thing in any context. For instance, we might refer to a red car, red flower or red door. For theists, of course, univocal language is unacceptable, because it means that God must be physical and limited, just like human beings.

> **Univocal language:** A word has only one meaning.

Aquinas rejects univocal language by making the statement that:

> Nothing can be said univocally of God and creatures. For effects that do not measure up to the power of their cause resemble it inadequately, not reproducing its nature, so that what exists in simple unity in the cause exists in the many forms in the effects: the uniform energy of the sun, for example, produces manifold and varied forms of effect on earth. And in the same way, as we have said, all the many and various perfections existing in creatures pre-exist in God in simple unity.
>
> (Aquinas, *Summa Theologica*, 1, 13, 5)

> **Equivocal language:** A word can have different meanings in different contexts.

When we talk equivocally, however, we may use the same word to mean different things in different contexts. It has a variety of meanings. For instance, the word 'field' can refer to an area of land but is also a term in electronics, or the word 'Alsatian' can refer to a breed of dog or to an inhabitant of the area of Alsace in France. In terms of religious language, the term 'good' is used of God – 'God is good' – with a different meaning from when 'good' is used of a person. God's 'good' is of a different kind, extent and quality than human goodness. For theists, therefore, using equivocal language is also inadequate, because, when any characteristic is used of God, we would not know what it meant because we could compare it with many other uses of the same characteristic, all of which would have slightly different meanings and connotations. For example, if God were to be described as 'strong', this could be understood in a number of different ways – does God have strong muscles, strong opinions, strong health or strong athletic abilities? Very few theists would wish to attribute any of these possible characteristics to God, but, if language is used equivocally, this would lead to a great deal of misunderstanding about the nature of God because each individual would have his or her own opinion. There could be no objectivity.

In the face of these kinds of difficulties, Aquinas thought that using analogy would render it possible to make positive statements about God. We can talk meaningfully of God being the cause of everything, of being eternal, perfect, good, omnipresent, omnipotent and so on. Aquinas teaches that analogy can be used in two ways – **analogy of attribution** and that of proportionality.

> **Exercise**
> Explain why Aquinas believes that univocal and equivocal language are inappropriate for talking about God.

Analogy of attribution: Humans can talk meaningfully about God because there is a causal relationship between human understanding of concepts like 'love' or 'goodness' and the understanding of these concepts in the mind of God.

Analogy of Attribution

Aquinas says that, although there are problems with knowing anything substantial about God, humans can use analogies with confidence to attribute certain characteristics to the divine. This is because there is a causal relationship between the two characteristics being described and compared. Aquinas used the example of a bull's urine. If the urine is healthy, we can infer that the bull from which it came is healthy. Brian Davies uses the example of bread and a baker. If we taste a piece of bread and say that the bread is good, it must mean that the baker is also good, because the bread is the product of the baker and so his goodness spreads to the bread. But if we develop this a little further, we can say that the bread is light, tasty and suitably moist. This does not mean, of course, that the baker is also light, tasty and moist, but that the baker has all the qualities and skills to be a good baker.

When Aquinas calls God the 'creator', it means that he can say with confidence that God created everything that exists and that God reveals his nature through what he has created. This enables humans to understand what God is like and the relationship he has established with humans. Religious believers can use terms such as 'good', 'just' and 'loving' in the reliable knowledge that their understanding of these terms relates, in a meaningful way, to God's nature. The analogy is not perfect, of course, because God is not human, but it provides some understanding that creates a connection between humans and God.

Analogy of proper proportion: The view that God possesses all good qualities infinitely, whereas humans own these qualities in proportion to their abilities.

Analogy of proper proportion

Aquinas taught that, when religious believers talk about God, they are able to do so meaningfully. This is because the terms that can be applied to God – 'good', 'creator', 'loving', etc. – may also be applied to and understood by humans because humans experience these same characteristics, but in proportion to how God has them. Humans experience love, but God *is* love. God's love is greater than human love because God is the cause of human love. The effects resemble the cause, and so their love is related, but different. As Aquinas states:

> Our natural knowledge begins from sense. Hence our natural knowledge can go as far as it can be led by sensible things. But our mind cannot be led by sense so far as to see the essence of God; because the sensible effects of God do not equal the power of God as their cause. Hence from the knowledge of sensible things the whole power of God cannot be known; nor therefore can His essence be seen. But because they are His effects and depend on their cause, we can be led from them so far as to know of God 'whether He exists,' and to know of Him what must necessarily belong to Him, as the first cause of all things, exceeding all things caused by Him.
>
> Hence we know that His relationship with creatures so far as to be the cause of them all; also that creatures differ from Him, inasmuch as He is not in any way part of what is caused by Him; and that creatures are not removed from Him by reason of any defect on His part, but because He super-exceeds them all.
>
> (Aquinas, *Summa Theologica* 1, 12, 12)

Here, Aquinas is saying that, although humans are contingent and fallible creatures, there are points of correspondence between them and God that enable humans to bridge the gap between them and God. This means that meaningful communication may take place and humans have a real understanding of God's nature. For example, Aquinas describes God as being perfectly good, because he is unchangeable and eternal. By this, Aquinas does not restrict God's 'goodness' to moral goodness, but extends it to all aspects of the word 'goodness'. Human 'goodness' is proportional to that of God.

> **Exercise**
> Decide whether the following examples are analogies of attribution or of proper proportion:
> 1. God is good – Andrew is good
> 2. The dog is faithful to its owner – Dan is faithful to his wife
> 3. Ann is tall – the tree is tall
> 4. The grass is green – the building is green
> 5. Emily's eyes are twinkling – the stars are twinkling

An alternative view

British philosopher and Member of the Order of Preachers Fergus Kerr (1931–present) argues that Aquinas did not intend his Five Ways to prove the existence of God through unaided human reason:

> That God's existence is something that does need to be argued for, Thomas holds, is based on the fact that we do not know what God's nature is – as the doctrine of the divine simplicity will say. In other words, the God who is present in the world as source and goal of all things is so much more mysterious than those who see signs of divinity everywhere believe that argument is required. The point of insisting that argument for God's existence is required is, then, not to convince hypothetical open-minded atheists, or even to

persuade 'fools', so much as to deepen and enhance the mystery of the hidden God. From the start, the 'theistic proofs' are the first lesson in Thomas's negative theology. Far from being an exercise in rationalistic apologetics, the purpose of arguing for God's existence is to protect God's transcendence.

(Kerr, *After Aquinas*, p. 58)

Kerr argues here that the Five Ways are not intended by Aquinas to be definitive (rational) 'proofs' for the existence of God. Instead, they were meant to demonstrate that God is incomprehensible, i.e. that God cannot be understood – he says we do not know what God is, and that God is 'mysterious'. Aquinas's negative theology (*via negativa*) is shown in his descriptions of God as 'Being in and of itself', which means that God cannot be known apart from what it says in the Bible because he transcends all analogies.

> **Exercise**
>
> Look back to chapter 4 where Aquinas's arguments for God's existence are discussed. Now re-read the quote above and try to decide whether you think Kerr is correct about Aquinas's intentions in the Five Ways. Do you agree with him that they are really apophatic ways of describing God's most important characteristics?

Criticisms of analogy

For many religious believers, analogy is a very helpful way of thinking about God and their relationship with him. As we have said above, analogies help people to relate to concepts such as God's infinity or eternal nature, because, without analogies, they would not be able to have any understanding of them at all. This point was the basis for Aquinas's teaching on analogy. He believed in the supreme authority of the Bible as the source of Christian beliefs. He took it as true that God created the universe and that humans were created 'in the image and likeness of God' (Gen. 1:26). Aquinas's acceptance of this statement, however, has been refuted by evolutionary biology. The work of Darwin implicitly shows that the universe was not created in the way that Genesis proclaims, but in a very different way, with organisms developing by adapting to their surroundings over a very long period of time. Richard Dawkins has explicitly argued for the position that no God was necessary for the evolution of the world. The point here is that, if Aquinas's assumptions are not correct, then his conclusions about the helpfulness of analogy as a means of knowing what God is like are not valid.

There are a number of other important criticisms of the use of analogy, which lessen its usefulness.

It is claimed by some critics that using analogy can lead to anthropomorphism. This is where human characteristics are attributed to God. For instance, God is described as 'loving', 'powerful', masculine (God is always called 'He' in the Bible), walking (in the Garden of Eden), and so on. The danger of this is that God is seen as comparable to human beings, although invested with more power, more love, etc., than humans. This makes God a very attractive and friendly being, who listens to people's prayers, helps them in times of difficulty, guides them through their lives and rewards them for living a moral life. It is very rare for believers to anthropomorphize the other characteristics of God as described in the Bible. For instance, God is described as infinite, eternal and timeless, among others. How then, can these be anthropomorphized? If God is timeless, how can s/he relate to people within time? This raises serious problems for the use of analogy because anthropomorphizing God leads to contradictions – a God with human characteristics who is ultimately beyond humans. Analogy therefore becomes useless.

A further difficulty of analogy is that those who use it tend to use only positive/good characteristics, rather than negative ones. It is clear, for instance, that there is a lot of evil in the world, so does this mean that God is evil too? St Augustine attempted a refutation of this point in his theodicy, but it is not universally accepted that he was successful. (See chapter 7, pp. 120–3.)

Another criticism of analogy is that it is not empirically verifiable. If we say that 'X is like Y', and we have no physical experience of 'Y', then we cannot show that the claim is either true or false. It is unverifiable. Critics of the use of analogy assert that analogies are of no value because there is no trustworthy evidence. If someone were to claim that pixies live in Manchester but that they are extremely good at hiding from people and leave no evidence of their presence, we would not be able to give this any credence. It is therefore of no value. This is what critics of analogy say.

A modern version of analogy: I. T. Ramsey

A more recent addition to the discussion of analogical language was made by Ian T Ramsey (1915–72) in his book *Religious Language* in 1957. Ramsey had studied Theology at Cambridge and became Nolloth Professor of the Philosophy of Religion at Oxford before being made Bishop of Durham in 1966. In many ways, this book was written in the context of the academic discussion by analytic philosophers such as A. J. Ayer, concerning the argument that religious language had no meaning (see chapter 10). Ramsey argues against this and advances a new form of analogy, to show the difference between religious language and literal, empirical language. To do this, he uses the terms '**models**' and '**qualifiers**'.

> **Models and qualifiers:**
> A model is an ordinary term that everyone can understand. A qualifier helps to show that the model is being used in a 'special' religious way.

Ramsey observes that there are two kinds of language: 'ordinary language' and 'religious language'. The first kind of language is straightforward public language that everyone uses all the time. 'Religious language' is what he calls 'logically odd' because the theological terms it uses, such as 'God', are *outside* public language. While religious language may look and sound grammatically simple, its logical structure is not straightforward. Ramsey claims that the challenge for religious language is how to make it into what he calls a 'suitable currency' so that religious believers and non-believers can communicate meaningfully with each other.

A 'model' is a form of analogy that creates an image to help believers understand what they have experienced and to explain it coherently. For example, religious believers often describe God as 'eternal father'. For Ramsey, 'father' is the model of a concept that is widely known and understood in ordinary language and human experience. The term 'eternal' is what he calls the 'qualifier'. The qualifier moves the model on from being simply a human understanding of a 'father' and gives it an extra meaning so that it is clear that it refers to a quality possessed only by God.

Criticisms of Ramsey

While some scholars believe that this is a helpful way to show that religious language is meaningful, others have criticized it. First, Ramsey does not really make a new point; his idea of models and qualifiers is simply a restating of an old idea. It is very similar to Aquinas's doctrine of analogy. The second criticism was made by theologian **Karl Barth**, who argued that Ramsey's analogical approach (and all other analogical approaches) were doomed to failure because it is impossible to understand God by using human language. The only way that communication between humans and God takes place is by revelation, which is, by necessity, initiated by God:

> What we can represent to ourselves lies in the sphere of our own existence, and of existence generally, as distinct from God. If we do know about God as Creator, it is neither wholly nor partially because we have a prior knowledge of something that resembles creation. It is only because it has been given to us by God's revelation to know him.
> (Karl Barth, *Church Dogmatics*, T. & T. Clark, 1964, vol. II, I, pp. 76–7)

Religious language as symbol

A third way of lending understanding to the language of religion is the one developed by philosopher Paul Tillich (1886–1965). Tillich believed that the problems associated with religious language stemmed from the incorrect idea that such language concerned literal assertions about the world. He denied that this was the case and proposed instead that religious statements were symbolic statements.

> **Paul Tillich** was one of the most important Protestant philosophers of the twentieth century. He was born in Prussia and served as an army chaplain during the First World War, after which he suffered two mental breakdowns. He became a professor of theology at Frankfurt University but was expelled by the Nazis in 1933 and emigrated to the USA. He was very influential in attempting to make links between traditional Christian belief and secular modern culture, and making this belief intelligible to non-religious people while preserving its authentic and unique substance. By his use of correlation and symbols, he tried to show that the essential content of Christian revelation contained in the Bible arose from a particular culture that was far removed from his own. Each age had to use its own thought-forms to understand the nature of God, and different ages and societies look for the problems faced in their society. He believed that twentieth-century people were at a distance from their culture and afraid of what might happen in a century that had experienced two world wars. Tillich believed that, through participation in God, people could learn to have courage to thrive even in the face of danger and anxiety. His most influential work was the three-volume *Systematic Theology* (1951-64). He died in Chicago in 1965.

Tillich held that the traditional concept of God was inadequate because it was based on a pre-scientific view of the universe, and he believed that it ought to be abandoned. He said:

> The concept of a 'Personal God', interfering with natural events, or being 'an independent cause of natural events', makes God a natural object besides others, an object among

others, a being among beings, maybe the highest, but nevertheless a being. This indeed is not only the destruction of the physical system but even more the destruction of any meaningful idea of God.

(Tillich, *Theology of Culture*, Oxford University Press, 1959, p. 130)

Tillich rejected the God of the Bible – a tyrant who interfered with human freedom, just as human tyrants had created havoc in his own recent history. A God seen as a person in a world of his own was simply a being. Even if God were the Supreme Being, he would still be a being. The traditional concept of God, for Tillich, was an 'idol', a human construction that had been elevated to an absolute status. For Tillich, however, this was not a reality and should be dispensed with.

For many people across the centuries, the belief in 'God' as a reality had allowed them to have hope when their lives were poor, riddled with disease, suffering, hardship and death. Tillich argues that people had forgotten how to interpret the old symbolism and now thought of it as purely factual. These symbols had become blurred and the reality of what 'God' meant could not be seen clearly. The word 'God' ceased to have any meaning for religious observers because it had lost the reality of what it symbolized. When religious believers spoke about these symbols (e.g. God, Salvation, Revelation, etc.) in a literal way, they were actually making inaccurate and untrue statements. This is the reason why Tillich was able to declare that 'God does not exist. He is Being itself beyond essence and existence. Therefore to argue that God exists is to deny him' (*Systematic Theology*, vol. I, p. 205). He also states:

> the question of the existence of God can be neither asked nor answered. If asked, it is a question about that which by its very nature is above existence, and therefore the answer – whether negative or affirmative – implicitly denies the existence of God. It is as atheistic to affirm the existence of God as to deny it. God is being itself, not a being.

(Ibid., p. 262)

Tillich says that it is now very difficult to talk meaningfully about God, because the name 'God' has become widely misunderstood, even by theists. Most theists now use the term 'God' as referring to a real supernatural being, but in doing so, they are showing that the term has lost its original symbolism and is now meaningless. 'God' has, for Tillich, become just one among many objects in time and space that may or may not exist. Tillich believes that this is not the meaning of God at all.

> **Exercise**
> To help understand what Tillich means at this point, make a list of five non-religious things that have symbolic meaning and say what they symbolize in the world. For example, a flag is a symbol that represents a country.
> Then make a list of five religious symbols and say what they symbolize. For example, you might choose the use of water in Christian baptism. Discuss your findings with your classmates.

Signs and symbols

It is important to explain that Tillich makes a clear distinction between a 'sign' and a 'symbol'. Signs – such as road signs – and symbols – such as your school emblem – are both significant because they point beyond themselves. They both refer to things in the world, and both can be words, pictures, objects or actions. Both are also significantly different from each other. The principal way they differ is that, with signs, there is no necessary or organic connection between the sign and what it represents. For example, traffic lights show red, amber and green for stop, prepare to move, and go. There is no necessary connection between these three colours and what they represent; different colours could have been chosen to achieve the same effect. With symbols, however, there *is* a necessary connection. For example, the flag of a country or state can evoke strong emotions in people (positive or negative), because the colours or pictures relate to events or important ideas that citizens empathize with or have experienced. Another way of expressing the difference is that signs are pointers to something else, while symbols are more complex and have evolved to express the power behind them. People can 'participate' in symbols as there is a deep personal connection between an individual and the symbol. So, for example, pupils will normally have to wear a uniform of some sort, which will include, typically, the name of the school and a crest/badge that may have a bird or animal or some words on it. The symbols used will express important beliefs held by the founders or the institution and pupils will, over time, come to 'participate' in the symbolism. They 'own' the symbols of the institution and assent to what they stand for and this ownership may last throughout the person's lifetime. In this way, the symbol (school crest) participates in the pupil's life and permanently transfers its values to the person.

Tillich believed that religious beliefs could only be expressed through the use of symbolic language. He stated: 'The language of faith is the language of symbols and it points beyond itself whilst participating in that to which it points' (*Dynamics of Faith*, George Allen and Unwin, 1957, p. 42). So, in an example we used earlier, when a Christian reports that 'God gave Moses the 10 Commandments', God's act of 'giving' is a symbol, not of any physical action, but of a spiritual 'giving' to help humans develop a set of rules for living. For Tillich, religious symbols point towards the Holy, or, in a phrase he preferred to use, the 'ground of being'.

Tillich also referred to God as the 'object of ultimate concern', the being that humans strive to understand but struggle in grasping. The ultimate concern demands complete surrender of the person who accepts the ultimate. Faith in the ultimate concern holds the promise of total fulfilment, but sacrifices must be made if this is to happen. He refers to faith as a 'total and centred act of the personal self, the act of unconditional, infinite and ultimate concern'. He then continues to examine the sources of faith. Faith comes from human awareness that they are part of the infinite but do not own it. God is both the subject and object of faith in the sense that God is present as the subject of people's faith but also, at the same time, transcendent as people's ultimate concern. As a result of this difficulty, Tillich says that only symbolic language is sufficient to express faith in God. In fact, religious faith can only express itself in symbolic language. He says: 'Whatever we say about that which concerns us ultimately, whether or not we call it God, has a symbolic meaning.'

Tillich further says that myths are an important part of our ultimate concern. Believers must recognize that the way they talk about God is in terms of myth, but that myths are necessary because they form part of human consciousness. To remove them would have the result of blocking human understanding of the ultimate concern because myths are the symbolic language of faith. He warns that myths must not simply be accepted as literally true because they would then lose their symbolic meaning and rob God of his standing as the ultimate concern. For example, many religious believers accept the creation story of Genesis 1 as a literal account of how God brought the universe into existence. Tillich would argue vigorously against this literal understanding. To take it literally would be to ignore the type of literature it is (a myth) and to miss the point of the story (to teach about God's omnipotence and his desire to have a relationship with humans). Tillich's hope was that, as more people came to have a better understanding of the nature of religion, there would be a more intelligent questioning of religious phenomena.

Criticisms of Tillich

Scottish-born theologian and philosopher, **John Macquarrie (1919–2007)**, disagreed with Tillich's use of the term 'symbol'. Tillich had used it in a very broad sense to mean any idea that stood for something else. Macquarrie argued that this made the term almost meaningless. He also thought that Tillich's use of the term was not consistent with its use in English. He says:

> We notice first that words (and even the letters out of which written words are made up) are symbols, so that in the broad sense, all language has a symbolic character. When, however, we speak of 'symbolic language', we generally have a fairly definite kind of language in mind, a kind in which the words are not understood in their direct or proper reference but in which they, so to speak, bounce off that to which they properly refer so as to impinge at a distance on a more remote subject-matter, to which the speaker wishes to refer.
>
> (Macquarrie, *Principles of Christian Theology*, SCM Press, 1966, p. 135)

Macquarrie proceeds to criticize Tillich's idea that symbols 'participate' in the things that they symbolize. In Macquarrie's view, Tillich is not clear about what he means by 'participate' and exactly how the symbol might share in the reality of the thing it symbolizes. Macquarrie uses the example of mathematical symbols, which are chosen without having any obvious connection or 'participation' with what they represent. He makes a distinction between a 'conventional' symbol and an 'intrinsic' one: 'The conventional symbol has no connection with what it symbolizes other than the fact that some people have arbitrarily agreed to let it stand for this particular symbolizandum. The intrinsic symbol, on the other hand, has in itself a kinship with what it symbolizes' (ibid., p 135).

Macquarrie did not see these as separate and distinct categories, as any symbol might contain elements of both. Different symbols can complement each other, even though they may initially appear to be contradictory. For instance, Christians believe that God is transcendent, but also that God is immanent. These may appear to be contradictory because transcendence means that God is not connected with the world and is completely beyond human understanding. Immanence, on the other hand implies that God may be known by humans and even be in relationship with them. Macquarrie's point here would be that these two symbols complement each other because they are both central aspects of the nature of God and together add to our understanding of the divine.

> **Exercise**
> Choose one religious tradition, make a list of its most important symbols, then write a sentence for each explaining what they symbolize and whether they are 'conventional' or 'intrinsic' (in Macquarrie's terms).

English philosopher John Hick agrees with Macquarrie's criticism of Tillich's use of the term 'participation' in connection with symbols. He raises a further issue:

> Is it really plausible to say that a complex theological statement such as "God is not dependent for his existence upon any external reality" has arisen from the unconscious, whether individual or collective? . . . And in what sense does this same proposition open up both "levels of reality which are otherwise closed to us" and "hidden depths of our own being"? These two characteristics of symbols seem more readily applicable to the arts than to theological ideas and propositions. Indeed, it is Tillich's tendency to assimilate religious to aesthetic awareness that suggests the naturalistic development of his position.
> (Hick, *Philosophy of Religion*, 4th edition, Prentice Hall, 1990, p. 87)

Hick is here saying that Tillich's ideas concerning symbols may feasibly have some relevance in some areas of knowledge and discourse, but they do not work for every example of religious language.

Stretch and challenge: myth as a form of religious language

In the twenty-first century, the word 'myth' is commonly used to mean a story or idea that is deliberately false – something that is non-factual, made up. We hear it today in the phrase 'urban myths', which are stories usually spread on social media that are intended to shock, frighten or 'enlighten' people. Examples from the past include:

- 'news' (*Express* newspaper, 29 June 2016) that singer Elvis Presley (whose death was reported in 1977) is still alive
- Area 51, a US Air Force base in Nevada, has been alleged for many years to be a haven for extraterrestrial life forms and is linked with time travel and sinister conspiracies
- the 'fact' that raw onions can cure people who suffer from flu, pneumonia and several other illnesses by somehow absorbing the relevant germs/bacteria from the ill person.

The word 'myth' is also often used in religious language, where its meaning is of great importance but disputed. New Testament scholar I. H. Marshall wrote: 'Myth is a confusing and slippery term in theology; it is used in so many ill-defined ways by individual theologians that it would be no bad thing if its use were to be prohibited'

('Myth', in S. B. Ferguson and D. F. Wright (eds.), *New Dictionary of Theology*, Inter Varsity Press, 1988, pp. 449–51).

Marshall goes on to describe four aspects of theological myth, which may be used either on their own or together:

- It may be a story that tries to explain the origins of things without the use of modern scientific thinking. This may lead to a negative evaluation.
- It may depict an aspect of human experience using the form of a story.
- It may be a story presented using symbolism and have emotional or poetic appeal, and be open to reinterpretation.
- It can be any kind of story that involves gods or supernatural agents.

> **Exercise**
>
> Read the story of the Fall in Genesis 3, and try to find an example of each of the four usages of 'myth'. Does seeing this account as a 'myth' add to the importance of the understanding of the story? If so, why? If not, why not?
>
> It is recognized by many scholars that Genesis 1–11 are written in the literary form of myth. Genesis 2, for instance, the story of Adam and Eve, is an **aetiological myth**, designed to explain the origins of several aspects of human life – why humans are mortal, why they have to work for a living, why women experience pain in childbirth, why there is sin in the world, and so on. It can be seen that, in a pre-literate society, stories like this would catch the imagination of the hearers and would be memorable ways of explaining some important everyday concepts.

Aetiological myth: A myth that attempts to explain the origin of something.

The difficulty with using myths to explain important theological ideas lies in how they are interpreted by people in cultures and times far distant from when they were originally produced. For religious believers, there is an additional problem that involves the authority of biblical texts. For Fundamentalist Christians who believe that God authored the Bible, the literary form of Genesis 1–11 will play little or no part in their understanding of the stories. Many Fundamentalists will believe that God actually created the universe in 7 days (of 24 hours) and that all humanity developed from Adam and Eve, and that Noah's flood actually happened. Other Christians, however, who do not take the words of the Bible as literally true, will understand these texts as having profound importance even though they were written many thousands of years ago and are in a particular literary form that is not used today to express or explain truths.

The recognition that religious truth could be expressed through the medium of myth only came with the expansion of European imperialism in the eighteenth and nineteenth centuries, opening up new countries to explore their natural resources, to discover their indigenous populations and their cultures. Other creation stories came to light from Israel's Near Eastern neighbours: Egypt, Canaan and Mesopotamia. Several parallel mythological stories of the creation of the world were discovered – for instance, the Babylonian *Enuma Elish*. The story of Noah and the flood was paralleled in the Sumerian myth of Ziusudra and also in the Akkadian versions of this myth in the *Epic of Atrahasis* and the *Epic of Gilgamesh*.

These discoveries sparked a new wave of scholarship, which began in Germany with **F. W. J. Schelling (1775–1854)**. He was very important in developing the idea that myths were not just bad science but were a valid literary expression of 'the struggle between the rational and the irrational in the human psyche, which in turn formed humanity's deepest intuitive knowledge of the divine' (Hugh S. Pyper, 'Myth', in A. Hastings, A. Mason and H. Pyper, *The Oxford Companion to Christian Thought*, Oxford University Press, 2000, p. 462). Schelling's basic ideas filtered into German biblical scholarship through theologians such as **Julius Wellhausen (1844–1918)**, who undertook a major study of the Pentateuch (Genesis–Deuteronomy) and discovered at least four schools of thought and authorship within it. This clearly opened up questions about whether God had written these books – and, by extension, the rest of the Bible – or they had been authored by humans. This debate ultimately led to a questioning of the nature of the Bible and its authority. Perhaps the most important outpouring of 'biblical criticism' came when the New Testament came under critical scrutiny. The investigation of 'the historical Jesus' spawned a huge number of books arguing either for or against the factual basis of the Gospel stories of Jesus. One of the most important Christians to engage with this question was the German theologian **Rudolph Bultmann (1884–1976)**. After extensive work on the question, Bultmann declared: 'I do indeed think that we can now know almost nothing concerning the life and personality of Jesus, since the early Christian sources show no interest in either, are moreover fragmentary and often legendary; and other sources about Jesus do not exist' (Bultmann, *Jesus and the Word*, C. Scribner, 1934, p. 8).

After much further study and debate by biblical scholars and theologians on the question of the historical Jesus and its implications for Christian belief, a group of British scholars, under the editorship of John Hick, published *The Myth of God Incarnate*. This was first published in 1977. It was a radical book authored by academic theologians and biblical scholars and called into doubt the literal truth of the Bible. The preface of the book stated:

> The writers of this book are convinced that another major theological development is called for in this last part of the twentieth century. The need arises from growing knowledge of Christian origins, and involves a recognition that Jesus was . . . 'a man approved by God' for a special role within the divine purpose, and that the later conception of him as God incarnate . . . is a mythological or poetic way of expressing his significance for us.

The Incarnation of Jesus Christ, a central theological belief in Christianity, was declared to be a myth and had no basis in history. Jesus had been a human being. Calling him 'God Incarnate' was 'just one interpretation of the significance of Jesus' (ibid., p. 2). If one looks at the language used in the Bible, and the ancient culture in which it was written, it is necessary to re-cast the meaning of the biblical words and thought-forms for the modern, scientific, world. This was claimed not to be a destruction of the central beliefs of the Christian faith, but rather a legitimate questioning of the language and ideas of its origins for the modern world. The language of the Bible could not be taken literally, but must be interpreted according to the type of language and literature it is, so that the correct theological meaning could be brought out and understood.

Exercise

If the concept of 'myth' is taken seriously by religious believers, do you think it would make any difference to the way they understand biblical stories?

For instance, what might they conclude about the stories of the Virgin Birth, Jesus' miracles or the Resurrection? Choose one of these examples, or one of your own choice, and study two contrasting interpretations of it.

Do you think taking 'myth' seriously is a positive aid for religious believers in their beliefs and the way they practise their religion? Give reasons for your answer.

FURTHER READING

Thomas Aquinas, *Summa Theologica*. 1, 13

Karen Armstrong, *The Case for God: What Religion Really Means*. Bodley Head, 2009

Fergus Kerr, *After Aquinas: Versions of Thomism*. John Wiley and Sons, 2002

Vladimir Lossky, *The Mystical Theology of the Eastern Church*. James Clarke & Co. Ltd., 1957

Andrew Louth, *Introducing Eastern Orthodox Theology*. SPCK, 2013

John Macquarrie, *God-talk: an Examination of the Language and Logic of Theology*. Harper & Row, 1967

Ian Ramsey, *Religious Language*. SCM Press, 1957

Rupert Shortt, *God is No Thing: Coherent Christianity*. Hurst, 2016

A. Spearing (ed.), *The Cloud of Unknowing*. Penguin, 2001

Paul Tillich, *Systematic Theology*, vols. I–III. University of Chicago Press, 1951, 1957, 1963

Thought Points

1. Compare and contrast the main points of apophatic and cataphatic uses of language.

2. Explain the main points of analogy of attribution, analogy of proportion and Ramsey's 'models' and 'qualifiers' to a classmate.

3. Explain Tillich's view of language as symbolic.

4. 'Religious language points to truths that elude scientific treatment, but this should not render it invalid by definition' (Shortt, *God is No Thing,* p. 35). Explain what you think this statement means and whether you agree with it.

5. To what extent is analogy more successful than symbolism in discussing religious language?

6. 'Religious language is meaningless.' Discuss.

7. To what extent do you agree that symbolism is the most effective way of explaining religious belief?

CHAPTER 10
Challenges to Religious Language

LEARNING OUTCOMES

In this chapter, you will be learning about:
- how views of religious language have changed over time –
  - Logical Positivism
  - Wittgenstein's views on language games and forms of life
  - discussion about the factual quality of religious language in the falsification symposium

You will also be able to assess critically:
- whether or not any version of the Verification Principle successfully renders religious language as meaningless
- whether or not any participant in the falsification symposium presented a convincing approach to the understanding of religious language
- a comparison of the ideas of Aquinas and Wittgenstein, including:
  - whether a cognitive approach (such as Aquinas's thinking on analogy) or a non-cognitive approach (such as the language games concept of Wittgenstein) presents a better way of making sense of religious language
  - the influence of non-cognitive approaches on the interpretation of religious texts
  - how far Aquinas's analogical view of theological language remains valuable in philosophy of religion

RELIGIOUS LANGUAGE

During the twentieth century, there were major developments in the study of religious language. These came about largely as a reaction to secular philosophical debates on what meaning religious language had. British philosopher of religion John Hick says:

> Modern work in the philosophy of religion has been much occupied with problems created by the distinctively religious uses of language. The discussions generally centre around one of two main issues. One, which was familiar to medieval thinkers, concerns the special sense that religious terms bear when they are applied to God. The other question, which also has a long history but which has been given fresh sharpness and urgency by contemporary analytical philosophy, is concerned with the basic function of religious language.
>
> (Hick, *Philosophy of Religion*, p. 82)

Logical Positivism

Logical Positivism is the name given to a group of philosophers, mathematicians and scientists who, in the 1930s, held a series of discussions surrounding the differences between scientific language and the use of language in non-scientific subject areas. Its leader was **Moritz Schlick (1882–1936)**, who had been appointed Professor of Science at the University of Vienna in 1922.

One of the roles Schlick was asked to take on here was to convene a group of scientists and philosophers each Thursday to discuss the links between the sciences and philosophy. The link with Vienna was the main reason why this group became known as the 'Vienna Circle', though they did not always meet in Vienna (and did not sit in a circle!). Other prominent members included Friedrich Waismann, Rudolph Carnap, Kurt Gödel and Otto Neurath. In 1925–6, the group discussed groundbreaking work in the foundations of mathematics by Gottlob Frege, Bertrand Russell and **Ludwig Wittgenstein**. The group became particularly interested in Wittgenstein's book *Tractatus Logico-Philosophicus* (1918, 1921 in German). Wittgenstein's aim in the book was to explore the relationship between language and the real world and to produce a definition of the limits of science (*Tractatus*, 4, 113).

Ludwig Wittgenstein (1899-1951) was born into one of the wealthiest families in Austria. He travelled to Manchester to study Aeronautical Engineering, but moved to study the Philosophy of Mathematics with Bertrand Russell in Cambridge. Russell considered him to be 'the most perfect example of genius' he had ever known. Wittgenstein also studied the Philosophy of Mind and Philosophy of Language. He published only one book (*Tractatus Logico-philosophicus*) during his lifetime (this period is now known as the 'early period'), but the *Philosophical Investigations* were published posthumously (this period is now known as the 'later period'). The writings of the later period are significant because, in them, he disagrees with much of his work in the early period. His theory of language games comes from the later period.

Challenges to Religious Language

Verification Principle: The idea that statements are meaningful only if they can be verified, i.e. shown to be true by empirical evidence.

The group developed what is now known as the **Verification Principle**. This stated that the meaning of a proposition (statement) was the mode of its verification (its meaningfulness), which enabled a person to count as meaningless any and all statements that could neither be verified nor falsified by sense experience. The English philosopher A. J. Ayer was heavily influenced by this principle and is responsible for bringing it to the English-speaking world through his influential but much-criticized book *Language, Truth and Logic*, originally published in 1934 when Ayer was just twenty-four years of age.

A. J. Ayer (1910–89) (known as Freddie) was one of the foremost English philosophers of the twentieth century. He studied at Eton College and at Oxford University (where he was taught by Gilbert Ryle). Ayer was initially influenced by Wittgenstein's analytic philosophy, but quickly stepped out on his own path. His reputation was made with the publication in 1936 of his first book, *Language, Truth and Logic*. Here he popularized for an English-speaking readership an analytic approach to philosophy, combining a British tradition stretching from David Hume to Bertrand Russell with the emerging European philosophical method of Logical Positivism formulated by the Vienna Circle. Ayer was a very popular speaker and undertook lecture tours in Britain, the USA, Japan, China and several countries in Europe. He took part in several radio broadcasts on the BBC. One of the most famous of these was the debate between Ayer and the Jesuit philosopher F. C. Copleston in June 1949: 'Logical Positivism – A Debate'. He published his autobiography, *A Part of My Life: The Memoirs of a Philosopher* in 1977. He was knighted in 1970.

Key ideas of Logical Positivism as expressed in Ayer's work

Ayer's starting point is the question: 'What makes statements meaningful as opposed to mere nonsense?' His aim is to provide some criteria by which we may judge whether a statement fulfils any useful function or whether it should be dismissed as an irrelevant distraction. The task of philosophy should be to show why statements such as 'All spligs have splogs' can have no possible function in our discourse, and therefore why they should be dismissed as irrelevant. In the context of the nonsense example just given, Ayer says: 'We need only formulate the criterion which enables us to test whether a sentence expresses a genuine proposition about a matter of fact, and then point out that the sentences under consideration fail to satisfy it' (*Language, Truth and Logic*, p. 35).

Since 'spligs' and 'splogs' are imaginary words, they do not refer to matters of fact that could be tested in the real world to determine whether, in fact, 'spligs' do have 'splogs'. Consequently, the sentence is meaningless. By contrast, a statement like 'water boils at 100 degrees Celsius' refers to a real situation in which tests could be performed, and could consequently be found to be a meaningful statement.

Ayer developed his criterion of judgement in more detail into 'the criterion of verifiability'. To 'verify' something in this context means to judge whether it is true or false. Each statement humans make must be capable of being judged true or false – i.e., of being 'verified'. So, the statement 'my good friend has ginger hair' is capable of verification (you could meet her) while 'my good friend comes from a time/space dimension beyond all human knowledge' is not capable of verification. According to the 'criteria of verifiability', therefore, the latter sentence is devoid of meaning and should be excluded from any sensible conversation.

Ayer expressed the central idea of verifiability as follows:

> The criterion which we use to test the genuineness of apparent statements of fact is the criterion of verifiability. We say that a sentence is factually significant to any given person, if and only if, he knows how to verify the proposition which it purports to express – that is, if he knows what observations would lead him, under certain conditions, to accept the proposition as being true or reject it as false . . . We enquire in every case what observations would lead us to answer the question, one way or the other; and if none can be discovered, we must conclude that the sentence under consideration does not, as far as we are concerned, express a genuine question.
>
> (Ibid.)

Ayer draws a distinction between 'practical verifiability' and 'verifiability in principle'. One could practically verify the statement 'my good friend's hair is ginger' by visiting her or looking at a photo of her. It is not possible to verify the statement (Ayer's example) 'there are mountains on the farther side of the moon' because 'no rocket has yet been invented which would enable me to go and look at the farther side of the moon'. Nevertheless, the statement is not meaningless since, as Ayer wrote, 'I do know what observations would decide it for me, if, as is theoretically conceivable, once we are in a position to make them' (ibid., p. 49).

He also distinguishes between 'strong' and 'weak' verification. If a statement could be strongly verified, it would be shown to be 'conclusively established in experience'. Many statements, however, while they may be highly probable, cannot be shown to be conclusively demonstrated by any experience. Ayer gives the example of 'all men are mortal'. Clearly, experience would suggest that this is very probably true, but unless all men in the past, present and future were 'checked', we could not be absolutely certain. This is true of all statements concerned with 'facts' based on inductive inferences. Ayer seems to conclude by the end of the book that all statements concerned with 'facts' established by experience are only capable of the weak form of verification, i.e. their *absolute* truth or falsity cannot be established.

Following Kant, Ayer describes statements or propositions like 'water boils at 100 degrees Celsius' or 'all men are mortal' as synthetic statements. In a synthetic statement, something is added to ('synthesized with') another thing, when that extra thing was not already logically contained in the initial thing. In grammatical terms, some 'predicate' is added to the subject, when that predicate was not logically part of the concept of the subject already. The question, therefore, of whether the 'synthesis' is true or false can only be decided by experiment or experience.

Ayer argues that the Verification Principle cannot establish the truth or falsity of any meaningful factual proposition as logically certain. It can only establish probability.

Ayer is, of course, aware that statements like 'A is bigger than B. Q is bigger than A, therefore Q is bigger than B', 'All bachelors are unmarried men' or 'All quadrilateral figures have four sides' are true with absolute certainty, and are immune from the verification process he sets out for other statements. This leaves Ayer with a problem: statements of the sort above cannot be about 'facts', otherwise they would be capable of a verification process which would yield judgements of relative probability. So the question is: what are these statements about? As Ayer puts it:

> As Hume conclusively showed, no general proposition whose validity is subject to the test of actual experience can ever be logically certain. No matter how often it is verified in practice, there still remains the possibility that it will be confuted on some future occasion. . . . And this means that no general proposition referring to a matter of fact can ever be shown to be necessarily and universally true. . . . Whereas a scientific generalization is readily admitted to be fallible, the truths of mathematics and logic appear to be necessary and certain. . . . Accordingly, the empiricist must deal with the truths of logic and mathematics in one of the two following ways; he must say that they are not necessary truths . . . or he must say that they have no factual content, and then he must explain how a proposition that is empty of all factual content can be true and useful and surprising.
>
> (Ayer, *Language, Truth and Logic*, pp. 96f.)

Ayer believes that non-synthetic propositions which are immune to verifiability can be true and useful, because they reveal the way our languages (whether of mathematics or of English conversation, etc.) work, or the meaning which different symbols have. He gives the following example – 'either some ants are parasitic or none are'. He comments: 'one need not resort to observation to discover that there either are or are not ants which are parasitic. If one knows what is the function of the words "either", "or" and "not", then one can see that any proposition of the form "either p is true or p is not true" is valid, independently of experience' (ibid. p. 105).

Importantly, Ayer emphasizes that the ant example makes no statement about the actual observed behaviour of ants; it is 'entirely devoid of factual content'. He gives another example that says nothing about any observed factual situation, but is nevertheless true and useful because it illustrates 'the way in which we use certain symbols': 'Nothing can be coloured in different ways at the same time with respect to the same part of itself' (p. 106). Two final examples Ayer gives are 'every oculist is an eye doctor' (p. 113) and '7+5=12' (p. 113). Once again, no reference need be made to experience to affirm or confute these statements; instead they reveal the way in which we use these symbols (i.e. words) of our language.

Ayer's conclusion is that, if a statement (proposition) is not verifiable, it has no meaning or purpose.

The implication for religious language from Ayer's Verification Principle is that it has no meaning, as it cannot be verified.

The death of religious language after the Verification Principle?

Implications for religious language

All Logical Positivists believed that the application of the Verification Principle to religious language about God rendered such language meaningless. They were not necessarily atheists who had wanted to establish the non-existence of God – this was not their aim or intention. Rather, they believed that their conclusions had made the question 'Is there a God?' a pointless question to ask, because the answer could not be verified as either true or false. It was literally 'non-sense'. There was no empirical test that would yield or fail to yield the necessary observations to show the existence of God. For Ayer, the existence of God is not verifiable, even 'in principle', because God is defined as beyond or transcending the natural world in which our experiences, experiments and observations take place. Consequently, no hypothesis stating that in X circumstances God will appear in some way is possible, in the way that it would be possible to say, for example, in X circumstances we would predict that water will boil at 100 degrees Celsius.

Ayer summarizes:

> [The theist] would say that in talking about God he was talking about a transcendent being who might be known through certain empirical manifestations, but certainly could not be defined in terms of those manifestations. But in that case, the term 'god' is a metaphysical term. And if 'god' is a metaphysical term, then it cannot even be probable that a god exists. For to say that 'God exists' is to make a metaphysical utterance which cannot be either true or false . . . No sentence which purports to describe the nature of a transcendent god can possess any literal significance.
>
> (Ayer, *Language, Truth and Logic*, p. 152)

Ayer is aware that someone might respond with something like the Teleological argument that, while God cannot be apprehended directly, he can be observed through seeing his effects, i.e. the order and purpose in the world. Ayer admits that, to some extent, the design and order in the world are open to observation, but points out that God is still held to exist *beyond* those effects in some super-sensory or metaphysical realm. God is clearly not identical with the world since, in order to create or design it, he needs to be separate from it, to transcend it. As long as this is the case, the question of God's existence remains beyond verification and is therefore meaningless.

Someone might ask, however, whether religious language (i.e. questions like 'is there a God?') can be preserved within Ayer's scheme, within the a priori analytic section of legitimate, meaningful statements? Ayer says 'No', because religious language is fundamentally concerned with questions of the existence of God, and as all criticisms of the Ontological argument demonstrate, questions of existence can only be verified empirically, i.e. by experience, experiment and observation.

Exercise

Complete the grid below with brief definitions of the key terms in Ayer's version of the Verification Principle.

Verification	
Falsification	
Verification in principle	
Practical Verification	
Strong Verification	
Weak Verification	

The challenge of falsification

In *Language, Truth and Logic,* Ayer mentions the criterion of falsifiability as a possible way out of one of the difficulties raised by the Verification Principle. The difficulty was that, according to Ayer's criterion, almost all statements are incapable of strong verification. We would have to test 'every human who has or ever will exist to conclusively show the truth of the otherwise accepted statement "all humans are mortal"'. Ayer mentions Karl Popper's falsification criterion as a possible solution.

Karl Popper

> **Karl Popper (1902–94)** was an Austrian-born Jewish-British scientist and philosopher and is regarded as one of the greatest philosophers of science of the twentieth century. He made a major breakthrough in the Philosophy of Science when he rejected the inductive method in the empirical sciences. He followed Hume in asserting that only an infinite number of observations could prove the theory correct and this was not achievable. Popper's view was that hypotheses are shown to be correct or incorrect by use of the 'falsifiability criterion'. This meant that just one exception to the rule was enough to disprove it. The absence of contradictory evidence means that the theory is correct. This criterion meant that some 'sciences', such as astrology, metaphysics and Freudian psychoanalysis, could not count as empirical sciences.
>
> Popper's most famous book was *The Open Society and its Enemies* (1945), which he wrote while teaching in New Zealand during the Second World War. This is a defence of liberal democracy, achieved by showing the weaknesses of Plato and Marx in a sustained critique. This book has been very influential. Popper continued his academic work until two weeks before his death at the age of ninety-two.

Popper claimed that the reason why scientific hypotheses are sound, despite not being verifiable, is that they are falsifiable. This means that we can suggest under what hypothetical circumstances they could be falsified. Science progresses because we make hypotheses that can be falsified, we test them, and when they are not falsified we regard them as strong hypotheses.

English philosopher **Anthony Flew**'s explanation of Popper is:

> Popper's contention was . . . that, whereas no theory and no proposition may be accounted scientific even when it is known to be false, no theory and no proposition can be properly presented as even a possible contribution to science unless its proponents are prepared to specify what would have to happen, or to have happened, for it to be falsified; that is, shown to be false.
> (Flew, *Introduction to Western Philosophy: Ideas and Argument from Plato to Popper*, revised edition, Thames & Hudson Ltd, 1989, p. 482)

Unfalsifiable hypotheses were regarded as weak because, if we cannot even explain how in theory a statement could be falsified, then it can never be truly tested. In science, evidence ought to shape a hypothesis. If no evidence could ever count against a hypothesis, then the hypothesis is not scientifically grounded. It is wrong to hold on to a hypothesis regardless of the evidence pointing against it, yet this is what unfalsifiable theories do.

Popper gave the example of astrology. He argued that astrologers made very vague predictions that mean that they cannot be proven wrong and they reinterpret all evidence to fit with their predictions. For example, if I predict that I will become rich and happy, and this does not happen, the astrologer may argue that I have not interpreted 'richness' and 'happiness' correctly and I have failed to see that my horoscope did in fact come true. I cannot possibly falsify what the horoscope said. That does not mean that it is true; it means that it is a weak, untestable and unfalsifiable claim.

> **Exercise**
>
> Given that a statement or proposition is only meaningful if we can imagine an experience or observation that would falsify (i.e. show to be inaccurate or false) the statement in question, consider the following propositions and decide whether they are falsifiable.
> 1. My mother has red hair
> 2. All humans are mortal.
> 3. There are mountains on the other side of the moon.
> 4. Traffic jams are caused by goblins.
> 5. Jane is in league with the Devil.
> 6. A loving and powerful God sustains the world.

Anthony Flew

Anthony Flew famously took up the falsifiability criterion and applied it to the question of God's existence. He argued that religious believers will not allow any evidence to count against religious statements. For Flew, this suggested that these statements are unscientific and therefore have no bearing on reality. They are meaningless. He says that it can appear to non-religious people that there is no event that could convince religious believers that God does not exist. A powerful hurricane that devastates thousands of acres of land and kills many people will not change the beliefs of religious believers. Flew says:

> Someone tells us that God Loves us as a father loves his children. We are reassured. But then we see a child dying of inoperable cancer of the throat. His earthly father is driven frantic in his efforts to help, but his Heavenly Father reveals no obvious sign of concern. Some qualification is made – 'God's love is not merely human love' or it is 'an inscrutable love' perhaps – and we realise that such suffering is quite compatible with the truth of the assertion that 'God loves us like a father (but of course. . .)'. We are reassured again. But then perhaps we ask: what is this assurance of God's (appropriately qualified) love worth, what is this apparent guarantee really a guarantee against? Just what would have to happen not merely (morally and wrongly) to tempt but also (logically and rightly) to entitle us to say 'God does not love us' or even 'God does not exist'?
> (Anthony Flew, 'The Presumption of Atheism', in *God, Freedom and Immortality*, Prometheus Books, 1984, p. 74)

Flew states that the constant qualifications and modifications that believers give to statements about God to make them fit in with evidence in the world render the statements vacuous – in reality, such statements do not tell us anything at all. He claimed that such statements die the 'death of a thousand qualifications'.

The Parable of the Gardener

Flew illustrated this criticism powerfully with the story of an imaginary situation taken from John Wisdom's story of the gardener:

> 'Let us begin with a parable. It is a parable developed from a tale told by John Wisdom in his haunting and revelatory article 'Gods'. Once upon a time two explorers came upon a clearing in the jungle. In the clearing were growing many flowers and many weeds. One explorer says, 'Some gardener must tend this plot'. The other disagrees, 'There is no such gardener'. So they pitch their tents and set a watch. No gardener is ever seen. 'But perhaps he is an invisible gardener'. So they set up a barbed-wire fence. They electrify it. They patrol with bloodhounds. . . . But no shrieks ever suggest that some intruder has received a shock. No movements of the wire ever betray an invisible climber. The bloodhounds never give cry. Yet still the Believer is not convinced. 'But there is a gardener, invisible, intangible, insensible to electric shocks, a gardener who has no scent and makes no sound, a gardener who comes secretly to look after the garden which he loves'. At last the Sceptic despairs, 'But what remains of your original assertion? Just how does what you call an invisible, intangible, eternally elusive gardener differ from an imaginary gardener or even from no gardener at all?''

The point that Flew makes from this story is that, just as the explorer's claim 'there is a gardener' has become meaningless because it is unfalsifiable and bears no relation to reality, so God, by definition, is beyond any experience that could falsify that God exists. God is like the 'invisible, intangible. . .' gardener. Furthermore, religious statements about God are non-falsifiable. For example, the statement 'God is good'. Would not the experience of a child dying in a cancer hospital falsify this proposition? Flew says 'no' because the believer would always say something like 'God's ways are beyond our limited human understanding; God is inscrutable and cannot be known by mere mortals.'

At the heart of Flew's thinking is the logical point that to know the meaning of the negation of an assertion is as near as makes no difference to knowing the meaning of that assertion. For example, the meaning of the assertion 'there is a lion approaching' is equivalent to knowing the situation in which the assertion would not be true – i.e., that the person who 'saw' the lion was hallucinating or playing a trick. So, when we know that the negation of the assertion does not apply (i.e., the person was not seeing things or is known not to play tricks), we know that the assertion is true (and we should escape). Crucially, in the absence of any such possible negations, according to Flew, the original assertion is meaningless. To know that a lion is approaching, we need to know the relevant situations in which a lion was not approaching, i.e. the evidence that would count against such an assertion – we are not in a zoo or in a known habitat for lions, there had been no warnings of escaped lions, etc.

In the case of the gardener, then, if there is no possible evidence that could count against the existence of the gardener, then the assertion 'There is a gardener' has no meaning. All meaningful statements must be capable of falsification. For Flew, then, for a statement really to assert something, it must be possible to describe the circumstances in which it could be demonstrated to be false. If I say, for example, 'My car is in the car park', I am asserting something definite is the case, and I can describe the circumstances in which the statement could be false – my car is actually in the garage or is at home or has been stolen or I do not actually own a car. When a religious believer asserts 'God exists / loves me', she is unable to describe under what circumstances the statement could be shown to be false. For Flew, this means that it is not a genuine assertion at all.

> **Exercise**
> Decide whether the following assertions can be falsified:
> 1. All cats sit on mats.
> 2. God is the ultimate creator of the physical universe.
> 3. There will be a row of three consecutive 7s in the infinitely long mathematical description of Pi.

Responses to Flew on falsification: Hare and Mitchell in defence of religious language

In what became known as 'The University Debate', **R. M. Hare (1919–2002)** and **Basil Mitchell (1917–2011)** published articles in response to Flew's arguments against the meaningfulness of religious language.

Hare's 'Bliks' and the lunatic student

Hare agreed with Flew that falsification was a sound principle for testing the scientific value of claims that attempt to convey factual information. He disagreed, however, that this was what religious language was trying to do.

Hare argued that, although the unfalsifiability of religious language means that it cannot be regarded as making factual claims, it does not necessarily follow that it is absolutely devoid of meaning. Hare suggested that religious language does have meaning – not because it conveys knowledge of the world, but because it helps to shape the way that people think about the world. He gave the following example to clarify his view:

> A certain lunatic is convinced that all dons want to murder him. His friends introduce him to all the mildest and most respectable dons that they can find, and after each one of them has retired, they say: 'You see, he doesn't really want to murder you; he spoke to you in a most cordial manner; surely you are convinced now?' But the lunatic replies: 'Yes, but that was only his diabolical cunning; he's really plotting against me the whole time, like the rest of them; I know it, I tell you.' However many kindly dons are produced, the reaction is still the same.
>
> (Hare, *Essays on Religion and Education*, p. 37)

Although the student's statements are unfalsifiable, Hare denies that they are meaningless. These assertions are significant within the life and worldview of the student. Hare coined the term **blik** to refer to this kind of belief.

Hare describes a blik as a frame of reference in which all evidence is interpreted. A blik is not based on evidence, so it cannot be either verified or falsified. This does not mean, says Hare, that bliks are meaningless, as they could still be true or false in reality. As the lunatic example demonstrates, his blik is insane, as opposed to other bliks that may be sane.

Blik:
Blik is the name given by R. M. Hare to an unfalsifiable conviction that was still meaningful.

The use that religious believers make of religious language to make assertions about their beliefs is also a blik and, according to Hare, is meaningful because it makes an impact on the ways in which believers view the world and live their lives. They cannot be discarded as meaningless because they have profound effects on the individuals who believe them. Religious language does not assert facts but demonstrates matters of deep personal conviction.

Responses to Hare

Flew dismissed Hare's argument. He said that Hare has merely developed the blik concept as a 'fraudulent substitute' to disguise the meaninglessness of unfalsifiable assertions. Flew maintained that such assertions, whether called 'bliks' or not, were still meaningless for the reasons he had already given. Flew believed that Hare had not addressed his own original arguments but had tried to sidestep them with the concept of bliks.

Furthermore, many religious believers would disagree with Hare and claim that their use of religious language aims to express truths about reality rather than expressing a worldview.

John Hick commented that, although Hare suggests that there are sane/insane or correct/incorrect bliks, there is no way to differentiate between them and so they must remain unfalsifiable and meaningless.

Mitchell's freedom fighter

The English philosopher of religion Basil Mitchell responded to Flew in a rather different way from Hare.

He suggested that, although religious language may not be straightforwardly falsifiable, religious believers can and do allow things to count against their beliefs. In Mitchell's view, this could be a gradual process based on an accumulation of evidence over time. A religious believer may not always accept that evidence falsifies their assertions, but Mitchell argues that this does not mean that these beliefs would always be maintained regardless of the evidence. His point is that evidence is not irrelevant to religious language claims. In this sense, such claims can be viewed as meaningful.

Mitchell provided the following story to demonstrate how faith can be shaken by a gradual accumulation of evidence:

> In time of war in an occupied country, a member of the resistance meets one night a stranger who deeply impresses him . . . The partisan is utterly convinced at that meeting of the Stranger's sincerity and constancy and undertakes to trust him. They never meet in conditions of intimacy again. But sometimes the Stranger is seen helping members of the resistance, and the partisan is grateful, and says to his friends, 'He is on our side.' Sometimes he is seen in the uniform of the police handing over patriots to the occupying power. On these occasions his friends murmur against him: but the partisan still says, 'He is on our side.' He still believes that, in spite of appearances, the Stranger did not deceive him . . . Sometimes his friends, in exasperation, say, 'Well, what would he have to do for you to admit that you were wrong and that he is not on our side?' But the partisan refuses to answer.
> (Basil Mitchell, *The Philosophy of Religion*, Oxford Readings in Philosophy. Oxford University Press, 1971, pp. 18–19)

'The partisan admits that many things may and do count against his belief', even though he maintains it. Mitchell attempts to demonstrate that religious believers do accept that there may be evidence against their beliefs. Believers may still hold on to the original belief, as the partisan and many religious believers do, but that does not mean that they think that no evidence could ever possibly show their belief to be false. Some religious believers might accept that there may be evidence or circumstances whereby their claims about God could be shown to be false. According to Mitchell, this means that statements of religious language can be seen to be meaningful truth-claims, because they are therefore open to falsification.

Flew's response to Mitchell

Flew's response was predictably negative. He thought that the partisan was open to the possibility of evidence that was contrary to his belief in the stranger, but Flew argued that it is different for the faith that religious believers demonstrate. Knowing that humans are fallible, the partisan has reason to question his trust in the stranger. Religious believers' trust in God is different because it is predicated on the acceptance that God is perfect but works in mysterious ways that are not easily understood. This, for Flew, is why religious believers will not allow any evidence to count against their religious language claims.

Interestingly, in 2007, when Flew was seventy-eight, he published a book entitled *There is a God: How the World's Most Notorious Atheist Changed His Mind*. He wrote that he had become convinced, by looking again at all the evidence, that there was a God. He had earlier (2003) declared that he had become a deist, and believed in an impersonal god of the Aristotelian type, but was not a Christian. There was some controversy when the book was published, because it was the product of his old age and he also had a co-author, Roy Abraham Varghese. Flew confirmed, however, that the book was an accurate reflection of his own views.

> **Exercise**
> 1. Summarize Flew's argument against the validity of religious belief.
> 2. Explain what Flew meant when he called statements about God as dying 'the death of a thousand qualifications'.
> 3. Explain how the falsification principle applies to religious language.
> 4. Show how Hare attempted to explain religious language as a blik.
> 5. Evaluate Mitchell's contribution to the debate on religious language.
> 6. Choose one of the philosophers in this section and prepare a presentation for the class, having researched their life, work, main ideas and contribution to the religious language debate.

Non-cognitive accounts of religious language

The challenge of verification and falsification was aimed at cognitive accounts of what it means to believe in God. According to these accounts, belief in God involves

Challenges to Religious Language

a statement about what is objectively the situation in reality. For example, to say 'God loves me' is to say that there is a God who really exists and that his existence will beneficially affect me because he loves me. Cognitivist accounts are very closely related to Realist accounts and rely on a **correspondence theory of truth**.

> **Correspondence theory of truth:** The theory that whether a statement is true or false is judged only on how it relates to the world and whether it actually describes (i.e. corresponds with) the world.

It is possible to apply a Cognitivist/Realist approach to all statements of belief, from the mundane to the supernatural. For example, the statement 'there is a rabbit over there' means that there is a rabbit over there, independent of my experience of seeing it and interpretation of it. My statement corresponds to the actual truth. To say in the same context, however, 'there is a rabbit-shaped tuft of grass over there' would be to say something contrary to reality. So, a statement is true if it corresponds with reality as it is, independent of my perception of it. Our language must reflect reality – otherwise, it fails.

This theory of language, when applied to statements about God, makes religious language vulnerable to Logical Positivist-type attacks. If statements correspond to reality, then we should be able to test reality in order to verify or falsify the statements.

Since the later philosophy of Ludwig Wittgenstein, however, expressed most clearly in his books *On Certainty* and *Philosophical Investigations*, a very different explanation of how language works has developed. This is a non-Cognitivist account that is closely related to an anti-Realist view, both of which rely on a coherence theory of truth.

Wittgenstein, using illustrations like the famous 'Duck/Rabbit', highlighted that people can live within different worlds of meaning, or what he called 'language games'. So, an individual may make statements about the duck or the rabbit according to their interpretation of the same data, i.e. the lines on the page. As they do so, they inhabit different frameworks of interpretation. Wittgenstein gives another example: 'If someone is ill and he says "This is punishment" and I say "If I'm ill I don't think of punishments at all". . . it is entirely different from what we would normally call believing the opposite' (*On Certainty*, Wiley-Blackwell, 1974, p. 57). The two people have different interpretations of the same data and there is no way in which anyone could persuade either to change their mind, because both 'truths' exist in a sense independently of the phenomenon (i.e. pain) that both share. Both live within different worlds of meaning or 'language games'.

The Duck–Rabbit of Illusion

When applied more widely, this view of language has far-reaching implications. For example, seeing a rabbit is no longer a case of believing that a rabbit exists independently of my perception of it, but rather that there is some experience which we interpret as being a rabbit. Normally, we might think it possible to misperceive a tuft of grass as a rabbit, i.e. we are getting our interpretation wrong. According to this account, however, there is no objective truth about which we can be wrong. Even perceiving a rabbit as a rabbit (in the normal way of speaking) is to interpret reality in an ultimately arbitrary way.

John Hick, in discussing Wittgenstein in *God and the Universe of Faiths* (Oneworld Publications, 1993, pp. 41–2) makes the point that, within the post-Wittgensteinian account of language, a statement is true if it fits in with the way you normally interpret experience – i.e. if it is coherent with the overall way that you understand the world. There is no reality that our language must reflect because our language – in a sense – creates reality. In a famous quote, philosopher **John Oman (1860–1939)** summarizes this position: 'knowing is not knowledge as an effect of an unknown external cause, but is knowledge as we so interpret our meaning as the actual meaning of our environment' (*The Natural and the Supernatural*, Cambridge University Press, 2014, p. 175).

Implications for religious language

What, then, are the implications of this non-Cognitivist/anti-Realist view for religious language? Wittgenstein began to develop them when he wrote, 'Whatever believing in God may be it can't be believing in something we can test or find any means of testing' (*On Certainty*, p. 21). Just as we cannot test whether pain is or is not a punishment from God (or any other being), so statements like 'There is a God' or 'God loves me' or 'God is the ultimate reason for the existence of the universe' are not reflections of reality, but interpretations of reality. We cannot take them and measure them against a reality that exists independently of them because they form that reality.

For example, take the following religious statements:

1. 'God had a purpose in creating the universe – to produce humans who loved him and each other'
2. 'God is love'
3. 'God will ultimately conquer evil'

Each of these is taken from the Judaeo-Christian language game and fits within that context. They are true, therefore, for believers in Judaism and Christianity. Importantly, they are immune from any challenges or criticisms that might come from other language games.

For example, a scientist may claim that recent cosmological theories (i.e. the Big Bang) contradict the first statement above because the cosmological theories replace any need for a God to explain the existence of the world. A believer, however, could reply that God explains *why* there is a universe, not *how* it came into being. By contrast, scientific theories tackle the *how* questions and must be silent on the *why* questions. Science and religion are both playing language games, or providing different interpretations for the same experience of the universe. The scientist is making a mistake in his criticism of religious belief, which is rather like the mistake someone would be making if they were asked 'why did you come to school today?' and replied 'by bus'.

Taking the second statement above, someone suffering a terrible injustice might say that, in light of their experience, 'God is love' cannot be an accurate reflection of reality (i.e. the truth). Within their world of meaning, however, a religious believer could reply with a particular explanation of suffering which reconciled its existence with the existence of God. For example, your current suffering will lead to a higher good within God's plan for your life. This will sound like nonsense within the non-believer's language game, but make great sense to the believer and thus pass the coherence test of the truth of propositions.

Challenges to Religious Language

> **Exercise**
>
> Work out, using the information in this section, whether the third statement above ('God will ultimately conquer evil') would pass the coherence test.

So, the problem of applying the criteria of verification and falsification to religious language arises from taking principles that are useful within one world of discourse, e.g. science, and trying to apply them to a different discourse, e.g. religion, which operates according to different rules.

D. Z. Phillips's contribution

Welsh philosopher **D. Z. Phillips (1934–2006)** did much work to apply Wittgenstein's thought to religious language.

He gave the following illustration of how the language game works and how it can be immune to challenges from other ways of looking at the world. He writes about a boxer who makes the sign of the cross every time before a fight to ensure God's presence with him in the ring. By this action, the boxer is not establishing a testable hypothesis like 'If I survive this fight, God loves me.' Rather he is in effect saying within a religious language game: 'Whatever happens in this fight, I will interpret it in the light of a God who died for me.' His worldview, therefore, is immune to verification or falsification. For Phillips, God is real in the sense that he functions within this game in the same way that 'beauty' functions in art criticism or 'tasty' functions in the group of people eating a school lunch. None of these words refer to anything that could be empirically tested or which could be recognized by someone outside the language game; they have no 'extra-linguistic' meaning. God, then, does not exist outside religious language. Phillips, a non-Cognitivist, says: 'To have the idea of God is to know God' (*The Concept of Prayer*, Wiley-Blackwell, 1981, p. 18), and 'What the believer learns is religious language, a language which he participates in along with other believers. What I am suggesting is that to know how to use this language is to know God' (p. 50).

Interestingly, Phillips applies this anti-Realist non-cognitivism to aspects of religious language, particularly the belief in the immortality of the soul, and the belief in petitionary prayer. He gives accounts of these sub-games within the larger religious language game, which remove any idea that there is either an objective eternal life beyond human language, or a God independent of humanity who answers prayers.

Two different applications of Wittgenstein's thought to religious language

1. A non-Cognitivist approach in the light of Wittgenstein will state that religious language is not making any statements about reality beyond and independent of the language, because all we have is the language. It would be like trying to find the real Platform 9¾ in Kings Cross Station in London existing beyond

J. K. Rowling's *Harry Potter* novels. There is no way of knowing anything beyond the religious language game, so the only test we can apply to particular religious statements is whether they fitted together with other pieces of the jigsaw. Apart from D. Z. Phillips, **R. B. Braithwaite (1900–90)** was an important thinker in this category.

Braithwaite denies that religious language is the making of statements about an objective, extra-linguistic God. He follows in the footsteps of Logical Positivism, saying that, since there is no way of testing for such a conception of God, it is meaningless to hold such a concept as God, in particular, and religious language in general. Unlike the Logical Positivists, however, Braithwaite still sees a use for religious language if it is re-understood as a way of making *moral* statements. The Christian statement that 'God is Love' is not a statement about some realist concept of a God who loves, but an expression of 'the intention to follow an **agapeistic** way of life' (Braithwaite, *An Empiricist's View of the Nature of Religious Belief*, Cambridge University Press, 1955, p. 336).

> **Agapeistic:** The adjective from the Christian word for selfless love: 'agape'.

Similarly, Braithwaite states more generally, 'A religious assertion for me is the assertion of an intention to carry out a certain behaviour policy, subsumable under a sufficiently general principle to be a moral one' (ibid., p. 336). In particular, one distinctive feature of religious language is that it involves stories that picture and reinforce the moral way of life, such as the tale of the Good Samaritan. While these religious stories may appear to be direct assertions of fact, they actually serve to express the intention of the one uttering them to live morally. Just as it is not necessary for an objective God to exist, so it is not necessary that the stories be true or that they even be believed for them to fulfil their primary purpose.

2. Some scholars have tried to apply Wittgenstein's theories, but maintain that religious language is still making meaningful statements about some really existing objective reality, i.e. something beyond our different language games, to which those games correspond. John Hick seems to come within this category, particularly in his early work. He summarizes the purpose of one chapter ('Religious Faith as "Experiencing-as"') in his *God and the Universe of Faith* as: 'I have now, I hope, offered a very rough outline of a conception of faith as the interpretative element within our cognitive religious experience.' Hick is unhappy with a fully non-cognitive account of religious language.

Criticisms of the non-Realist/non-Cognitivist account of religious language

1. If anti-Realist/non-Cognitivist accounts claim to describe how religious believers use religious language, they are wrong, since most religious believers maintain that there is an objectively existent being independent of them. Non-Cognitivist accounts fail, therefore, to describe the meaning that religious people attach to religious language.
2. If religion is a self-contained language game making no statements about objective reality, the believer is being irrational if she continues to use religious

language about some existent, independent being, in the same way as someone who talked and tried to behave as though she had inherited £1,000,000, when she knows in fact that she has not, would be irrational.
3. Religious belief may be useful, but humans have an insatiable desire to know whether it is true, i.e. whether it corresponds to reality. Anti-realism leaves this desire unfulfilled. As a result, anti-realism writes off almost the entire history of the philosophy of religion, which has comprised arguments for and against the existence of God.
4. Anti-Realists may be able to define what sort of sensation is objectified when we describe an ice-cream as 'tasty' – i.e. sugary, vanilla, creamy . . . However, they disagree as to what subjective response to the world is being objectified when religious language is used.
5. Anti-Realists like Don Cupitt appear to say that that we can never get beyond our subjective, personal responses to the world to some objective, Realist sphere of what really is. We can never get beyond our own perspective upon the objective truth: a way of looking at the world that is sometimes called 'perspectivism'. As a result, Realist statements are impossible. However, perspectivism claims to be a conclusive account of how things really are, i.e. hidden from us. The response to Cupitt is that he does not have the authority to claim a privileged standpoint when most people are trapped in subjectivity. Essentially, Cupitt's theory destroys itself – it is 'self-stultifying'.

Why Logical Positivism ultimately fails

1. Clearly, according to the criterion of 'strong verifiability', which was held by some Logical Positivists, there is no such thing as a meaningful statement, even though many such statements would be considered factually valid and intelligible by many people. For example, 'All people spend part of their lives asleep.' This statement seems to be meaningful and true, but no sense experience could conclusively verify it since it is always possible that one person has lived, is living or will live, who does not sleep.
2. Similarly, many statements accepted as valid by most people could not be conclusively falsified. For example, 'All cats are mortal.' The empirical situation necessary to show that this statement was false would be the discovery of an immortal cat. But how would we know that we were encountering an immortal cat, since even a remarkably old cat may die at some point in the future. Nevertheless, while this statement is not conclusively falsifiable, most people would accept it as true.
3. If all statements are either verifiable or falsifiable or tautological/analytic, what status does the statement 'All statements are either verifiable or falsifiable or tautological/analytic' have? Clearly, the statement is not analytic because many people do attach meaning to statements that are neither verifiable/falsifiable nor analytic. For instance, religious adherents believe in a concept (God) whose existence is neither verifiable nor analytical. Clearly, the belief is not

empirically verifiable since no sense experience could possibly prove it to be true. Consequently, the very assertion 'All statements are either . . .' seems to defeat itself, since the statement itself falls outside these two categories.

4. The verifiability criterion claims to be closely related to the scientific method, in which sense experience judges hypotheses through experimentation. However, this may conceal a simplification of scientific method. Scientists will posit the existence of entities that they cannot observe in order to explain what they can observe. Richard Swinburne gives an example: 'S is moving in a way which is to be expected if Newton's laws . . . are the true laws of motion . . . only if there is an unobserved planet P which is exerting an attractive force on S. It is far simpler to postulate P . . . than to change Newton's laws which account well for other phenomena' (*The Existence of God*, p. 81). Similarly, physicists will postulate unobservable fundamental particles (photons, positrons, neutrinos . . .) to explain the behaviour of observable material objects.

5. John Hick focuses his attack on the Logical Positivists not by questioning their principles, but by arguing that religious statements are verifiable in principle at some stage beyond death. Hick calls this 'eschatological verification'. He also argues that it will never be possible to falsify religious statements, but that religious statements are similar to many other statements that are generally considered to be meaningful in this regard.

6. The Logical Positivists sought to explain why some statements are meaningful and others are not. Yet they exclude many statements that people do find meaningful, even though they are fully aware that they cannot describe any empirical situations that would verify or falsify those statements. Take, for example, the following statements:

    - This classroom really exists independently of my perception of it (a Realist view)
    - Event A (a white ball hitting a red ball in snooker) caused event B (red ball to move), rather than Event B happening simultaneously and completely independently of Event A
    - Action X (e.g. murder) is objectively wrong, independently of any human judgement about it.

7. The implication of the falsifiability challenge in particular is that no piece of evidence could constitute evidence against the assertion that God exists. Clearly, though, many theists do struggle with observable phenomena which seem to cast doubt on the existence of God. For example, the existence of suffering in the world. This is illustrated in Basil Mitchell's 'Parable of the Stranger', in which he concluded:

    > The partisan of the parable does not allow anything to count decisively against the proposition 'the stranger is on our side'. This is because he has committed himself to trust the stranger. But he, of course, recognizes that the stranger's ambiguous behaviour does count against what he believes about him. It is precisely this situation which constitutes the trial of his faith.
    > (B. Mitchell, *The Justification of Religious Belief*, Macmillan, 1973, p. 346)

Mitchell's arguments seem to do more justice to the actual act of belief than Flew's argument that nothing could possibly count against the assertion that 'God exists'.

Furthermore, the Logical Positivist position would render inductive, a posteriori arguments (e.g. teleological, cosmological) for the existence of God absolutely meaningless, which contradicts the evident fact that many people have found such arguments, at the very least, intelligible.

Perhaps, overall, it is not surprising that A. J. Ayer seems eventually to have rejected the possibility of formulating the verification or falsifiability principle as unsatisfactory.

Comparison of Aquinas's and Wittgenstein's views on religious language

In some ways, it is not easy to compare Aquinas and Wittgenstein. Aquinas was a Christian, Wittgenstein an agnostic. Aquinas lived during the Middle Ages, Wittgenstein in the twentieth century. Their knowledge of the world and the philosophical frameworks in which they operated were very different. Aquinas wrote almost entirely for practising Christians, especially priests, who could use his teaching to help them live their lives in the service of God, while Wittgenstein had no particular audience for which he wrote and made no assumptions about any religious beliefs they might hold.

In other ways, there are similarities to be seen between Aquinas and Wittgenstein. Both men understood the fundamental importance of religious language. For example, Wittgenstein famously said that there were no philosophical problems, only problems of language. Both held that human language was inadequate to express the true nature of God and that God was thus essentially unknowable. Both believed that religious language must be understood in a particular way if it was to convey any meaning, though they disagreed on what this way might be.

Thomist scholar Fergus Kerr, who was influenced by Wittgenstein's philosophy of language, has studied the links between Aquinas and Wittgenstein in his book *Theology after Wittgenstein* (Blackwell, 1989, pp. 151–60). He argues that the key to understanding the relationship between them is Wittgenstein's phrase 'theology as grammar', which he used in his *Philosophical Investigations*. Wittgenstein says that, if we are to understand ideas, we must know what kind of language is being used by the speakers and how that language is understood by the participants. Words have to be used before any meaning becomes clear. Kerr says:

> Whether I mean the same thing by saying 'I believe in God' as other people do when they say the same thing will come out at various places in our lives: our practices, aspirations, hopes, virtues, and so on. It will show in the rest of what we do whether we have faith in God. It will not be settled by our finding that we make the same correlation between our words and some item of metaphysical reality . . . Faith, in appropriate circumstances, is visible in one's behaviour; it is not some undetectable inner object.
>
> (Kerr, *Theology after Wittgenstein*, p. 152)

Aquinas used analogy as the most appropriate way to understand religious language. In contrast to the way humans normally use language with each other, where words have only a single meaning (i.e., univocally), language about God must be used equivocally and analogically. This is the only way that God's teaching and commands may be understood. Of course, humans will not be able to comprehend everything about God by analogical understanding, but it will allow humans to have some understanding of the divine nature. (See chapter 9, pp. 171–3, for more on Aquinas and analogy.)

Wittgenstein argued that religious language is best understood when considered as a 'language game' within the 'form of life' of religion. Religious believers operate within a religious 'language game' and can gain understanding of and meaning from religious terms like 'infinite', 'holy' or 'immanent' within this context. As we have seen, D. Z. Phillips, who was heavily influenced by Wittgensteinian philosophy, sees religious language not as true or false, but as meaningful for believers in their attempt to understand what God is like and what their relationship is with God. (See above, p. 199.)

As should be expected, Aquinas's analogical understanding of religious language has been much more influential than the relatively recent and agnostic position of Wittgenstein. Most religious believers take a Cognitivist view of religious language, and this has been the case for many centuries because of the influence of Aquinas. When believers make statements about their understanding of God, they tend to take statements like 'God created the universe' and 'Jesus was the son of God' as referring to empirical facts. For these believers, God exists as a real entity – sometimes, but not always, as a physical being – who inhabits a space outside and beyond human space. God is in some ways similar to human beings but much greater in all respects – moral goodness, perfection, power, love, compassion, and so on.

The main problem with this view is that believers who make claims like this about God have no evidence to verify them. This was the point made by Ayer and Flew and, before the believers' truth-claims can be accepted by non-believers, their criticisms would have to be met.

For Wittgenstein and his followers, there is nothing inherently either meaningful or meaningless in religious believers' truth-claims. Believers' statements concerning God must be viewed in the context of the 'form of life' that religious believers live in. Claims such as 'God protects me from sin' are simply part of the language game of religion and have no intrinsic meaning. For anyone outside that particular language game, these words and expressions of belief have no meaning, for they are outside the context of the 'game' which is inhabited by non-believers. In some sense, therefore, all religious statements are of no value. The consequence, if this is true, is that there can be no meaningful interaction between believers and non-believers. Further, as there are many other language games – history, economics, sport, dance, music . . ., it follows that there can be few if any meaningful conversations between the different groups that make up society, and so 'society' cannot exist.

> **Exercise**
>
> Do you agree that, if Wittgenstein's ideas are valid, society cannot exist? Explain your reasons.

Does Aquinas's use of analogical language have any value for religious believers in the twenty-first century?

For many Christians in the twenty-first century, the analogical approach set out by Aquinas to understanding language about God is still the default position. Many believers continue to find understanding and meaning in thinking of the Bible as a largely factual account of God's interaction with humans. This is a cognitive approach and they extend this to the major doctrines of the church such as the Trinity, the Incarnation and Salvation. This view is held by many Roman Catholic Christians, but also by many conservative Protestants as well.

The analogical approach to religious language can and does lead to problems for those believers who hold it. When talking to other Christians who take a different approach, and to non-believers, fundamental questions will be raised about the authority by which they hold their cognitive beliefs and what evidence they can present in support of their views.

There is long-standing tension between Fundamentalist Christians and more liberal believers. This stretches back beyond the twentieth-century debate about cognitive versus non-cognitive language to the nineteenth century, when biblical scholars, particularly in Germany, began to look seriously at the nature of the text of the Bible. For example, Julius Wellhausen, Professor of Old Testament Studies at Göttingen University, noticed that there were two 'creation' accounts, two versions of Noah's flood, and four different names used for God. This made him study the Bible as an ancient text, without assuming that it was 'the word of God'. His discoveries (later known as the Documentary Hypothesis) led to the development of biblical criticism, which in turn led to the view that various authors over a long period of time were responsible for the authorship of books in the biblical canon. In some ways, this may be seen as the initiation of a non-cognitive approach within Christianity, rather than understanding them symbolically or as ancient myths that conveyed fundamental truths about the nature of God.

Another aspect of this approach to the Bible was developed by the German biblical scholar and theologian, Rudolph Bultmann, Professor of New Testament at Marburg University.

Bultmann published a radical essay in 1941, 'The New Testament and Mythology', which argued that the supernatural elements in the New Testament, such as the virgin birth of Jesus and the miracles he performed, could not be taken seriously by a modern readership. Christians, therefore, should read biblical stories as ancient myths that attempted to speak about God's nature and relationship with humans. They should '**demythologize**' the stories in order to distill their essential meaning.

Bultmann's essay was seen as shocking by many Christians, but as a great step forward in our understanding by others. It sparked a great deal of argument and discussion in the years that followed its publication, and a number of books that developed the issues Bultmann had raised and their implications for Christian believers. The American philosopher **Paul van Buren (1924–98)** wrote *The Secular Meaning of*

> **Demythologize:**
> 'Demythologize' was Bultmann's word to describe the process that needs to be undertaken with the biblical texts so that the 'original' meaning(s) can be understood by modern readers.

the Gospel in 1963 and, in the same year, British theologian and Bishop **John Robinson (1919–83)** wrote *Honest to God*. Both authors took a non-cognitive approach in their exploration of the relevance of the biblical texts in the twentieth century.

In 1965, **Harvey Cox (1929–present)** published *The Secular City: Secularization and Urbanization in Theological Perspective*. In the introduction, he wrote:

> This is the age of the secular city. Through supersonic travel and instantaneous communications its ethos is spreading into every corner of the globe. The world looks less and less to religious rules and rituals for its morality or its meanings . . . For fewer and fewer does [religious belief] provide an inclusive and commanding system of personal and cosmic values and explanations . . . if we are to understand and communicate with our present age, we must learn to love it in its unremitting secularity . . . it will do no good to cling to our religious and metaphysical versions of Christianity in the idle hope that religion or metaphysics will one day regain their centrality. They will become even more peripheral and that means that we can now let go and immerse ourselves in the new world of the secular city.
>
> (Cox, *The Secular City*, Princeton University Press, 2013, p. 3)

The debate about the nature and importance of the Bible in the modern world continued and, in 1977, John Hick edited a volume provocatively called *The Myth of God Incarnate*. The authors claimed that a new (non-cognitive) view of the origins of Christianity and the biblical texts was necessary in the last quarter of the twentieth century if Christianity was to continue to have any meaning or relevance. It shocked many readers in its central suggestion that Jesus was a 'man approved by God' rather than God incarnate, and that the biblical stories should be read as poetic ways of expressing the significance of Jesus to modern people, rather than as historical facts.

The book caused an immediate evangelical (Cognitivist) response, *The Truth of God Incarnate* edited by **Michael Green (1930–present)**, which defended the traditional doctrine of the Incarnation. There has been a stream of books in the generation since these formative books were published, and the debate continues to excite passions on both sides. Sometimes the discussion is framed in terms of 'traditional values' (the Cognitivist approach) and 'making Christianity relevant' to 21st-century life (the non-Cognitivist approach).

FURTHER READING

A. J. Ayer, *Language, Truth and Logic*. Penguin, 1934

R. M. Hare, *Essays on Religion and Education*. Oxford University Press, 1998

J. Hick, *Philosophy of Religion*, 4th edition. Prentice Hall, 1990

B. Magee, *Popper*. Fontana Modern Masters, 1977

A. O'Hear (ed.), *Karl Popper: Philosophy and Problems*. Cambridge University Press, 2008

D. Z. Phillips, *Wittgenstein and Religion*. Palgrave Macmillan, 1994

K. Popper, *The Open Society and Its Enemies*, 2 vols. Routledge, 1945

Thought Points

1. Summarize the development of the Logical Positivist movement.

2. Explain the Verification Principle.

3. Explain why falsification was a challenge to religious language.

4. Explain the importance of Hare's theory of bliks in the religious language debate.

5. 'A non-cognitive approach is ultimately successful in retaining meaning for religious language.' Discuss.

6. 'A God that cannot be tested is no different from no God at all' (Anthony Flew). Explain and evaluate this statement.

7. 'All religious language, whether cognitive or non-cognitive is literally nonsense.' Discuss how far you agree with this statement.

Study Skills and Assessment

A Level is a step up from GCSEs and the essay writing at its heart calls for a range of skills and techniques, as well as fluency in your style. Mastering technical terms, providing examples and having a good grasp of the strengths and weaknesses of theories are all part of the mature essayist's work. In short, taking the mystery out of exam success is our aim in this chapter.

Planning lots of skeleton outlines to exam-style questions will help you to take a broad question and focus it down to a relevant and well-crafted argument. Practice trains you to select examples, reasons and evidence. It also keeps you focused, stops you going off on tangents and avoiding fallacies, and helps you to spot gaps in your revision. Writing timed essays in class will also train you to allocate minutes in proportion to the marks available and to work out how many paragraphs you can reasonably write in the 2 hours available for planning and writing three essays (if you are doing A Level) or the 75 minutes available for planning and writing two essays (if you are doing AS Level).

This chapter will give you a good idea of what examiners are looking for in the answers of top candidates, and it should serve as a guide as you learn to research and plan your essays. Irrelevance and running out of time are two major reasons for under-performance, so essay skills are at the heart of your success in this subject. Making essay plans and structuring them in paragraphs will help to hone your skills as an essay writer. We begin by flagging up some key elements in essay writing.

Crafting your essay argument

- Interpret the focus of the question together with any terms or value judgements implicit in it.
- Decide on your thesis (the broad argument you are going to advance, taking into account any qualifications you might offer to the terms of the question – e.g. 'In my assessment, this is not an either–or situation, but a both–and one').
- Weigh up the *extent* to which you agree with any assertion made in the question – is it true of all or some forms? Are you aware of other *perspectives* or *viewpoints* that could be taken?

- Be clear on the counterargument, key reasons and examples opposed to your thesis + evaluation of strengths and weaknesses. Showing your awareness of these increases the credibility of your own position.
- Then set out the reasoning of key thinkers and arguments *for* your thesis and evaluation of their strengths and weaknesses.
- Evaluate arguments and counterarguments and (if you have time) bring them into dialogue.
- Make your personal response explicit, with phrases like 'it is my contention that', or 'in my assessment, there are obvious strengths in Aquinas's view of the Cosmological argument because. . .'
- Summarize the reasons for your concluding judgement.

Dialogue not monologue

Aristotle commented that 'it is a mark of the educated mind to be able to entertain a thought without accepting it'. One of the lessons to learn as you move from GCSE/IGCSE to A Level is that arguments that oppose your own conclusion deserve a fair hearing, and their criticisms of your position require you to respond to them. Avoid setting up straw-men opponents that are easy to demolish. Try to understand the weaknesses of your position and arrive at a well-reasoned and balanced conclusion.

Essential skills and strategies for success

Please note that all comments concerning techniques, strategies and skills necessary for success at AS and A Level are the views of the authors, not of OCR.

Interpretation

Analysis

Evaluation

Personal response

One of the important ways in which AS and A Level differ from GCSE is in the technique for formulating and writing essays. At GCSE, there is much more of a focus on knowledge learning. To some degree, it is possible to prepare answers in advance, remember the information, then write it in the examination. This is a strategy that will not work at AS or A Level.

If you wish to achieve high marks in the essays you write at this level, you will need to learn a number of important new skills and techniques.

Reading and planning your essay

Homework essays are time-consuming and labour intensive. It is tempting to skim-read in preparation or even to write them straight off without research and planning. But teachers and examiners can tell apart those students who have taken the time to read and plan their essays from those who have not done so. Reading builds your vocabulary and understanding of concepts. It sharpens your writing style and offers you a wider range of examples. If this all seems too much like hard work, there are lots of good online audio resources to listen to.

Essay strengths

- Your own personal response as you analyse and evaluate arguments and demonstrate independent reasoning and judgement
- Close attention to the wording of questions and key words.
- Clear, practical examples and a sound ability to engage critically with theory.
- Good grasp of concepts and distinctions, e.g. a clear understanding of philosophical grammar in distinguishing 'infer' from 'imply', 'refute' from 'deny', or 'a priori', 'a posteriori', etc.
- Achieving a balance between breadth and depth as required by the demands of the question.
- Logical structure and tightly argued paragraphs that are relevant to the question.
- Clear analysis of strengths and weaknesses of rival positions when assessing their merits.
- Excellent engagement between philosophical theory and its implications

Essay weaknesses

- Pre-rehearsed answers that ignore the specific wording of the question. Irrelevance and poor timing are the key reasons why students underperform.
- Generalizations – e.g. 'all Christians believe the Bible is literally true' – or lists of ideas without explanation.
- Incoherent or long-winded arguments that do not develop the essay thesis from paragraph to paragraph. Your essay should weave the threads of the argument together coherently.
- Evaluation left until the conclusion rather than woven throughout the essay in the analysis of strengths and weaknesses.
- Confusion or conflation of ideas belonging to two distinct thinkers, e.g. Aquinas and Ayer.

Elements of essay writing: consider how you can sharpen these in making an informed, coherent and persuasive argument

- A *sentence* is a grammatical structure ending in a full stop. Try to put just one idea into each sentence, to keep it clear and straightforward. This will make it easier for your teacher and examiner to understand and will help you to explain ideas properly.
- A *paragraph* is a collection of sentences grouped around one purpose or theme. Single-sentence or full-page paragraphs sound alarm bells when examiners scan essays because it usually means that you do not fully understand what you are writing about. You should organize your argument into a step-by-step logical sequence.
- To do this, it is best to structure your essay into a series of steps and then to shuffle your paragraphs to find the most logical order for your essay. For example, you might begin with the weaker position or the one you disagree with, noting its strengths and the critical questions it raises for the position you wish to advance.
  Every view deserves a fair hearing, so do not be too quick to dismiss opposing positions and to assert the strengths of your own view. A critically considered conclusion will carry more credibility.
- *Introduction*. Interpret the question's key words/phrases and set out your broad position in the essay. Unpack the question and set out your thesis point by point.
- Think of essays as dialogues between ideas – not monologues or, much worse, rants. Be concise and clear in your structure.
- *Links/transitions* between paragraphs. Avoid a repetitive style. Try to avoid the same stock phrases – your style of writing is important.
- *Evidence*. Your general argument needs specific examples, both to illustrate it and to give the reasons weight. These can take the form of academic authorities who advance a position, or demonstrations of how a theory proves to be more or less workable in practice. Balanced arguments can give you more credibility through your impartial handling of the evidence.
- *Include examples*. These illustrate your essay and develop a more engaging style.
- *Quotations* are important. For each essay topic, learn a few short quotes that will enhance your style by showing a familiarity with primary sources.
- *Paragraphs*
  - *Signposts at the beginning* – This will help the marker get a clear sense of your structure. State your main argument in the opening sentence of the essay.
  - *Intermediate conclusions at the end* – Stay on course with the focus of the question. Recapping what your examples, evidence and reasons have established in a sub-conclusion (one or two sentences) allows you to move the argument forward. You may even take a different course, persuading the reader that, though the initial position had its merits, it was mistaken,

inadequate or needed revision. *Sub-conclusions* establish shifts in the argument, like switches that move your train onto a new set of tracks.
- *Fluency with technical vocabulary.* Be aware of key vocabulary from glossaries and indexes in your textbook and have a clear idea of trigger words in questions (see below).
- *Scholars, textual sources, statistics.* Be accurate and selective – let the reasoning drive the essay. Evidence and examples ought to make an essay's reasoning more persuasive and engaging. Read textbooks – they will make you more fluent with ideas.
- *Arguments and counterarguments.* These should form a dialogue in your essay. At times this can lead to a layering of a weakness identified, a response, then a further weakness that clinches the argument in favour of one side. If you were asked whether Augustine was more successful than Irenaeus on the Problem of Evil, for example, you could present strengths and weaknesses separately but also have a paragraph where some dialogue and debate entered into the argument. This layering of reasons and responses creates a dialogue rather than a monologue, and builds more credibility for your evaluative conclusions.
- *Theory summaries – the way to tame the abstract.* Bullet-point the key elements of abstract theories in your revision notes and define the meaning(s) of key concepts clearly. Use these concisely in exam essays. Do not ramble because this only shows that you do not know the material well.
- *Conclusion.* This is where you summarize your argument rather than embarking on a new one. Every paragraph in the essay should lead logically to the conclusion.
- *Review your homework essays.* It may seem like a novel idea, but if it is a homework essay, do not hand it in without first re-reading it! When you do this, check it for spelling and grammar errors. Then ask yourself whether your explanations are clear in their understanding of concepts and theories. Also try to be self-critical about whether you have addressed the question relevantly, reflected a range of perspectives, and structured a well-evidenced argument in the right order. If not, then edit it. It is tempting to think that it is your teacher's job to rewrite your essay for you, but this is not their job – it is yours! You are learning to be an INDEPENDENT thinker, so critical self-review is the way to mature as an essay writer.

Transitional phrases

As mentioned above, one element of becoming a good essay writer is to move from one paragraph to the next in such a way as to lead your reader through the steps in your thought. This avoids repetition, makes your logic clearer and ought to make it more persuasive. Structure, substance and style all help to engage an examiner and make their job easier. Whilst you do not need to have a formal stock of transitional phrases up your sleeve, you do need to work on the style and structure of your homework essays so that you mature as an essay writer, offering a logical progression from one paragraph to another. Below is a list of exemplar phrases that illustrate this process. But be sure to select from, and deploy, your pre-rehearsed material in the right way, so that you address the exact terms of the question presented to you, otherwise you will lose marks.

Scaffolding your essay

To facilitate this, it is useful to have in mind some scaffolding to your essay. Structure shows through in paragraphing (with signpost sentences at the start, and sub-conclusions at the end).
Interpret the key terms in the question.
Set up the contrasts and comparisons in your mind.
Weave evaluative judgements about strengths and weaknesses into every sub-conclusion of your essay – do not leave it until the final concluding paragraph.

If you find it helpful, here are some examples of transitional phrases to bring your personal response to the forefront of:

- *your opening thesis statement*
- *sub-conclusions at the close of each of your paragraphs*
- *your main conclusion.*

Introductions

The key terms of the question are contested by different philosophical ideas / philosophers, and it is my contention that . . .
My thesis in this essay will be that the terms in the question . . .
At the outset of this essay, I wish to clarify the contested terms in the essay title.
Various theories interpret the phrase 'X' in the essay title differently . . .
With respect to the term 'useful' / 'helpful' / 'successful', I would judge that X theory is, in comparison with Y theory, preferable because . . .
In this essay, I will argue that . . .

Setting out your personal thesis/assessment

I agree with Philosopher X who makes a strong case for . . .
Personally, I would argue that a weakness of X's theory is that . . .
I find the argument of X more persuasive than that of Y because . . .
In my view, X's example of . . . is a useful starting point for considering the . . .
Although this is a matter of debate, and is certainly unprovable, I would argue that . . . because . . .
I am persuaded by X's more radical approach to this issue because . . .
Regardless of the individual criticisms that can be made of X's proposal, I still think that it holds up under scrutiny.

In my assessment, this theory has the advantage(s) that . . .
In my judgement, X cogently defends the view that . . .

Expressing what you see to be difficulties with a position / positions

In my estimation, X does not properly account for . . .
It may be objected to X's position that . . .
I consider X's position to be indefensible at the point at which . . .
X's assumption that . . . does not, in my judgement, hold up to criticism and is easily disproved.
In applying this theory to the issue at hand, its weaknesses become evident.
Not all arguments presented by X have survived scrutiny. . .
Several problems appear with this position.
That argument needs to be made cautiously, given the . . .
The argument is undermined by the fact that . . .
A more fruitful line of argument is . . .

A different position / contrasting view

While all of this may be logically valid, I side with the opposing position set out by X . . .
After evaluating the evidence, I would argue that X is correct in asserting that Y was wrong when he insisted that . . .
On the other side of the issue, X contends that . . ., and I find her argument persuasive.
As for Y . . . I am still more persuaded by X's argument.
In my judgement, while this is a strong argument, it ultimately fails because . . .
This may initially sound like a plausible idea, but I would argue that it fails to explain . . .
In contrast, an alternative argument, which, in my opinion, is a stronger one, is put forward by X . . .

Conclusions/summaries

The contrasts and comparative assessment that I have set out lead me to conclude that the position/theory of X is more useful / practical / principled / consistent and rational / ethically robust than that of . . .
In concluding, it has been my contention in this essay that . . .
Despite the counterarguments to my opening thesis, I see no compelling reason to doubt the view that . . .
In summary, I have tried to make a case for . . .

Note-taking throughout the course

As you work through the course, keep brief notes on comparisons and contrasts, similarities and differences, between theories. You need to be conversant with these. Also write down questions you have regarding the material your teacher covers, or that you would ask of theories and thinkers. Bring these up in lessons for discussion. Much of evaluative essay writing involves the requirement to:

- compare common ground between theories, and
- contrast distinctive features / contested approaches to practical ethical issues to form evidence-based judgements

Evaluate strengths and weaknesses throughout the essay

Strengths	Weaknesses
Reasons + evidence and examples	Reasons + evidence and examples
Similarities	**Differences**
Reasons + evidence and examples	Reasons + evidence and examples

Exercise

Photocopy several opinion or editorial pieces from quality newspapers, then...

(1) Ask yourself whether the writer has been fair in assessing different or opposing viewpoints, rather than misrepresenting them (the straw-man fallacy).
(2) Highlight key words and phrases from each paragraph to identify the basic outline of the argument.
(3) Critically evaluate whether you think other evidence or information about context or more specific examples / case studies are necessary to support the author's argument – are more conclusions made than are justified by the evidence produced?

Be strategic about your planning and preparation

- Think about your style – be concise and target the focus of the question.
- Make sure your information is accurate and relevant. Arrive at your concluding judgement(s) only after a balanced comparison of the strengths and weaknesses of theories.
- In preparing revision diagrams on topics, collect as many past-paper questions together as possible (here it may even be worth looking up past papers from other exam boards or the previous OCR Specification to see whether there could be a broader range of questions to test your knowledge)
- Work through mark schemes and level descriptors to see precisely what examiners were looking to reward in past exam questions.

- Search books and web links for examples and case studies to illustrate your essays (though let the reasoning drive the essay, not the examples).
- Use mind maps or other diagrams to select the essential terms or ideas on a topic that can be seen in an easily memorable way.

Why essays make you employable

Essay writing might seem like a real chore. Yet in developing transferable skills of persuasiveness, analysis and creative thinking, you are becoming more employable. As you read around theories, you will understand them better and consequently your confidence and fluency will improve. It is precisely these skills in selecting and deploying relevant and precise evidence and arguments that make graduates in the humanities so employable.

Not losing sight of the wood for the trees – seeing the big picture of your argument

To use an analogy, you can get lost in the woods of concepts and abstract arguments with no visible way out. Equally, you might feel the need to airlift your wayward argument out of the forest in the concluding paragraph as you realize that you have not relevantly addressed the terms of the question. Yet a safer way out of the forest may be to leave stores of food there: to have well-rehearsed key points ready to go once you have selected what is relevant to the question. Excellent selection and deployment of relevant reasons, examples, thinkers, strengths and weaknesses are crucial in achieving a high grade.

Before you actually start writing an essay, whether as homework or in an exam, it is important to think carefully about both the content and its structure. This will be easier if you have used mind-mapping techniques or some similar way of noting the information for a topic. Set out key terms, examples, key quotes, relevant thinkers, arguments and analytical points. Doing this will prepare you for any essay on any topic that you may be set.

Doing well in exams is a feat of memory – use bullet points, acronyms and mnemonics to help your recall become exam-proof.

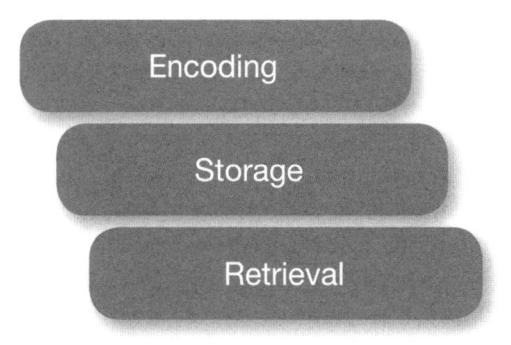

Encoding

Storage

Retrieval

Exams are not just about understanding theories and being able to explain them. They are also timed tests of your recall. Under such pressure, you need to find a process or system for encoding the information that will make it easy to retrieve. Lists of key principles and concepts in theories, as well as evaluative lists of strengths and weaknesses, should be memorized. This is best done in a concise orderly way using mind maps or bullet points, or with the aid of acronyms and mnemonics.

The two websites listed below may assist you in generating acronyms and mnemonics.

Acronym	*Mnemonic*
An acronym is an abbreviation using the first letter of each word. For example AIDS is an acronym for Acquired Immuno-Deficiency Syndrome	A mnemonic is a short phrase that you use to help remember something. So 'Richard Of York Goes Battling In Vain' helps me to remember the colours of the rainbow – red, orange, yellow, green, blue, indigo, violet
Acronym generator: www.cs.uoregon.edu/Research/paracomp/anym/	Phonetic mnemonic generator: www.remarkablemarbles.com/memory/phonetic-mnemonic-generator

Assessment

AS Religious Studies and A Level Religious Studies

You will choose to study either AS Religious Studies **OR** A Level Religious Studies. These are two separate qualifications that are self-contained. In both cases, the AS and A Level Philosophy of Religion component of Religious Studies amounts to 33.3 per cent of the course alongside the other two other sections of the course, namely Religion and Ethics, and Developments in Religious Thought.

A summary of the major differences is provided here:

	AS Level	*A Level*
Course studied over	1 year	2 years
% of marks for AO2 Analysis and evaluation	50%	60%

For students taking an AS Level course, the end-of-course exam will be made up of 30-mark questions (they answer two questions from three options). A possible question for the AS Level Philosophy of Religion component of the course could be:

1. Assess the effectiveness of Aristotle's four causes in explaining the world. [30]

Study Skills and Assessment

For students taking an A Level course, the end-of-course exam will be made up of 40-mark questions (they answer three questions from four options). A possible question for the A Level Philosophy of Religion component of the course could be:

1. 'Religious experience shows that we can be united with something greater than ourselves.' Discuss. [40]

The key difference between AS and A Level questions is that, whereas at AS Level the descriptors only go to level five (for Very Good), at A Level, there is an extra descriptor – level six (for Excellence). This recognizes the greater level of maturity that students may have developed in their second year of study. The weighting also shifts from 50–50 to 60–40 in favour of AO2 (assessment and evaluation).

There are two Assessment Objectives (AO1 and AO2). Learning to understand what these assessment objectives mean will help you a great deal in the way you write essays. They will help you to interpret and analyse information and to assess and evaluate theories. You will need to develop an independent mind and critical awareness of strengths and weaknesses so that you can make your own response to the question you have been asked.

AS Level	75 minutes	Two 30-mark questions	60 marks in total
A Level	120 minutes	Three 40-mark questions	120 marks in total

Assessment Objectives

AS Level	A Level
AO1 50%	AO1 40%
AO2 50%	AO2 60%

Getting to grips with AO2 skills

You will have to sharpen your skills of interpretation and analysis of the terms in the question. Thorough knowledge and understanding ought to be the foundation of your success. But experience of doing past-paper questions will sharpen your skills in:

- interpreting key terms, trigger words and value judgements over rival positions
- selecting and deploying relevant theories and thinkers, examples and arguments
- seeing how your judgement may rest on interpreting the question precisely
- evaluating the strengths and weaknesses of rival positions concisely
- making focused and concise comparisons and contrasts and supplying good relevant examples.

- identifying fallacies, assumptions, errors or claims that are scientifically or
- coming to a personal response regarding, for example, whether a theory is the
- using technical language fluently

So, after you have learned each section of the course, you need to practise, practise, practise essay technique. Test and homework essays are not just for consolidating your knowledge. Rather, they are where you develop as a thinker and sharpen your skills of selection and structuring a coherent argument. Essays are where you learn the discipline of sifting, sequencing and assessing the material in front of you. In guiding the reader/examiner through the process of your thinking, it is helpful to use transitional phrases that *explicitly* set out your *personal response* to the question for the reader, together with *your own* interpretation, analysis, argument and evaluation of the question. Setting out a clear plan and structure to your argument avoids repetition, makes your logic clearer and ought to be more persuasive. The use of good examples or astute analysis and comparison of theories and ideas identify high-grade candidates. Whilst you do not need to have a formal stock of transitional phrases up your sleeve, you do need to bring *your personal response* to the question to the forefront of your essay.

For AO1

An **excellent** demonstration of knowledge and understanding in response to the question:

- fully comprehends the demands of, and focuses on, the question throughout
- demonstrates excellent selection of relevant material which is skilfully used
- shows accurate and highly detailed knowledge which demonstrates deep understanding through a complex and nuanced approach to the material used
- uses technical terms and vocabulary in context thoroughly, accurately and precisely
- uses an extensive range of scholarly views, academic approaches and/or sources of wisdom and authority to demonstrate knowledge and understanding

For AO2

An **excellent** demonstration of analysis and evaluation in response to the question:

- provides excellent, clear and successful argument
- develops confident and insightful critical analysis and detailed evaluation of the issue
- contains views skilfully and clearly stated, coherently developed and justified
- answers the question set precisely throughout
- uses technical terms and vocabulary in context thoroughly, accurately and precisely
- uses an extensive range of scholarly views, academic approaches and/or sources of wisdom and authority to support analysis and evaluation

Assessment of extended response: There is an excellent line of reasoning, well-developed and sustained, which is coherent, relevant and logically structured.

A Level candidates achieving excellence in their answers (the level six descriptors listed above) show a familiarity with scholarship informed by wider reading. This gives them fluency with technical vocabulary and allows for an intelligent interpretation of the question to produce a thoroughly relevant answer that pays close attention to its wording. Level six candidates will show skill in selecting and deploying material, along with a nuanced understanding of thinkers. These candidates understand classic philosophers and their contemporary interpreters so well that they can present a nuanced account of how their thought may apply to modern debate.

Accomplished essay writers exhibit accuracy, precision and depth of understanding together with a breadth of perspective that allows for a variety of views to be compared and contrasted in a sophisticated way. They have fingertip familiarity with a range of scholarship, but have digested it to the extent that they can advance their own thesis and position on any given question, arguing cogently for their own judgements in a persuasive way. Most importantly, they understand that assessment and evaluation should be woven through the whole essay, not just restricted to the concluding paragraph.

A discerning writer makes informed judgements as to the relative strengths and weaknesses of theories throughout the essay. Their critical analysis is coherent and persuasively argued from a clear thesis statement to a successful conclusion.

Glossary of Key Terms

A posteriori A type of argument that reaches a conclusion based on observation and experience.
A priori A type of argument that reaches a conclusion based only on reason.
Aetiological myth A myth that attempts to explain the origin of something.
Agapeistic The adjective from the Christian word for selfless love: 'agape'.
Analogy A comparison of one thing with another to help explain something.
Analogy of attribution Humans can talk meaningfully about God because there is a causal relationship between human understanding of concepts like 'love' or 'goodness' and the understanding of these concepts in the mind of God.
Analogy of proper proportion The view that God possesses all good qualities infinitely, whereas humans own these qualities in proportion to their abilities.
Analytical School of Philosophy A movement beginning in the early twentieth century that sought clarity in language and thought.
Anthropic Principle The idea that the universe is fine-tuned so that humans can live in it.
Anthropocentric Human centred. The idea that words and ideas are focused on human ideas and characteristics.
Anthropomorphism The idea that God may be understood by attributing human characteristics to him.
Apophatic theology (*via negativa* in Latin) Also known as 'Negative theology', attempts to come to a knowledge of God indirectly, by removing those things that God is not.
Behaviourism All mental states are simply descriptions of behaviour that can be observed.
Blik The name given by R. M. Hare to an unfalsifiable conviction that is still meaningful.
Cataphatic theology (Greek) / *via positiva* (Latin) Comes from the Greek word *kataphasis*, meaning 'affirmation'. It attempts to come to knowledge of God by using positive and direct language.
Category Error To confuse items or ideas from different categories.
Cause *in esse* A cause that sustains the being or existence of an effect.
Cause *in fieri* A cause that causes something to become what it is.
Cogito ergo sum 'I think, therefore I exist.'
Contingent existence Something that is capable of not existing at some point.
Conversion An experience that brings about a (usually) radical change in an individual, typically from atheism to theism.

Glossary of Key Terms

Correspondence theory of truth   The theory that whether a statement is true or false is judged only on how it relates to the world and whether it actually describes (i.e. corresponds with) the world.

Cosmological   A type of argument that looks at the world (cosmos), searching for evidence of God's existence.

Deductive argument   An argument where the premises lead to the only possible conclusion.

Demythologize   Bultmann's word to describe the process that needs to be undertaken with the biblical texts so that the 'original' meaning(s) can be understood by modern readers.

Design *qua* purpose   Aquinas's term for the way the parts of the universe fit together for a purpose.

Design *qua* regularity   Aquinas's term for the way that the order and regularity in the world are proof there is a designer.

Dualism   The view that humans consist of two substances – body and mind/soul.

Efficient Cause   How an object comes into being.

Empirical   Making use of evidence from the world.

Empiricism   The theory that all our knowledge of the world is based on sense experience. It is particularly associated with Bishop George Berkeley and David Hume.

Epistemic distance   The idea that there is a gap between God's knowledge and human knowledge. Because they do not have innate knowledge of God, humans must seek God through faith.

Equivocal language   A word can have different meanings in different contexts.

Euthyphro Dilemma   The question of whether certain acts are classed as good/bad because God has chosen them to be so, or because they are intrinsically good or bad.

Ex nihilo   '*Ex nihilo nihil fit*' – 'Nothing comes from nothing.'

Fallacy of composition   The mistaken assumption that the whole must share the same properties as its parts.

Final Cause   The purpose of an object.

Form of the Good   This Form is seen to be the ultimate object of enquiry and is far superior to all other Forms in terms of reality and perfection in Platonic thinking.

Forms   Plato's doctrine that there was an ideal, eternal, spiritual world that is 'real' and that existed above our world. The Forms are found in the Realm of the Forms, and included Forms of Beauty, Justice and Truth, among other ideals.

Four Causes   The term given to Aristotle's theory that there are four different kinds of cause to explain why things exist.

Idealistic Monism   Only the mind exists and consequently the external, physical world is an illusion created by the mind.

Immanent   God existing within and sustaining the universe.

Incarnation   The Christian view of Jesus as 'wholly human' and yet 'wholly God'.

Inductive argument   An argument in which the premises lead to a conclusion that is probable, not conclusive.

Ineffability   The idea that God cannot be spoken of truly or described accurately.

Invalid   An argument that does not make logical sense.

Glossary of Key Terms

Material Cause The substance from which a thing is made or created.

Materialism The philosophical idea that matter is the fundamental substance in the universe and that everything, including consciousness and mental activity, consists of material interactions.

Materialistic Monism The single reality is matter, made up either only of atoms or of some world-forming substance. The essential view is that all states may be reduced to the physical.

Mind–Body Problem The question of how the mind, a non-physical property, can interact with the body, a physical property.

Models and qualifiers A model is an ordinary term that everyone can understand. A qualifier helps to show that the model is being used in a 'special' religious way.

Monism The view that humans are made up of only a single (material) substance.

Mysterium tremendum et fascinans For Otto, this was the effect that a religious experience had on an individual.

Mysticism Where a person feels that he/she is gaining spiritual truth beyond normal understanding as he/she is drawn into an ever-closer union with God.

Natural Theology The attempt to use rational, scientific evidence about the world to argue for the existence of God.

Necessary existence Something that is not capable of not existing.

Numinous Otto's term for an individual's encounter with 'the Holy', or God.

Ockham's Razor The logical principle that 'entities should not be multiplied beyond necessity', i.e. that the explanation with fewer assumptions is the correct one.

Omniscient All-knowing.

Ontology The study of 'being' – that is, the nature of the properties of something.

Predicate A predicate is a property or attribute of something.

Prime Matter Anything that lacks a well-defined form – it is not organized into any particular structure.

Principle of Sufficient Reason Based on the premise that there must be an explanation (rather than a cause) for the existence of the universe and every thing in it. Argues towards there being sufficient reason for the universe.

Proof There can be only one conclusion from the argument, so it must be true.

Qualia The name given to individual, subjective experiences that people have.

Quantifier shift fallacy The mistaken assumption that because everything (plural) has a cause there is a cause for every thing (singular).

Religious experience Any experience of the sacred in a religious context, including visions, and mystical and conversion experiences.

Revealed Theology In contrast to Natural Theology, this is the belief that God is known through the sacred texts of a religion.

Revelation A divinely given disclosure of information to humans.

Sound A valid argument that is also factually correct.

Substance The material from which things are made.

Teleology The English word 'teleology' comes from the Greek word *telos*. *Telos* means 'aim' or 'purpose', or the 'result' of a course of action.

Theodicy The idea that God allows evil to occur because he has a just reason for it.

Theory of Evolution Living organisms developed from simpler to more complex form gradually over time and through the purely natural processes of random variation, natural selection and the survival of the fittest.

Theory of Forms Plato's key idea, one of the earliest and most famous attempts to explain certain kinds of knowledge

Therefore Signals the conclusion of an argument.

Univocal language A word has only one meaning.

Vale of Soul Making Hick's attempt to justify both moral and natural evil, saying that evil will disappear at the end of the world.

Valid An argument in which the premises lead to a logical conclusion.

Verification Principle The idea that statements are meaningful only if they can be verified, i.e. shown to be true by empirical evidence.

Via eminentiae ('Way of eminence') Aquinas's way of arguing that humans can talk positively about God, but acknowledging that our knowledge is only partial.

Illustration Credits

Introduction
p. 4, Carlo Crivelli / Yorck Project

Chapter 1
p. 10, Wikimedia Commons; p. 15, iStock/ilbusca; p. 20, https://thesiseleven.wordpress.com/philosophy/platos-republic/simile-of-the-divided-line

Chapter 2
p. 25, Wikimedia Commons; p. 27, iStock/yayayoyo; p. 27, Wikimedia Commons; p. 27, iStock/darrenplatts123; p. 27, Wikimedia Commons

Chapter 3
p. 48, Wikimedia Commons; p. 50, Wikimedia Commons

Chapter 4
p. 60, Wikimedia Commons; p. 62, iStock/kurga; p. 64, Wikimedia Commons

Chapter 5
p. 85, Wikimedia Commons; p. 87, Wikimedia Commons; p. 89, Wikimedia Commons; p. 90, Author

Chapter 6
p. 99, Wikimedia Commons; p. 101, Wikimedia Commons; p. 103, Wikimedia Commons; p. 107, iStock/clu

Chapter 7
p. 120, Wikimedia Commons; p. 125, Wikimedia Commons; p. 126, Wikimedia Commons

Chapter 8
p. 146, iStock/GeorgiosArt

Chapter 9
p. 167, iStock/bennyb; p. 168, Wikimedia Commons; p. 176, Wikimedia Commons

Chapter 10
p. 186, Wikimedia Commons; p. 187, Wikimedia Commons; p. 189, iStock/MaryValery; p. 191, LSE Library / Flickr; p. 197, Wikimedia Commons

Index

a posteriori 4, 5, 21, 59, 65, 73, 77, 79, 203, 210
a priori 4, 5, 17, 20, 21, 53, 71, 84, 86, 88, 91, 190, 210
Al-Ghazali 72
Al-Kindi 61, 72
Analytical School of Philosophy 50
Anselm, Saint 84–8, 89–90, 91, 92, 93, 150, 151, 154–5
  four-dimensionalist approach to eternity 154–5
  Ontological argument 85, 86
anthropomorphism 66, 140, 174
Aquinas, Thomas 4, 33, 58, 73, 88, 150, 163, 166, 170
  Cosmological argument vii, 5, 33, 57, 72–8
  design qua purpose 59
  design qua regularity 59
  First Way 72–3, 76, 91
  Second Way 73–6
  Soul 47
  Third Way 73, 77
argument Cosmological 5, 33, 57, 72, 73, 76, 78–81, 85, 88, 198, 203, 209
  deductive 5, 6
  inductive 4, 6
  Ontological 4, 48, 84, 86, 89–93, 190
  proof 3, 4, 5, 6, 33, 34, 59, 63, 66, 68, 73, 76, 80, 81, 85, 86, 109, 110, 174, 216
  teleological 57–71, 190
Aristotle vii, 4, 24–37, 39, 42, 45, 46, 47, 55, 72, 74, 75, 134, 135, 137, 171, 209
  four causes 24, 27–30, 33, 75
  Prime Mover 24, 30–2, 33, 36, 37, 58, 73, 134, 135
  teleology 29
Augustine, Saint 22, 59, 85, 108, 115–17, 120–7
Ayer, A. J. 110, 175, 187, 203

behaviourism 41–2
Boethius 88, 133, 150
  on God's eternity 151–3
  on God's foreknowledge 153–4
bliks 194–5, 196
Braithwaite, R. B. 200
Bultmann, Rudolf 182, 205
  on demythologization 205
  on myth 182

Calvin, John 116, 118, 146–7
Churchland, Paul 41
Cicero 58
Cosmological argument 72–82
  Aquinas on vii, 5, 33, 57, 72–8
  criticisms of 76, 79, 80, 81
Cox, Harvey 206
Craig, William Lane 72, 153

d'Holbach, Baron 52
Darwin, Charles 36, 52, 67, 174
  and design argument 67–8
Davies, Brian 43, 44, 73–4, 131, 144–5, 172
Dawkins, Richard 52–3, 68, 126, 150, 174
  on God's goodness 150
  on religious language 174
Descartes, Rene 42, 47, 48–50, 75, 84, 89–92, 142
  Cogito ergo sum 48
  Ontological argument 89–90
  Substance Dualism 48–9
Dualism 103, 135, 166
  Cartesian 48–9
  Platonic 23, 39, 42–4
  Substance 39, 48, 50

Empiricism 25, 32, 89, 97
evil 33, 34, 59, 66, 67, 71, 115, 141, 145, 146, 154, 175, 212
  Augustine on 22, 120, 122–4
  definition of 116
  evidential problem of 118–19
  free will defence 120, 130–1
  Hick/Irenaeus on 125–30
  inconsistent triad 119
  Leibniz's Best of All Possible Worlds 118, 120
  logical problem of 116–17
  moral 119–20, 130
  natural 67, 119, 123, 130
  non-moral 119
  Plotinus on 117, 122
  Spinoza on 118

evil (*cont.*)
  theodicy 117, 120, 121, 122, 123, 125, 127–30, 175
evolution 36, 41, 48, 52, 53, 57, 64, 67, 68, 124, 129, 170, 174

fallacy 44, 91
  of composition 35, 80
  quantifier shift 80
falsification principle 196
Flew, Anthony 169, 191, 192, 207

God's characteristics 86, 120, 133–57, 165, 169
  Calvin and the doctrine of double predestination 118, 146–7
  eternity 133, 146, 147, 151, 154, 155
  Euthyphro Dilemma 149
  free will 71, 85, 117, 118, 120, 127, 135–7, 139, 140, 144, 165, 172, 176, 194
  God as craftsman 139–40
  God as Creator 58, 66, 70, 82, 87, 116, 118, 120, 127, 135–7, 139, 140, 144, 165, 172, 176, 194
  omnibenevolence 120, 133, 141, 149
  omnipotence 81, 120, 128, 130, 131, 133, 140–3, 144, 145, 148, 149, 179
  omnipresence and immanence 148
  omniscience 71, 81, 120, 124, 133, 144–8, 151
Gray, Asa 67, 68

Hare, R. M. 194–5
Hawking, Stephen 81, 82
Hick, John 1, 61, 94, 122, 125, 127, 180, 182, 186, 195, 197, 200, 202, 206
Hobbes, Thomas 41
Hume, David 2, 32, 57, 64–7, 71, 80, 81, 89 162, 187, 189, 191

Kant, Immanuel 2, 5, 80, 84, 99, 129, 188
  on apparent design 66
  on Ontological argument 89–92
Kenny, Anthony 49, 73
Kerr, Fergus 173, 174, 203

Leibniz, Gottfried 41, 72, 76, 118, 120
  Principle of Sufficient Reason 78–9
Logical Positivism 185, 186–7, 200
Lossky, Vladimir 163, 168, 183

Macquarrie, John 179–80
Mill, John Stuart 26, 67, 71
Mind--Body Problem 40
Minucius Felix 59
Mitchell, Basil 194, 195, 196, 202, 203
Monism 41, 42, 103
  idealistic 41, 42
  materialistic 41, 42

Nietzsche, Friedrich 39, 40, 144

Ockham's Razor 70, 71
Ontological argument 4, 48, 84–94, 154, 190
  Anselm on 85–8
  Descartes on 89, 90
  Gaunilo on 87
  Kant on 89–92
  Malcolm, Norman on 92–3
  Russell on 91
  Southern, R. W. on 84–5

Paley, William 60–4
  criticisms of 64–6
  eye analogy 62
  Teleological argument 60–4
  watch analogy 59–60
Palmer, Michael 71, 76, 77
Parable of the freedom fighter 195–6
Parable of the Gardener 169, 193
Paul, Saint 59, 109, 126, 164, 169
Persinger, Michael 42
Phillips, D. Z. 199, 200, 204
Plantinga, Alvin 1
Plato 9–23, 24–9, 32, 33
  Dualism 42–4
  soul 39–44
Popper, Karl 21, 191–2
Pythagoras 11

Qualia 52

Ramsey, Ian 175–6
  on analogy 175
  criticisms of 176
religious experience 33, 47, 52, 58, 97–114, 200
  conversion 97, 100, 101, 104–8, 120
  Cruz, Nicky 105–6, 107
  Dame Julian of Norwich 103–4
  Feuerbach, Ludwig 111–12
  Freud, Sigmund 112–13, 191
  Honderich, Ted 103
  ineffability 102, 164
  James, William 101
  Muggeridge, Malcolm 107–8
  mysterium tremendum et fascinans 99
  mysticism 22, 97, 99, 100, 101, 103
  noetic 102
  numinous 99, 100, 101
  Otto, Rudolf 99, 100, 101
  passivity 102
  Saul of Tarsus 106, 107
  Schleiermacher, F. D. E. 98, 99, 101
  Swinburne on 109
  temporal lobe epilepsy 111
  transciency 102
religious language 161–84, 185–207

analogy 166, 170, 171–3
  criticisms of 174–5
apophatic way 161, 168
  criticisms of 168–9
Ayer on 187–9, 190, 191, 203, 204
cataphatic way 161, 166, 169
cloud of unknowing, the 163, 167, 183
comparison of Aquinas and
  Wittgenstein 203–4
falsification principle 185, 191, 193, 194, 196, 199
Hume on language 162, 187, 189, 191
Lossky, Vladimir on negative language 168
myth as a form of religious language 180–2
non-cognitive accounts of religious
  language 196–7
Pseudo-Dionysius on negative language 163, 165–6, 167
Tillich on 178–80
Verification Principle 110, 185, 187, 188, 189, 191
Wittgenstein on 185, 186, 187, 197, 199, 203, 204
Robinson, John 206
Rowe, William L. 62, 72, 82, 131, 143
Russell, Bertrand 22, 36, 41, 50, 79, 80, 91, 186, 187
Ryle, Gilbert 50, 52, 187
  Category Error 51

Schlick, Moritz 186
Socrates 9, 10, 11, 15, 18, 24, 25, 43, 44, 58, 149

soul 13, 16, 19, 23, 26, 48, 49, 51, 101, 104, 123, 127, 128, 160, 167, 199
  Aristotle on 47
  Dawkins on 52–3
  Plato on 39–44
Swinburne, Richard 63, 110, 202
  on design 70–1
  on evil 126
  on God's timelessness and free will 135, 155
  on religious experience 109

Teleological argument 57–71, 84, 190
Tennant, Frederick R. 68–70
  Anthropic Principle 68–70
    criticisms of 69–70
    Strong version 69
    Weak version 69
Theory of Forms 9, 10, 15, 21
  Form of the Good 14, 16, 19–20, 21–2, 32–3, 134–5
  the Cave 9, 15–20
  the Divided Line 9, 14, 19–20
  the Sun 9, 14, 19–20
Tillich, Paul 99
  criticisms of 178–9
  on symbol 176–8

van Buren, Paul 205
Verification Principle 110, 185, 187–91
Vienna Circle 186, 187
Wittgenstein, Ludwig 50, 185, 186, 187, 197–8, 199–200, 203–4
Wolff, Christian von 41